OXFORD

take off in

Japanese

Lynne Strugnell

OXFORD
UNIVERSITY PRESS

OXFORD
UNIVERSITY PRESS

Great Clarendon Street, Oxford OX2 6DP

Oxford University Press is a department of the University of Oxford.
It furthers the University's objective of excellence in research, scholarship,
and education by publishing worldwide in

Oxford New York

Auckland Bangkok Buenos Aires Cape Town Chennai
Dar es Salaam Delhi Hong Kong Istanbul Karachi Kolkata
Kuala Lumpur Madrid Melbourne Mexico City Mumbai Nairobi
São Paulo Shanghai Taipei Tokyo Toronto

Oxford is a registered trade mark of Oxford University Press
in the UK and in certain other countries

Published in the United States
by Oxford University Press Inc., New York

British Library Cataloguing in Publication Data

Data available

Library of Congress Cataloging in Publication Data

Data available

ISBN 0-19-860278-2 (Books and cassettes)
ISBN 0-19-860300-2 (Books and CDs)
ISBN 0-19-860301-0 (Book only)

5

Commissioning, development, and project management: Tracy Miller
Audio production: Gerald Ramshaw
Music: David Stoll
Design: Keith Shaw
Editorial: Helen Wilson
Teaching consultant: Jenny Ollerenshaw

Printed in Great Britain by
Clays Ltd, St Ives plc

Contents

Introduction

Oxford Take Off In Japanese is designed to help the beginner develop the basic language skills necessary to communicate in Japanese in most everyday situations. It is intended for learners working by themselves, providing all the information and support necessary for successful language learning.

How to use the course
The book and the recording are closely integrated, as the emphasis is on speaking and listening. The recording contains step-by-step instructions on how to work through the units. The presenter will tell you when to use the recording on its own, when to use the book, and when and how to use the two together. The book provides support in the form of transcriptions of the recording material, translations of new vocabulary, and grammar explanations. You'll find this icon ⓐ in the book when you need to listen to the recording.

1 (recording/book) Read the unit objectives on the first page telling you what you will learn in the unit, and then begin by listening to the **dialogue** on the recording. You may not understand everything the first time you hear it, but try to resist the temptation to look at the transcript in the book. The first activity on the recording will help you develop your listening skills by suggesting things to concentrate on and listen out for. You'll be given the opportunity to repeat some of the key sentences and phrases from the dialogue before you hear it a second time. You may need to refer to the vocabulary list (book) before completing the second activity (book). Listen to the dialogue as many times as you like, but as far as possible try not to refer to the dialogue transcript (book).

2 (book) Once you have listened to all the new language, take some time to work through the **transcript, Vocabulary, Language Building**, and **activities** in the book to help you understand how it works.

3 (recording) Then it's time to practice speaking: first **Pronunciation practice** and then the **Your turn** activity. You will be given all the instructions and cues you need by the presenter on the recording. The first few times you do this you may need to refer back to the vocabulary and language building sections in the book, but aim to do it without the book after that.

4 (book) The fourth learning

section, **Culture**, concentrates on reading practice. The course provides an introduction to reading katakana and hiragana, as well as some simple kanji. The activities which accompany the text will help you develop reading comprehension skills.

5 (recording/book) For the final learning section, return to the recording to listen to the **Story**. This section gives you the opportunity to have some fun with the language and hear the characters in the story use the language you have just learnt in different situations. The aim is to give you the confidence to cope with authentic Japanese. There are activities in the book to help you.

6 (book) Return to the book, and work through the activities in the **Test** section to see how well you can remember and use the language you have covered in the unit. This is best done as a written exercise. Add up the final score and, if it is not as high as you had hoped, try going back and reviewing some of the sections.

7 (recording/book) As a final review, turn to the **Summary** on the last page of the unit. This will test your understanding of the new situations, vocabulary and grammar introduced in the unit. Use the book to prepare your answers, either by writing them down or speaking aloud, then return to the recording to test yourself. You will be given prompts in English on the recording, so you can do this test without the book.

8 (book) At the very end of each unit you will find some suggestions for **revision** and ideas for further practice.

Each unit builds on the work of the preceding units, so it's very important to learn the vocabulary and structures from each unit before you move on. There are review sections after units 3, 7, 10, and 14 for you to test yourself on the material learnt so far.

Other support features
If you want a more detailed grammar explanation than those given in the Language Building sections, you will find a *Grammar Summary* at the end of the book. For a definition of the grammar terms used in the course, see the *Glossary of Grammatical Terms* on page 241.

The *Answers* section at the end of the book will give you the answers to all the book activities. Some activities require you to give information about yourself, so you may also need to check some vocabulary in a dictionary.

At the end of the book you'll find a comprehensive *Japanese–English Vocabulary*.

About Japanese

Japanese is generally considered one of the easier languages for a beginner to speak. The pronunciation is straightforward, and the grammatical rules are regular with few exceptions. There are only a few verb tenses, and no articles, plurals or masculine/feminine endings; nor do the verbs change for person, so you do not have to worry about making words agree.

Japanese uses different speech levels for formal and informal occasions, and to show the relationship between speaker and listener, so the speaker needs to choose his words carefully in consideration of his listener. In this course we have used the everyday polite forms which are appropriate for most situations at the beginner's level, but towards the end of the course we have also introduced examples of more formal and informal speech.

The Japanese writing system

The complexity of the Japanese writing system makes it a difficult language to read and write. It is made up of three different sets of characters, **hiragana**, **katakana**, and **kanji**, which are used in combination. Kanji are ideograms originally brought in from China several thousand years ago. There are perhaps 50,000 different kanji, although around 3,000 are in daily use in Japan. Kanji characters are not phonetic, but represent meanings, and are commonly used for nouns, verb roots, and adjectives. Hiragana and katakana are

phonetic systems: the characters represent sounds rather than meanings. There are 46 of each. Hiragana is used to write words which have no kanji representation, and for verb and adjective endings and auxiliary verbs to show the tense, etc. Katakana characters are used to spell loan words imported into Japanese from other languages.

Within the scope of the course, it is not possible to teach such a complex writing system, so a form of romanized script has been used. However, the writing system is fascinating, and we hope the inclusion of some reading practice in the Japanese Culture section of each unit will give you a useful and interesting introduction to it.

Pronunciation

To achieve good pronunciation, there is no substitute for listening carefully to the recording and, if possible, to Japanese native speakers, and trying to reproduce the sounds you hear. Here are a few guidelines for you to keep in mind when doing so. You will find this section most useful if you listen to the Pronunciation section on the recording as you read it.

Pronunciation

Vowels

Sound short vowels	Phonetic symbol	English approximation	Example
a	/a/	cat	Yokohama, karate
i	/i̥/	treat	kimono, sushi
u	/ɯ/	good	sushi, samurai
e	/ɛ/	pen	hen, desu
o	/ɔ/	hot	otoko, tomato

Long vowels are pronounced in the same way as short vowels, but are written as **ā, ii, ū, ē, ō**.

long vowels			
ā	/a:/		obāsan
ii	/i̥:/		chiizu
ū	/ɯ:/		pūru
ē	/ɛ:/		sētā
ō	/ɔ:/		kōkō

In vowel combinations, each vowel is pronounced separately.

Vowel combinations (examples)			
a + i	/ai/		samurai
e + i	/ɛi/		geisha

Consonants

Most consonants are pronounced as in English, with the following exceptions.

Sound	Phonetic symbol	English approximation	Example
f	/ɸ/	*softer than in English*	Fuji san, tōfu
r	/ɾ/	*between l and r*	biiru, gorufu

Double consonants are held longer than single consonants.

Double consonants (examples)			
tt	/t:/	*held for an extra beat*	chotto, matte
kk	/k:/	*held for an extra beat*	yukkuri, gakkō
nn	/n:/	*held for an extra beat*	konnichiwa, onna

Hiragana

	a	i	u	e	o
	あ a	い i	う u	え e	お o
k	か ka	き ki	く ku	け ke	こ ko
g	が ga	ぎ gi	ぐ gu	げ ge	ご go
s	さ sa	し shi	す su	せ se	そ so
z	ざ za	じ zi	ず zu	ぜ ze	ぞ zo
t	た ta	ち chi	つ tsu	て te	と to
d	だ da	ぢ ji	づ zu	で de	ど do
n	な na	に ni	ぬ nu	ね ne	の no
h	は ha	ひ hi	ふ fu	へ he	ほ ho
b	ば ba	び bi	ぶ bu	べ be	ぼ bo
p	ぱ pa	ぴ pi	ぷ pu	ぺ pe	ぽ po
m	ま ma	み mi	む mu	め me	も mo
y	や ya		ゆ yu		よ yo
r	ら ra	り ri	る ru	れ re	ろ ro
w	わ wa				を wo
n	ん				

Katakana

	a	i	u	e	o
	ア a	イ i	ウ u	エ e	オ o
k	カ ka	キ ki	ク ku	ケ ke	コ ko
g	ガ ga	ギ gi	グ gu	ゲ ge	ゴ go
s	サ sa	シ shi	ス su	セ se	ソ so
z	ザ za	ジ zi	ズ zu	ゼ ze	ゾ zo
t	タ ta	チ chi	ツ tsu	テ te	ト to
d	ダ da	ヂ ji	ヅ zu	デ de	ド do
n	ナ na	ニ ni	ヌ nu	ネ ne	ノ no
h	ハ ha	ヒ hi	フ fu	ヘ he	ホ ho
b	バ ba	ビ bi	ブ bu	ベ be	ボ bo
p	パ pa	ピ pi	プ pu	ペ pe	ポ po
m	マ ma	ミ mi	ム mu	メ me	モ mo
y	ヤ ya		ユ yu		ヨ yo
r	ラ ra	リ ri	ル ru	レ re	ロ ro
w	ワ wa				ヲ wo
n	ン				

Starting out
Hajime ni

OBJECTIVES

In this unit, you'll learn how to:

✓ greet people

✓ meet people and give your name

✓ get a drink and something to eat

And cover the following grammar and language:

✓ the verb **desu** ('am', 'is', 'are')

✓ question forms

✓ polite requests

✓ forms of thank you

LEARNING JAPANESE 1

Always remember that you can go a long way with just a little language. Even if you're not sure how to form a complete sentence, try using the few words or phrases you do know, and you'll be surprised by how much you'll be able to communicate.

Above all, don't worry about getting things wrong. Of course you should aim to speak perfect Japanese, but you can learn a lot from the mistakes you make along the way. And even with some errors, people will still be able to understand you.

🎧 Now start the recording for Unit 1.

1.1 Greetings

Aisatsu

ACTIVITY 1 is on the recording.

ACTIVITY 2

What is the weather for each time of day mentioned?

1	day	a	cold and horrible
2	evening	b	good weather
3	morning	c	hot

DIALOGUE 1

○ Shimada san, konnichiwa.
■ Itō san! Konnichiwa.
○ Ii tenki desu ne.
■ Sō desu ne. Ii tenki desu ne.

■ Yoshida san, konbanwa.
○ Konbanwa. Atsui desu ne.
■ Ē. Atsui desu ne.

○ Yamada san, ohayō gozaimasu.
■ Ohayō. Iya-na tenki desu ne.
○ Sō desu ne. Samui desu ne.

VOCABULARY	
hajime ni	first of all, at first
aisatsu	greetings
... san	Mr, Mrs, Ms ...
konnichiwa	hello, good afternoon
ii tenki	nice weather
desu	am, is, are
sō desu	that's right; it's so
ne	isn't it!
konbanwa	good evening
atsui	hot
ē	yes (informal)
ohayō gozaimasu	good morning
ohayō	morning! [*informal*]
iya-na tenki	horrible weather
samui	cold

Answers to the activities are in the Answer section on page 213.

✓ desu – am, is, are

The word **desu** is very versatile. It can mean '(I) am', '(you) are', '(we) are', or '(he/she/it) is'. The words for 'you' or 'I', etc., are often omitted when it's obvious from the context who or what you're talking about.
Like all Japanese verbs, **desu** generally comes at the end of the sentence.

Ii tenki **desu**. It's nice weather.
Yoshida san **desu**. That's Yoshida san.

✓ ne – isn't it?

You can add **ne** to the end of a sentence to make a tag question ('isn't it?', 'aren't they?', etc.).

Atsui desu **ne**.   It's hot, isn't it?
Ii desu **ne**.   It's nice, isn't it?
Sō desu **ne**.   It is, isn't it? / That's right, isn't it?

✓ Talking about the weather

Japanese people do not often use the equivalent of 'How are you?' when they meet, except when they haven't seen each other for a while, or are genuinely enquiring after someone's health. Instead, they tend to comment on the weather when greeting each other.

ACTIVITY 3

Which of these comments on the weather would you make where you are today?

1 Ii tenki desu ne.
2 Iya-na tenki desu ne.
3 Samui desu ne.
4 Atsui desu ne.

🎧 Now do activities 4 and 5 on the recording.

First meetings

Dōzo yoroshiku

ACTIVITY 6 is on the recording.

ACTIVITY 7

Can you say which of these names were mentioned in the conversations?

Yoshida san	Koyama san
Yamada san	Kimura san
Shimada san	Yoshimura san

DIALOGUE 2

○ Kimura san desu ka.
■ Hai, Kimura desu.
○ Shimada desu. Dōzo yoroshiku.
■ Dōzo yoroshiku.

○ Yoshida san! Yoshida san!
▼ Shimada san! Konnichiwa! Atsui desu ne.
○ Ē, atsui desu ne. Yoshida san, Kimura san desu.
■ Kimura desu.
▼ Yoshida desu. Dōzo yoroshiku.

VOCABULARY	
ka	*[indicates a question]*
hai	yes
dōzo yoroshiku	pleased to meet you

⊘ Asking questions with *ka*

To ask a question, simply add **ka** to the end of a sentence. As **ka** always indicates a question, it's not usually considered necessary to use a question mark.

Ikeda san desu **ka**. Are you Ikeda san?
Atsui desu **ka**. Is it hot?

⊘ Using *san* with people's names

The word **san**, used after names, is similar to Mr, Mrs, and Ms in English – in general, the context should make it clear which is intended. As it is a term of respect to other people, don't use it when saying your own name. **San** can be used after family names or first names, although you won't hear Japanese people use first names often, except within the family or between close friends.

ACTIVITY 8

Imagine you've just been introduced to someone. How would you give your own name and say 'Pleased to meet you'?

ACTIVITY 9

Match each Japanese sentence with the correct English translation.

1 Koyama desu.   a That's Koyama san.
2 Koyama san desu.   b I'm Koyama.
3 Koyama san desu ka.   c Is he Koyama san?

 Now do activities 10 and 11 on the recording.

1.3 At the coffee shop
Kissaten de

ACTIVITY 12 is on the recording.

ACTIVITY 13

Can you say what the two people ordered?

Woman: _____ _____

Man: _____

DIALOGUE 3

▼ Irasshaimase!
○ Orenji jūsu o kudasai.
▼ Orenji jūsu desu ne.
■ Remon tii o kudasai.
▼ Hai, orenji jūsu to remon tii desu ne.
○ Sumimasen.
▼ Hai.
○ Chiizu sando mo kudasai.
▼ Hai, chiizu sando desu ne.

▼ Hai, orenji jūsu to chiizu sando desu. Dōzo.
○ Arigatō.
▼ Remon tii desu.
■ Dōmo.

VOCABULARY	
kissaten de	at the coffee shop
irasshaimase!	welcome!
orenji jūsu	orange juice
... o kudasai	I'd like ... / could I have ...?
remon tii	lemon tea
to	and
sumimasen	excuse me / sorry
chiizu sando	cheese sandwich
mo	too, also
dōzo	here you are / here it is [also go ahead]
arigatō	thank you
dōmo	thanks

ACTIVITY 14

Japanese has borrowed many words from other languages. Can you guess what these items of food and drink are? It might help to try saying them aloud – think about the sound rather than the spelling.

1	tomato jūsu	7	piza
2	kōhii	8	supagetti
3	aisu kuriimu	9	koka kōra
4	mikkusu sando	10	biiru
5	kuriimu soda	11	hanbāgā
6	miruku tii	12	sarada

LANGUAGE BUILDING

⊘ Asking for something with ... *o kudasai*

Use the phrase ... **o kudasai** ('I'd like ...' / 'Could I have ...?') when you want to ask for something, for example in a shop, coffee shop, or restaurant. The word **o** highlights the item you want by coming just after it.

Kōhii o kudasai.	Could I have a coffee?
Biiru o kudasai.	I'd like a beer, please.
Kōra to piza o kudasai.	A coke and a pizza, please.

⊘ Saying thank you

As in English, the longer the phrase when saying thank you, the more formal and polite.

Dōmo	Thanks
Arigatō	Thank you
Dōmo arigatō	Thank you very much

You may hear the even more formal phrases **dōmo arigatō gozaimasu** and **dōmo arigatō gozaimashita** from people such as sales clerks and hotel staff, but you don't need to use these phrases yourself.

Now do activities 15 and 16 on the recording.

Japanese Culture
Nihon no bunka

CULTURE

COFFEE SHOPS

A Japanese coffee shop, or **kissaten**, is much more than just a place to stop for a coffee when you need a rest. People go to a **kissaten** to meet friends, to read, to have informal business meetings, even to have English lessons when no classroom is available. The coffee may be expensive, but you can stay as long as you like in a **kissaten**.

Many **kissaten** specialize in different kinds of music or decor, so customers may choose a particular coffee shop for its classical music, or its jazz, or its modern paintings. Whichever you choose, you will always be met with a friendly cry of **Irasshaimase!** (Welcome!), and be given a glass of iced water (**mizu**) and often an **oshibori**, a moist handtowel, for you to wipe your hands and refresh yourself while you look at the menu.

If you're worried about understanding what is available in a **kissaten**, you can always check the display window outside. All restaurants and **kissaten** show amazingly realistic wax models of all the food and drink on the menu, so you can see if they have something you want. And as a last resort, you can always ask the waiter or waitress to come outside and point to what you want in the display window, using **... o kudasai**.

	a	i	u	e	o
	ア a	イ i	ウ u	エ e	オ o
k	カ ka	キ ki	ク ku	ケ ke	コ ko
g	ガ ga	ギ gi	グ gu	ゲ ge	ゴ go
s	サ sa	シ shi	ス su	セ se	ソ so
z	ザ za	ジ zi	ズ zu	ゼ ze	ゾ zo
t	タ ta	チ chi	ツ tsu	テ te	ト to
d	ダ da	ヂ ji	ヅ zu	デ de	ド do

ACTIVITY 17

Written Japanese is complicated, but there are a few situations where a little knowledge can go a long way.

As you've seen, the words for drinks and snacks in a **kissaten** are mostly western in origin – sandwiches, hamburgers, coffee, etc. They are written in the menu in **katakana**, the script used for writing words of non-Japanese origin (see page viii) and it's not difficult to decipher them if you have the **katakana** chart to help you. Using the chart on page 8, see how many of the items on this menu you can read and understand.

コーヒー ショップ アーケード

コーク	¥400	トースト	¥380
ココア	¥420	ケーキ	¥420
アイスココア	¥430	チーズケーキ	¥520
ソーダ	¥380	ソーセージ	¥500

1.5 Midori-ya

It's the middle of the evening, and Itō san welcomes two of the regular customers, Harada san and Ikeda san, to his small neighbourhood bar, called Midori-ya.

onegai shimasu	please [*when asking a favour*]
irasshai!	welcome! [*informal version of* **irasshaimase!**]
kanpai!	cheers!
Ii desu ka	is it OK? [*when asking permission*]
dōzo	go ahead
sumimasen ga ...	excuse me, but ..., I'm sorry, but ...
sō desu ka	I see [*also* is that right? really?]
ja	well, in that case
... ja nai yo!	it isn't ...! [*very informal*]
oishii	delicious, tastes good

ACTIVITY 18

Listen to the conversation, and then put the following events into the correct order.

1 __ someone asks for juice
2 __ two women order drinks
3 __ a woman asks a question
4 __ someone comments on the weather
5 __ a woman says 'cheers'

ACTIVITY 19

Decide if the following statements about the conversation are true, false, or you don't know as not enough information has been given in the conversation.

1 It's a warm evening.	T / F / DK
2 Two friends come into the bar.	T / F / DK
3 The women drink beer.	T / F / DK
4 Itó san gives the newcomer a coke.	T / F / DK
5 The newcomer is a businessman.	T / F / DK

ACTIVITY 20

In the story, how many questions do you hear, ending in **ka**?

ACTIVITY 21

Put these words in the order you hear them in the story.

arigatō / atsui / onegai shimasu / dōmo / oishii

STORY TRANSCRIPT

Itō	Irasshaimase! A, Harada san, konbanwa.
Harada	Konbanwa.
Itō	Biiru desu ka.
Harada	Hai, onegai shimasu.
Itō	Dōzo. Irasshai! Ikeda san, konbanwa.
Ikeda	Konbanwa. Atsui desu ne.
Itō	Sō desu ne. Biiru desu ka.
Ikeda	Hai, biiru o kudasai.
Itō	Dōzo.
Ikeda	Arigatō. Kanpai!
Stranger	Ii desu ka.
Itō	Hai, dōzo dōzo, irasshaimase. Biiru desu ka.
Stranger	Sō desu ne ... Kōra o kudasai.
Itō	Kōra?! Sumimasen ga ...
Stranger	Sō desu ka. Ja, jūsu?
Itō	Jūsu?!! Jūsu desu ka?
Stranger	Sō desu ne. Sumimasen. Ja, biiru o kudasai.
Itō	Hai, biiru.
Stranger	Dōmo.
Ikeda	Oishii desu ka.
Stranger	A, oishii desu ne.

Test

Now it's time to test your progress in Unit 1.

1 Match the words and phrases to their Japanese translations.
(Be careful – there is one English phrase too many.)

1	good morning	a	arigatō
2	pleased to meet you	b	sō desu ne
3	thank you	c	konbanwa
4	yes, please	d	ohayō gozaimasu
5	it is, isn't it!	e	kanpai
6	good evening	f	dōzo yoroshiku
7	cheers!		

6

2 How would you ask for these things in a coffee shop?

1 a coffee and an ice cream
2 a plate of mixed sandwiches and a coke
3 a hamburger and an orange juice
4 a beer and a pizza
5 a salad and a tomato juice

10

3 Sort these items into food and drink, and write them on the
appropriate line. All these words have been imported from
other languages except one – which one?

kōhii, hanbāgā, orenji, miruku, biiru, mizu, sarada, chiizu,
tii

Food: _____

Drink: _____

Exception: _____

10

Answers to the Test sections are in the Answer section on page 213.

4 What's the Japanese for:

1 Are you Mr Shimada?
2 Nice weather, isn't it?
3 Good morning!
4 Yes, that's Ms Kimura.
5 Excuse me.

10

5 Pat Ross has to go to the airport to meet a visitor arriving from Japan. Look at their name cards below, and complete the conversation they had on meeting.

Ross   _____ san desu _____.

Koyama   _____, Koyama _____.

Ross   _____ _____. Dōzo _____.

Koyama   Dōzo _____.

8

TOTAL SCORE   **44**

If you score less than 34, look at the Language Building sections again before completing the Summary on page 14.

Summary 1

Now try this final test summarizing the main points covered in this unit. You can check your answers on the recording.

How would you:
1 greet someone in the morning? in the afternoon? in the evening?
2 comment that the weather is good?
3 agree with someone who says it's cold?
4 ask this woman if she's Koyama san?
5 say you're pleased to meet her?
6 order a coffee and an orange juice in a coffee shop?
7 say thank you?

REVISION

Before moving on to Unit 2, play Unit 1 through again and compare what you can say and understand now with what you knew when you started. Make a note of any vocabulary you still feel unsure of.

Remember that it will also be useful revision to listen to Unit 1 again after working through the next few units, in order to reinforce what you have learned here.

2

From time to time
Eiga wa nan-ji kara desu ka

OBJECTIVES

In this unit, you'll learn how to:

- ✓ ask and give the time
- ✓ state and understand when events start and finish

And cover the following grammar and language:

- ✓ numbers up to 99
- ✓ structures for giving the time
- ✓ the topic indicator **wa**
- ✓ **ja arimasen** ('isn't', 'aren't')

LEARNING JAPANESE 2

Don't try to do too much at one time. You will find you can learn more effectively if you study for half an hour or so at regular intervals, rather than try to do a whole unit in one sitting.

It also helps if you can learn with someone else. If you can persuade a friend or family member to study with you, it will give you an extra impetus to keep working. Agree times to meet and goals for the week, and test each other regularly.

Now start the recording for Unit 2.

Ima shichi-ji desu

🎧 **ACTIVITY 1** is on the recording.

ACTIVITY 2

1 What time is it?
2 What does Fukuda san order?
3 Why does she want a cold drink?
4 Why does Wada san suddenly ask for the bill?

DIALOGUE 1

○ Fukuda san wa osoi desu ne.
▼ Irasshaimase!
■ Konbanwa! Atsui desu ne! Sumimasen, aisu kōhii o kudasai. Ima 7.00 (shichi-ji) desu ne.
○ Iie, 8.00 (hachi-ji) desu.
■ Sō desu ka. 8.00 desu ka. Eiga wa nan-ji desu ka.
○ Eiga wa 8.00 desu. Sumimasen! O-kanjō, onegai shimasu.

VOCABULARY	
wa	*shows topic of sentence*
osoi	late
ima	now
shichi-ji	seven o'clock
iie	no
hachi-ji	eight o'clock
eiga	film
nan-ji	what time?
o-kanjō	bill, check

✓ Giving the time: hours

Here are the numbers 1 to 12. There are different ways of saying some of the numbers, depending on what you are counting. In the case of hours when giving the time, use **yo** (4), **shichi** (7), and **ku** (9).

1	ichi	5	go	9	kyū, ku
2	ni	6	roku	10	jū
3	san	7	shichi, nana	11	jū-ichi
4	yon, yo, shi	8	hachi	12	jū-ni

To give the time, add **-ji** ('o'clock') to the number.

Yo-ji desu. It's 4.00. **Hachi-ji han** desu ka. Is it 8.30?
Ku-ji desu ka. Is it 9.00? Iie, **ku-ji han** desu. No, it's 9.30.

For more information on numbers and counting, see the Grammar Summary at the end of the book.

✓ Indicating the topic with *wa*

The word **wa** has no equivalent in English, but its purpose is to highlight the main topic of a sentence by following directly after it. In general, Japanese sentences first state the topic under discussion, and then a comment is made about the topic. In effect, **wa** means 'as for, regarding'.

Nyūsu wa nan-ji desu ka. What time is the news? [*literally* Regarding the news – what time is it?]
Konsāto wa shichi-ji han desu. The concert is at 7.30.
Ikeda san wa osoi desu ne. Ikeda san is late, isn't she?

ACTIVITY 3

Can you give the Japanese for the numbers in: your car registration? your house number? your post code? Use **yon** (4), **nana** (7), and **kyū** (9).

ACTIVITY 4

Use the TV listing to answer the questions.

1 Sumimasen, eiga wa nan-ji desu ka.
2 Konsāto wa nan-ji desu ka.
3 Nyūsu wa hachi-ji desu ka.

film: 8.30
concert: 7.00
news: 9.00

🔊 Now do activities 5 and 6 on the recording.

Nan-ji kara nan-ji made desu ka

⊕ **ACTIVITY 7** is on the recording.

ACTIVITY 8

Can you say which times are mentioned? Circle the ones you hear.

3.00   3.30   5.00   7.30   8.30   9.00   9.30

DIALOGUE 2

■ Odeon eigakan desu.
○ Sumimasen, ashita wa *Sutā Wōzu* desu ne.
■ Hai, sō desu.
○ Nan-ji kara desu ka.
■ San-ji han kara desu.
○ San-ji han kara desu ne. Hai, arigatō.

▼ Hai, supōtsu sentā desu.
○ Sumimasen, pūru wa nan-ji kara, nan-ji made desu ka.
▼ Kyō desu ka.
○ Iie, kyō ja arimasen. Ashita desu.
▼ Ashita wa asa hachi-ji han kara yoru ku-ji made desu.
○ Sumimasen, mō ichido, onegai shimasu. Nan-ji made desu ka.
▼ Gogo ku-ji made desu.
○ Dōmo arigatō.

VOCABULARY	
eigakan	cinema, movie theatre
ashita	tomorrow
Sutā Wōzu	*Star Wars*
kara	from
supōtsu sentā	sports centre
pūru	swimming pool
made	until, to [*also* as far as]
kyō	today
ja arimasen	isn't, aren't
asa	morning, a.m.
yoru	evening
mō ichido	once more

✅ 'from' and 'to'

The words for 'to', 'from', 'by', 'with', etc. (in English *prepositions*), as well as **wa**, are known as particles and they always come after the word or phrase to which they refer.

> Konsāto wa **nan-ji made** desu ka. What time does the concert finish? [*literally* The concert - what time is it until?]
> Depāto wa **nan-ji kara nan-ji made** desu ka. What hours are department stores open? [*literally* Dept stores - from what time to what time are they?]

Notice that, in Japanese, words are often omitted if the meaning is obvious from the context. In the sentences above, there are no equivalents of the verbs 'open' or 'close' because the words **kara** and **made** are enough to convey the meaning.

✅ *ja arimasen* – 'isn't', 'aren't'

The negative of **desu** ('is', 'are') is the phrase **ja arimasen** ('isn't', 'aren't'), and like **desu** it comes at the end of the sentence. You may also hear the more formal **dewa arimasen** and the less formal **ja nai**.

> Iie, sō **ja arimasen**. No, it isn't.
> Kyō wa *Sutā Wōzu* **ja arimasen**. *Sutā Torekku* desu. It isn't *Star Wars* today, it's *Star Trek*.

ACTIVITY 9

Look at the times of the various activities below, and answer the questions with **Hai, sō desu** or **Iie, sō ja arimasen**.

Sports Centre	
POOL	8.30 a.m. – 9.30 p.m.
GYM	8.00 a.m. – 7.30 p.m.
SAUNA	11.00 a.m. – 8.30 p.m.

1 Pūru wa hachi-ji han kara desu ka.
2 Jimu wa hachi-ji kara roku-ji han made desu ka.
3 Sauna wa yoru jū-ichi-ji made desu ka.

🎧 Now do activities 10 and 11 on the recording.

San-ji jū-go-fun desu

ACTIVITY 12 is on the recording.

ACTIVITY 13

1 Ogawa san is in New York.	T / F
2 It's morning in New York.	T / F
3 It's 6.15 a.m. in Tokyo.	T / F
4 Takahashi san has to get up soon to go to work.	T / F

DIALOGUE 3

○ Moshi moshi.

■ Moshi moshi, Takahashi san? Ogawa desu.

○ Ogawa san? Chotto hayai desu ne.

■ Tōkyō wa hayai desu ka. Sumimasen. Nyū Yōku wa ima gogo desu. Gogo san-ji jū-go-fun desu. Tōkyō wa?

○ Tōkyō wa asa desu.

■ Ohayō gozaimasu. Nan-ji desu ka.

○ Asa roku-ji jū-go-fun desu.

■ Roku-ji jū-go-fun desu ka. Sumimasen! Demo kyō wa shigoto desu ne.

○ Iie, kyō wa shigoto ja arimasen. Yasumi desu.

VOCABULARY	
moshi moshi	hello? [*on the phone*]
chotto	a little, rather
hayai	early
Nyū Yōku	New York
gogo	afternoon, p.m.
jū-go	fifteen
fun	minutes
Tōkyō wa?	how about Tokyo?
demo	but, however
shigoto	work, job
yasumi	holiday, day off

✓ Numbers up to 99

Counting large numbers is very straightforward in Japanese. The tens are formed as follows.

10 **jū**	40 **yon-jū**	70 **nana-jū**
20 **ni-jū**	50 **go-jū**	80 **hachi-jū**
30 **san-jū**	60 **roku-jū**	90 **kyū-jū**

To count other numbers in between, simply add on the number to the tens.

21 **ni-jū-ichi**   47 **yon-jū-nana**   89 **hachi-jū-kyū**

✓ Giving the time: minutes

To give the minutes, use the number plus **-fun** (in some cases this changes to **-pun** – it's best to memorize these).

1-5 minutes   **ip-pun, ni-fun, san-pun, yon-pun, go-fun**
6-10 minutes   **rop-pun, nana-fun, hap-pun, kyū-fun, jup-pun**

Give the time with hours and minutes like this:

2.05	**ni-ji go-fun**
5.10	**go-ji jup-pun**
10.35	**jū-ji san-jū-go-fun**

✓ articles ('the, a') and plurals

In Japanese there are no words for 'a' or 'the'. Nor are there any plural forms, so **fun**, for example, may mean 'minute' or 'minutes'. It's usually clear from the context what's meant.

ACTIVITY 14

Match these times to the appropriate numbers.

1	san-ji jū-go-fun	a	6.40
2	jū-ji jup-pun	b	5.30
3	roku-ji yon-jup-pun	c	8.25
4	hachi-ji ni-jū-go-fun	d	10.10
5	go-ji han	e	3.15

🎧 Now do activities 15 and 16 on the recording.

2.4 Japanese Culture
Nihon no bunka

LEISURE AND ENTERTAINMENT

In the evenings and at weekends, city centres buzz with crowds of people meeting to go to cinemas, clubs, theatres, and concert halls. You can get information about what's on from a variety of sources. There are three English-language daily newspapers in Japan which have film and theatre reviews: the *Japan Times*, the *Daily Yomiuri*, and the *Asahi Evening News*. Most big cities also have monthly English-language magazines giving listings of what's on locally. These include not only films, plays, musicals, and concerts, but also festivals, sporting events, exhibitions, organized tours, and interesting places to visit.

Clubs (**kurabu**) and drinking places (**izakaya**) can be found open at all hours, but entertainments such as films, plays, and concerts tend to begin and end much earlier than you might expect. The first showing at cinemas is often as early as 9.00 a.m., and the last showing usually begins at around 6.30 p.m. Plays and concerts begin at about 7.00 p.m.

Some Japanese films to see:

Rashomon (1951): set in 12th-century Kyoto, four contradictory versions of an ambush, rape, and murder

Gojira [*Godzilla*] (1954): first in the series of Japanese monster movies that became popular around the world

Shichi-nin no samurai [*Seven Samurai*] (1954): Japanese samurai film, later remade in the US as *The Magnificent Seven*

Tōkyō Monogatari [*Tokyo Story*] (1953): study of a middle-class Japanese family that has come to Tokyo from the country

Kagemusha (1980): set in 16th-century Japan, a disreputable thief is spared and ends up standing in for a clan leader

Ran (1985): Japanese remake of *King Lear*, in which a warlord divides his kingdom between his three sons

O-soshiki [*Death Japanese-style*] (1985): black comedy about the family management of a funeral

Tampopo (1986): satire on the eating behaviour of the Japanese, in which a trucker wanders into a struggling noodle bar and says he can make the owner the best chef in Tokyo

Shall We Dance? (1998): humorous film about a middle-aged businessman who takes an interest in ballroom dancing.

ACTIVITY 17

Foreign films are generally shown in their original language, with Japanese subtitles, although the title will often be written in **katakana** on posters.

Using the **katakana** chart on page viii, can you work out what these videos are?

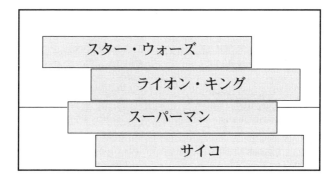

スター・ウォーズ

ライオン・キング

スーパーマン

サイコ

2.5 | Midori-ya

It's getting late, and the customers in Midori-ya are thinking
about going home. Only Fukuda san, Harada san, and the
stranger are left.

masutā	master [*form of address to owner of bar*]
mō	already
soro soro	it's time I was leaving [*literally slowly, gradually*]
pikunikku	picnic
Yoyogi Kōen de	at Yoyogi Park
mata ashita	see you tomorrow [*literally until tomorrow*]
oyasumi nasai	goodnight
watashi	I, me
Midori-ya no pikunikku	Midori-ya's picnic
daijōbu	all right
o-kyaku san	customer [*form of address used in bars, restaurants, etc.*]
namae	name
dōzo	go ahead, please do so

ACTIVITY 18

How many times do you hear the following words? Put a tick
each time you hear them.

soro soro _____   ashita _____

shigoto _____   onegai shimasu _____

ACTIVITY 19

Who said each of the following lines – Itō san (the owner of
Midori-ya), Ikeda san (one of the women customers), or
Hayashi san (the stranger)? Circle the appropriate names.
Then put the sentences in the order you hear them.

1	See you tomorrow. Goodnight.	Itō/Ikeda/Hayashi
2	It's 11.30.	Itō/Ikeda/Hayashi
3	What? You're closed?	Itō/Ikeda/Hayashi

4   Please come too, Hayashi san.   Itō/Ikeda/Hayashi
5   It's late, isn't it!   Itō/Ikeda/Hayashi

ACTIVITY 20

Here is an English summary of the conversation in Midori-ya, but there are four mistakes. Can you find them?

As Ikeda san leaves Midori-ya at 11.00, Itō san reminds her that tomorrow afternoon is the Midori-ya picnic, in Yoyogi Park.

Harada san is the next to leave. Itō san is concerned when he hears that Harada san has to go shopping tomorrow, but she says she'll be finished by midday.

The stranger, whose name is Hayashi san, decides to have one more beer. He was hoping to come for a drink tomorrow night too, so is disappointed to hear that Midori-ya will be closed. Itō san invites him to the picnic, but unfortunately Hayashi san is busy in the afternoon.

STORY TRANSCRIPT

Ikeda	Masutā, ima nan-ji desu ka.
Itō	11.30 desu.
Ikeda	Mō 11.30? Osoi desu ne. Ja, soro soro. O-kanjō, onegai shimasu.
Itō	Hai. Ikeda san, ashita wa pikunikku desu ne.
Ikeda	Hai, 2.00 desu ne. Yoyogi Kōen de.
Itō	Sō desu.
Ikeda	Ja, mata ashita. Oyasumi nasai.
Itō	Harada san, biiru wa?
Harada	Iie, watashi mo soro soro. Asa wa shigoto desu.
Itō	Shigoto desu ka. Demo ashita wa Midori-ya no pikunikku desu yo.
Harada	Daijōbu desu yo. Shigoto wa 12.00 made.
Itō	Sō desu ka. Ja, o-kanjō desu ka.
Harada	Hai, onegai shimasu. Ja, oyasumi nasai.
Itō	O-kyaku san, biiru wa?
Stranger	Sō desu ne. Iie, watashi mo soro soro.
Itō	Hai. O-kanjō.
Stranger	Hai. Ja, ashita ne.
Itō	A, o-kyaku san, sumimasen ga, ashita Midori-ya wa yasumi desu.
Stranger	E? Yasumi desu ka.
Itō	Ē, ashita wa Midori-ya no pikunikku desu.
Stranger	Sō desu ka. Ja ...
Itō	Sumimasen ga, o-kyaku san no o-namae wa?
Stranger	Hayashi desu.
Itō	Sumimasen, mō ichido.
Stranger	Hayashi desu.
Itō	Ja, Hayashi san mo dōzo.
Stranger	Ii desu ka.
Itō	Hai, ii desu yo.
Stranger	Arigatō. Ja, ashita. 2.00, Yoyogi Kōen de.

Test

Now it's time to test your progress in Unit 2.

1 Match the phrases and sentences to their Japanese equivalents. (There's one English phrase too many.)

1 Hello?
2 No, it isn't.
3 What time?
4 It's early, isn't it?
5 The bill, please.
6 It's late, isn't it?
7 Once more.

a Mō ichido.
b Osoi desu ne.
c Moshi moshi.
d O-kanjō, onegai shimasu.
e Hayai desu ne.
f Iie, sō ja arimasen.

6

2 How would you give these times in Japanese?

1　1.30

2　4.15

3　7.00

4　20.20

5　22.40

6　23.55

12

3 How would you tell someone the opening and closing times of the following places?

1 department store: 10.00 – 8.00

2 bank: 9.00 – 3.00

3 sports centre: 8.30 – 9.45

6

4 Put these words in order to make sentences.

    1 arimasen / yasumi / kyō / ja / wa
    2 desu / wa / nan-ji / konsāto / ka / kara
    3 wa / 10.00 / depāto / desu / asa / kara
    4 made / wa / pūru / 7.00 / gogo / desu
    5 shigoto / desu / wa / ka / ashita

`10`

5 Answer these questions about where you are now.

    1 Ima asa desu ka. Gogo desu ka.
    2 Ima nan-ji desu ka.
    3 Kyō wa yasumi desu ka.

`6`

6 How would you give the following in Japanese?

    1 What time does the concert begin?
    2 I work from 9.00 to 5.30.
    3 Today is rather cold, isn't it?
    4 The concert isn't today. It's tomorrow.
    5 Once more, please.

`10`

TOTAL SCORE `50`

If you scored less than 40, look at the Language Building sections again before completing the Summary on page 28.

Summary 2

 Now try this final test summarizing the main points covered in this unit. You can check your answers on the recording.

How would you:
1 count to ten?
2 ask what time it is now?
3 tell someone the film starts at 7.15?
4 say the pool closes at 5.00?
5 say you're not working tomorrow?
6 ask someone to repeat what he said?
7 ask if it's morning or afternoon in Tokyo right now?
8 comment that it's early, or late?

REVISION

Before moving on to Unit 3, which covers shopping and money, make sure you're familiar with the numbers up to 99. You'll need these for giving and understanding prices. Here are a few ways you might practise:

– count backwards from 10 to 1
– describe the opening and closing times of your local library, banks, shops, bars, etc.
– get someone to write down a random sequence of numbers and see how quickly you can say them

Money, money, money
Ikura desu ka

LEARNING JAPANESE 3

Always try listening to the recordings several times before looking at the audioscript in your book. When you first listen, it may feel as though you haven't understood very much, but try doing the activities anyway. The activities are structured to help you to understand the dialogues and to work out what's happening for yourself. Write down some kind of answer, and don't look at the answer key until you've had a go, even if you consider it only to be a guess. Guesswork is an important strategy in learning a new language and you'll probably be pleasantly surprised at how often you're right.

Now start the recording for Unit 3.

3.1 At the post office
Yūbinkyoku de

ACTIVITY 1 is on the recording.

ACTIVITY 2

1 Where does Fukuda san want to send the letter?
2 How much does it cost to send a postcard to the USA?
3 How many postcards does she send?

DIALOGUE 1

○ Kore, Igirisu made, onegai shimasu.
■ Hai, kōkūbin desu ne.
○ Hai, onegai shimasu.
■ Kore wa … ¥230 (ni-hyaku san-jū en) desu.
○ Sore kara, hagaki wa Amerika made ikura desu ka.
■ Hagaki desu ka. ¥150 (hyaku go-jū en) desu.
○ Ja, ¥150 kitte o san-mai kudasai.
■ Hai, san-mai desu ne. Ii desu ka.
○ Hai.
■ Zenbu de, ¥680 (rop-pyaku hachi-jū en) desu.

VOCABULARY

yūbinkyoku de	at the post office
kore	this item
Igirisu	England, Britain
kōkūbin	air mail
hyaku	hundred
en	yen
sore kara	and also, then
hagaki	postcard
Amerika	America, USA
ikura	how much?
kitte	stamp
-mai	*counter for flat objects*
zenbu de	altogether

✓ Counting in hundreds

The word for 'hundred' is **hyaku** but this sometimes changes to **-byaku** or **-pyaku** depending on the sound which comes before it.

100	**hyaku**	400	**yon-hyaku**	700	**nana-hyaku**
200	**ni-hyaku**	500	**go-hyaku**	800	**hap-pyaku**
300	**san-byaku**	600	**rop-pyaku**	900	**kyū-hyaku**

✓ Talking about 'this' and 'that' with *kore, sore, are*

In English we divide things into the two groups 'this' and 'that', but in Japanese there are three groups: **kore** 'this one near me', **sore** 'that one near you', and **are** 'that one over there'.

Kore o kudasai. I'll have this, please.
Sore wa ikura desu ka. How much is that?
Are wa Itō san desu ka. Is that Itō san over there?

✓ Counting flat objects with the suffix *-mai*

We sometimes use special counters in English depending on what we're counting, e.g. a **bar** of chocolate or soap, a **piece** of paper or cake. In Japanese there are many different counters for objects of different shapes. Flat objects such as stamps (**kitte**), letters (**tegami**), CDs (**shii dii**), pizzas (**piza**), and postcards (**hagaki**) are counted with the suffix **-mai**.

¥100 kitte o **san-mai** kudasai. Three 100-yen stamps, please.
Earoguramu o **go-mai** kudasai. Five aerograms, please.

ACTIVITY 3

How would you respond if someone asked you the price of these items?

1 postcard – ¥100
2 aerogram – ¥160
3 ice cream – ¥230

Now do activities 4 and 5 on the recording.

Going shopping

Kaimono

ACTIVITY 6 is on the recording.

ACTIVITY 7

Which of these activities occur?

1 Fukuda san suggests sunglasses as a birthday present.
2 Fukuda san points out some Italian sunglasses.
3 Maruyama san says they are rather expensive.
4 Maruyama san buys some children's sunglasses.

DIALOGUE 2

○ Uōkuman, iyaringu, wain. … A, kore wa dō desu ka.
■ Nan desu ka. Megane?
○ Iie, chigaimasu. Sangurasu desu.
■ Sangurasu desu ka. Ikura desu ka.
○ ¥20,000 (ni-man en) desu.
■ ¥20,000!? Chotto takai desu ne.
○ Demo Itaria no sangurasu desu yo.
■ Sore wa dō desu ka. Sore wa ¥4,500 (yon-sen go-hyaku en) desu. Ii desu ne.
○ Maruyama san, sore wa kodomo no sangurasu desu yo.
■ A, sō desu ka.

VOCABULARY	
kaimono	shopping
uōkuman	Walkman, personal stereo
iyaringu	earrings
wain	wine
dō	how about?
nan	what?
megane	glasses
chigaimasu	be different, incorrect
sangurasu	sunglasses
man	ten thousand
takai	expensive [*also* high, tall]
Itaria no	Italian
yo	you know [*emphasizes the speaker's strong opinion*]
sen	thousand
kodomo no	children's

✓ Counting in thousands and ten thousands

The word for 'thousand' is **sen**. Only the words for 3,000 and 8,000 change slightly: **san-zen** and **has-sen**. In Japanese there is also a unit of ten thousand: **man**.

¥10,000	**ichi-man en**
¥15,000	**ichi-man go-sen en**
¥33,500	**san-man san-zen go-hyaku en**

✓ Using *no* to show belonging

You can add **no** after a noun to show possession in much the same way that -'s is used in English.

| **Fukuda san no** tokei | Fukuda san's watch |
| **Tōkyō no** depāto | Tokyo's department stores |

It can also be used generally as a link word to show that the first noun gives more information about the following noun.

kodomo no uōkuman	a personal stereo for children
	[*literally* a children's personal stereo]
Rondon no o-miyage	a souvenir of London
	[*literally* a London's souvenir]

✓ Saying 'it isn't' with *chigaimasu* and *ja arimasen*

The verb **chigaimasu** means 'it's different' so it's an indirect way of correcting someone.

Furansu no wain desu ka. Iie, **chigaimasu**. Itaria no wain desu.
Is it French wine? No, it's not. It's Italian wine.

Or you can use **ja arimasen** ('isn't', 'aren't'). You need to include the subject with this expression.

Iie, **Furansu no wain ja arimasen**. Itaria no wain desu.
No, it's not French wine. It's Italian wine.

ACTIVITY 8

A friend needs ideas for a present. Suggest these items using the structure **... dō desu ka**.

1　French wine
2　a jazz (**jazu**) CD
3　a Japanese watch
4　a souvenir of Tokyo

🎧 Now do activities 9 and 10 on the recording.

3.3 Asking if something is available
Arimasu ka

ACTIVITY 11 is on the recording.

ACTIVITY 12

1 Fukuda san suggests buying a purse.	T / F
2 Maruyama san doesn't like the first one because it's too big.	T / F
3 There aren't any smaller purses.	T / F
4 The purse costs ¥23,000.	T / F
5 Maruyama san doesn't have enough money.	T / F

DIALOGUE 3

○ Saifu wa dō desu ka, Maruyama san?

■ Ii desu ne.

○ Iroiro arimasu yo. Kore wa dō desu ka.

■ Chotto ōkii desu ne.

○ Ōkii desu ka. Motto chiisai saifu wa takusan arimasu yo. Kore wa?

■ Sore wa chotto …

○ Maruyama san! Mō 5.30 desu yo!

■ Sō desu ka. Sumimasen. Ja, kore ni shimasu.

○ Hai. (*calling to sales clerk*) Sumimasen! Kore o kudasai.

▼ Hai, ¥23,000 (ni-man san-zenen en) de gozaimasu.

■ ¥23,000?! Arimasen yo.

VOCABULARY

saifu	purse, wallet
iroiro	all sorts of, many kinds of
arimasu	there is, there are
ōkii	big
motto	more
chiisai	small
takusan	many, lots of
… ni shimasu	I'll/We'll have …..
de gozaimasu	is, are [*polite version of* desu]
arimasen	don't/doesn't have

✅ Asking for something with *arimasu*

Use **arimasu** ('there is / are', 'have') to ask if a store has an item, or if a place has certain facilities. Verbs in their everyday, polite form always end in **-masu** in the present tense, and come at the end of the sentence. This verb ending is the same whoever is doing the action, unlike English ('you have', 'he has', etc.).

| Yūbinkyoku wa **arimasu** ka. | Is there a post office? |
| Firumu wa **arimasu** ka. | Do you have any films? |

In the negative, the ending changes to **-masen**.

| Kamera wa **arimasen**. | I don't have a camera. |

✅ Shop talk with *gozaimasu, de gozaimasu*

People who work in shops, hotels, and restaurants use very polite language to the customers. You will often hear **de gozaimasu** (the formal equivalent of **desu**) and **gozaimasu / gozaimasen** (equivalent to **arimasu / arimasen**). You won't need to use these forms yourself, but it is useful to be able to recognize them.

Motto chiisai T-shatsu wa **arimasu** ka. Do you have any smaller T-shirts?

Sumimasen ga, **gozaimasen**. I'm sorry, but we don't.

ACTIVITY 13

Imagine you're in the small shop in your Tokyo hotel. How would you ask if they sell these items?

> stamps
> postcards of Tokyo
> film
> children's T-shirts

ACTIVITY 14

The assistant in the shop has shown you various items to choose from. Tell her you've decided on:

1 the postcards of the hotel (*hoteru*)
2 the 'Godzilla' T-shirts

🎧 Now do activities 15 and 16 on the recording.

3.4 Japanese Culture
Nihon no bunka

SHOPPING JAPANESE-STYLE

Offices, banks, and post offices are all closed on Sundays, but for the department stores it's the busiest and most profitable day of the week. There are no barriers to Sunday trading, and the department stores are more than happy to cater to the huge number of people who choose to spend their free time shopping.

Japanese department stores are fascinating places, and there are lots of things to see and do even for those who don't like shopping. They cater for everyone. Of course, there are the usual floors devoted to clothing, electrical goods, food, toys, and sporting goods. But in addition, there may be a whole floor of restaurants, ranging from fast food and sandwich bars to the most elegant of expensive restaurants. On another floor there'll probably be an art gallery or museum where you can see famous works of art on loan from some of the finest art galleries in the world. On the roof you're likely to find a children's playground, a pet centre, and, in the summer, maybe a beer garden.

Some department stores also run culture centres, so there may be a floor devoted entirely to classrooms, and you can join courses to learn anything from French to flower arranging to pottery. There may even be tennis courts where you can take tennis lessons.

Wherever you go in a Japanese department store, you will be assured of the highest degree of service and courtesy, and every purchase will be carefully and beautifully wrapped. And of course, you will always know you are welcome from the number of times you hear **irasshaimase!** ('Welcome!').

Eight big department stores

Mitsukoshi	Matsuzakaya
Seibu	Isetan
Tōkyū	Tōbu
Takashimaya	Hankyū

ACTIVITY 17

Some of the larger department stores provide store guides in English for foreign visitors, but these may not always be available. Look at the store guide below, and first circle all the items which are in **katakana**. Then, using the **katakana** chart on page viii, see if you can work out what they mean.

R （ゲームコーナー、ビヤガーデン）

5 （アートギャラリー、レストラン）

  （着物、帯）

4 （おもちゃ、かばん）（水着）

  （テニスウェア、ゴルフウェア）

3 （紳士靴下）

  （スーツ、コート、シャツ）

2 （ブラウス、ジーンズ、ナイトウェア、エプロン）

1 （婦人靴、紳士靴、化粧品）

  （アクセサリー、ハンカチーフ、ネクタイ、ベルト）

B1 （肉、野菜、魚）

  （フルーツ、コーヒー、ティー）

THE PICNIC
MIDORI-YA NO PIKUNIKKU – 1

The owner of the bar Midori-ya has organized a picnic for his regular customers. He's now in the park unpacking the food and drink ready for the picnic, waiting for the others to arrive.

sushi	*bite-sized delicacies served on vinagered rice*
sukoshi	a little, small amount
mina san	everyone
(o-)sake	sake [*rice wine*]
kinō	yesterday
koko	here, this place
tsuyoi	strong
nen	year [*also counter for years*]
mada	not yet
tanoshii	fun, enjoyable
mata	again
hen-na	strange, peculiar
hito	person

ACTIVITY 18

Match the names to their characters.

1	Itō san	a	a cheerful young woman, a regular customer at Midori-ya
2	Harada san	b	a new male customer at Midori-ya
3	Ikeda san	c	the owner of Midori-ya
4	Hayashi san	d	a grumpy, older woman, a regular customer at Midori-ya

ACTIVITY 19

Listen to the story, and rearrange the following events in the order they occur.

1 ___ everyone has a beer
2 ___ Harada san decides that Hayashi san is very odd
3 ___ Ikeda san comments on how strong Itō san is
4 ___ Ikeda san arrives and greets everyone
5 ___ Hayashi san gives some information about the film *Picnic*

6 ___ Itō san introduces Hayashi san, the new customer at Midori-ya

7 ___ Hayashi san gives the date of the film *Superman*

ACTIVITY 20

These statements are all slightly wrong. Listen again and correct them.

1 Everyone drinks some sake.

2 Harada san thinks it's too cold to drink beer.

3 Ikeda san thinks picnics are interesting.

4 Hayashi san seems like a very interesting person.

STORY TRANSCRIPT

Harada	Konnichiwa.
Itō	A, Harada san. Dōzo, dōzo.
Harada	Arigatō. Kore wa watashi no jūsu desu. Dōzo. Sore kara, chiizu, piza, sushi. Sukoshi dōzo.
Itō	Arigatō.
Ikeda	Mina san, konnichiwa.
Itō	A, Ikeda san, konnichiwa.
Ikeda	Ii tenki desu ne!
Itō	Sō desu ne.
Hayashi	Konnichiwa!
Itō	A, are wa Hayashi san desu.
Ikeda	Hayashi san?
Itō	Hai, kinō no o-kyakusan. Namae wa Hayashi san desu.
Hayashi	Konnichiwa.
Itō	Konnichiwa. A, Ikeda san, Harada san, Hayashi san desu.
Harada/Ikeda	Dōzo yoroshiku.
Hayashi	Hayashi desu. Yoroshiku.
Itō	Sa, biiru to sake wa .... koko desu yo.
Ikeda	Masutā! Daijōbu desu ka. Masutā wa tsuyoi desu ne. Sūpaman desu ne.
Hayashi	1978-nen.
Harada	E? Nan desu ka, Hayashi san.
Hayashi	*Sūpaman*. Amerika no eiga desu. 1978-nen desu.
Itō	Hai. Ja, mina san, biiru wa dō desu ka. Harada san?
Harada	Biiru? Chotto hayai desu ne. Mada 2.00 desu yo.
Itō	Ii desu yo. Dōzo.
Harada	Hai, arigatō.
Itō	Mina san mo, dōzo.
Itō	Kanpai.
All	Kanpai.
Ikeda	A, pikunikku wa tanoshii desu ne.
Hayashi	Ii eiga desu ne.
Ikeda	E? Nan desu ka, Hayashi san.
Hayashi	*Pikunikku*. Eiga no namae desu. Amerika no eiga. 1955-nen desu.
Ikeda	Sō desu ka. Mata eiga no namae desu ka.
Harada	Hen-na hito.

Test

Now it's time to test your progress in Unit 3.

1 How would you tell someone how much these items cost?

    1   film – ¥850

    2   child's T-shirt – ¥3,450

    3   small wallet – ¥9,500

    4   large wallet – ¥14,200

    5   Italian sunglasses – ¥24,800

| 6 |

2 Choose the appropriate word from the brackets to complete the sentences.

1   ¥200 kitte (wa / o) san-mai kudasai.
2   Motto chiisai saifu wa (ja arimasen / arimasen).
3   Kodomo (wa / no) sangurasu wa ¥1,200 desu.
4   Sumimasen ga, firumu wa (arimasu / desu) ka.
5   Iie, kore wa watashi no uōkuman (ja arimasen / chigaimasu).
6   Nihon no tokei wa (dō / sō) desu ka.

| 5 |

3 Match the questions and answers.
(Be careful, there's one answer too many.)

1   Iyaringu wa ikura desu ka.   a   Iie, chigaimasu.
2   Sumimasen ga, motto chiisai   b   Ii desu ne.
    T-shatsu wa arimasu ka.   c   ¥750 desu.
3   Kore wa nan desu ka.   d   Hai, gozaimasu.
4   Are wa Ikeda san no kamera   e   Ōkii desu.
    desu ka.   f   T-shatsu desu.
5   Tōkyō no o-miyage wa dō
    desu ka.

| 10 |

4 Put these sentences in the correct order to make a conversation in a hotel souvenir shop.

1 Hai, gozaimasu.

2 Sumimasen ga, kitte wa gozaimasen.

3 Ja, san-mai kudasai. Kitte wa arimasu ka.

4 Ii desu ne. Ikura desu ka.

5 Sumimasen, hoteru no hagaki wa arimasu ka.

6 ¥100 de gozaimasu.

| | 6 |

5 Nothing goes right on today's shopping trip. How would you comment that:

1 the cameras are rather expensive?
2 the T-shirts are rather small?
3 the sunglasses are rather large?
4 the post office is rather hot?

| | 8 |

6 What's the Japanese for:

1 Excuse me, but do you have any smaller purses?
2 How much is that over there?
3 Three aerograms, please.
4 Are these your sunglasses, Fukuda san?
5 Is that French wine?
6 They aren't Japanese watches.

| | 10 |

TOTAL SCORE | 45 |

If you scored less than 35, look at the Language Building sections again before completing the Summary on page 42.

Summary 3

Now try this final test summarizing the main points covered in this unit. You can check your answers on the recording.

How would you:

1 ask for two ¥120 stamps?
2 ask how much it is to send a postcard to England?
3 say the price ¥25,000?
4 suggest T-shirts to someone who wants to buy souvenirs for her children?
5 comment that they're rather expensive?
6 say that someone is mistaken in what they've just said?
7 ask if this is a Japanese camera?
8 ask in a shop if they sell films?
9 say you'll have the small watch?
10 ask in a shop if they have any larger T-shirts?

REVISION

The next section is a review of the first three units, so now is a good time to go back and revise those areas you're not sure about. Try listening to the conversations from the first three units without looking at the text, and see how much you can now understand.

Test yourself on the vocabulary that's been introduced so far.

To review numbers, ask a friend to write out some prices, and see if you can read them aloud in Japanese as quickly as they are written.

Review 1

VOCABULARY

1 Look at these expressions. Which ones are for greeting people, and which ones are for saying goodbye?

ohayō gozaimasu

mata ashita

konnichiwa

konbanwa

oyasumi nasai

2 Look at the menu and decide whether the following statements are true or false. For those which are false, give the correct version in Japanese.

coffee ¥320	ice cream ¥280
milk ¥300	cheese sandwich ¥320
cola ¥290	hamburger ¥450
orange juice ¥350	spaghetti ¥560

1 Kōra wa ni-hyaku kyū-jū en desu.   T / F
2 Aisu kuriimu wa ni-hyaku yon-jū en desu. T / F
3 Kōhii wa ni-hyaku san-jū en desu.   T / F
4 Supagetti wa go-hyaku roku-jū en desu.   T / F
5 Orenji jūsu wa san-byaku go-jū en desu.   T / F
6 Chiizu sando wa ni-hyaku jū en desu.   T / F

Answers to the Review sections are in the Answer section on p. 213.

3 Which are the odd ones out in these groups?

1 sake / jūsu / hanbāgā / wain / kōhii
2 ikura / nan-ji / dō / ima / nani
3 kodomo / hoteru / ginkō / yūbinkyoku / depāto
4 oishii / tanoshii / takai / hayai / tegami
5 go / to / san / hyaku / sen

GRAMMAR AND USAGE

4 Choose the best response to these questions.

1 Igirisu made ikura desu ka.
  a Kōkūbin desu ka.
  b Hai, sō desu.
2 Nyūsu wa nan-ji desu ka.
  a Iie, sō ja arimasen.
  b Ku-ji han desu.
3 Kyō wa atsui desu ne.
  a Sō desu ne.
  b Iie, kyō ja arimasen.
4 Sumimasen, motto chiisai T-shatsu wa arimasu ka.
  a Gozaimasu.
  b Kore wa T-shatsu desu.
5 Ashita wa shigoto desu ka.
  a Iie, yasumi desu.
  b Iie, yasumi ja arimasen.

5 Complete these sentences with **desu**, **ja arimasen**, **arimasu**, or **arimasen**.

1 Shii dii wa takusan _____ ka.
2 Shii dii wa ichi-mai ikura _____ ka.
3 Sumimasen ga, hagaki wa _____.
4 Kyō wa atsui _____ ne.
5 Sumimasen ga, Itaria no wain wa _____ ka.
6 Watashi no namae wa Shimada _____. Yamada _____.

6 Choose the most appropriate word to complete these sentences.

1 Eiga wa nan-ji kara (desu / arimasu) ka.
2 Kōhii to chiizu sando o (kudasai / desu).
3 Eiga wa nan-ji (kore / kara) desu ka.
4 Rondon (no / wa) o-miyage wa takai desu ne.
5 Kodomo no namae wa (doko / nan) desu ka.

7 You've forgotten the time of the film you're going to see tomorrow. Call the cinema and listen to the recorded message, and then answer the questions.

1 What's the name of today's film?
2 How many times is it showing today?
3 What time does the first show begin?
4 What's the name of the film starting tomorrow?
5 What time does the second show begin?

8 Listen to two people out shopping, and mark any differences between what you hear and the dialogue below. (There are 5 differences altogether.)

A T-shatsu wa dō desu ka. Iroiro arimasu yo.
B Ii desu ne.
A Kore wa dō desu ka.
B Ikura desu ka. ¥5,000? Chotto takai desu ne.
A Sō desu ne. Ja, kore wa? A, kore wa chotto chiisai desu.
B Motto ōkii T-shatsu wa arimasu yo. Kore wa dō desu ka.
A ¥2,450 desu ne. Hai, kore ni shimasu.

🎧 **SPEAKING**

9 Here are some of the family names you have come across in the first three units. How do you pronounce them? Read them aloud, and then listen to the audio to check your pronunciation.

1 Shimada san	2 Ikeda san

3 Hayashi san	4 Kimura san

10 A friend has called to suggest meeting up tomorrow, Saturday. Use the cues below to prepare your side of the conversation, then use the recording to test yourself.

Fukuda	Moshi moshi, Fukuda desu.
You	(Greet Fukuda san – it's morning.)
Fukuda	Ashita wa yasumi desu ka.
You	(Say yes, it is.)
Fukuda	Ja, ashita, tenisu wa dō desu ka.
You	(Tennis? You think it's a bit cold for tennis.)
Fukuda	Un, sō desu ne. Ja, eiga wa dō desu ka. Ashita wa *Hoteru* desu.
You	(Say you think *Hotel* is a good film. Ask what time it begins.)
Fukuda	5.30 kara desu.

Now try that dialogue again, without referring to the book.

11 You're going to hear some questions on the recording. The questions will be about the following topics, but in a different order. You'll be asked about:

- your name
- if it's morning
- if you're working or not today
- if it's cold today
- if you have a Japanese camera
- the number of CDs you have

Use this list to prepare what you're going to say, then use the recording to test yourself.

4

Out and about
Asoko ni arimasu

OBJECTIVES

In this unit, you'll learn how to:

- ✓ get by when taking a taxi
- ✓ ask about the location of various places
- ✓ understand where places are

And cover the following grammar and language:

- ✓ **... arimasu** to show the location of objects
- ✓ **... imasu** to show the location of people
- ✓ **koko / soko / asoko** ('here' / 'there' / 'over there')
- ✓ **kono / sono / ano** ('this' / 'that' / 'that ... over there')
- ✓ prepositions
- ✓ the sentence subject indicator **ga**

LEARNING JAPANESE 4

To help you remember vocabulary, buy a small notebook and try organizing vocabulary in topic areas – some people find that a context for memorizing words makes it easier to remember them. Look at the notebook at spare moments during the day, and get someone to test you regularly.

Some people find they can remember vocabulary better when they hear it. Once you've made your list of related words, try recording yourself reading them, and then play the cassette in the car or at home whenever you have free time.

Now start the recording for Unit 4.

Taking a taxi

Takushii de

ACTIVITY 1 is on the recording.

ACTIVITY 2

1 The taxi driver isn't sure where the Plaza Hotel is. T / F
2 Fukuda san doesn't know the address. T / F
3 The hotel is near a station. T / F
4 The hotel is on the right. T / F

DIALOGUE 1

○ Nakano no Puraza Hoteru made onegai shimasu.
■ Hai, Nakano desu ne. Eki no chikaku desu ka.
○ Wakarimasen. Chotto matte kudasai. Dōzo. Hoteru no jūsho wa koko ni arimasu.
■ A, hai, wakarimashita. Eki no chikaku ni arimasu ne.

■ Nakano eki wa koko desu ga. ...
○ A, Puraza Hoteru wa asoko ni arimasu.
■ Doko desu ka.
○ Migi ni arimasu yo.
■ A, hai. Sō desu ne.

VOCABULARY	
takushii de	by taxi
eki	train station
chikaku	nearby, (in) the local area
wakarimasen	I don't know [*also* I don't understand]
chotto matte kudasai	just a moment, please
jūsho	address
ni	in, at
wakarimashita	I see [*also* I understand]
asoko	over there
doko	where?
migi	the right

✓ Giving location with *ni arimasu*

To say where something is, use the structure **... ni arimasu** ('It's located in ...'). The word **ni** ('in', 'at') follows directly after the word or phrase for the place.

Kaisha wa **Rondon ni** arimasu. My office is in London.
Uchi wa **Meguro ni** arimasu. My house is in Meguro.
Daigaku wa **hidari ni** arimasu. The university is on the left.

✓ 'Here' and 'there' with *koko / soko / asoko*

In Unit 3 we saw how things are divided into the three groups **kore**, **sore**, **are** depending on where they are. Another group of words beginning with **ko-**, **so-**, **a-** describe location: **koko** ('here', 'this place near me'), **soko** ('there', 'that place near you'), and **asoko** ('that place over there', at a distance from both of us').

Saito san no sangurasu wa **koko** ni arimasu yo. Your sunglasses are over here, Saito san.
Watashi no kamera wa **soko** ni arimasu ka. Is my camera there (by you)?
Tōkyō eki wa **asoko** ni arimasu. Tokyo station is over there.

ACTIVITY 3

Now it's your turn to take a taxi. You want to go to Maruzen, a bookstore which sells English books. Complete the conversation below.

You   1   Ask the driver to take you to Maruzen.

_____

Driver   Ginza ni arimasu ne.
You   2   You don't know if it's in Ginza or not.

_____

     3   Show him Maruzen's card and point out the address.

_____

Driver   Hai, wakarimashita.
You   4   Tell the taxi driver when you see Maruzen over there.

_____

     5   Tell him it's on the left.

_____

🎧 Now do activities 4 and 5 on the recording.

Describing where a place is
Eki no mae ni arimasu

ACTIVITY 6 is on the recording.

ACTIVITY 7

Which letters on the map below correspond to the police box and Nakano Hall?

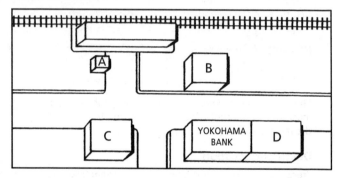

DIALOGUE 2

○ Mō 7.15 desu yo.

■ Daijōbu desu. Asoko ni Puraza Hoteru ga arimasu ne.
Nakano Hōru wa Puraza Hoteru no ushiro ni arimasu.

○ Wada san, are wa Puraza Hoteru ja arimasen. Depāto desu.

■ A, sō desu ne.

○ A, eki no mae ni kōban ga arimasu.
… Sumimasen, Nakano Hōru wa doko ni arimasu ka.

▼ Nakano Hōru desu ka. Asoko ni Yokohama Ginkō ga
arimasu ne. Nakano Hōru wa ginkō no tonari ni arimasu.

○ Hai. Dōmo arigatō.

■ Ogawa san! Chotto matte!

VOCABULARY	
ga	[*indicates subject of sentence*]
Nakana Hōru	Nakano Hall
Puraza Hoteru no ushiro	behind the Plaza Hotel
eki no mae ni	in front of the station
kōban	police box [*see 4.4*]
tonari	next to
chotto matte	just a minute!

✓ Indicating the subject with *ga*

The word **ga** is used to point out the subject of a sentence, especially when the information is being introduced for the first time and needs to be emphasized.

> Ano depáto ni **kissaten ga** arimasu. **Kissaten wa** totemo oishii desu.
> There is a coffee shop in that department store. The coffee shop is really good [*literally* delicious].

In the first sentence the subject of the coffee shop is introduced for the first time. In the second, we find out something more about the coffee shop (which was introduced in the first sentence).

Now compare these sentences.

> Asoko ni **eki ga** arimasu. Over there is **a station**.
> **Eki wa** asoko ni arimasu. **The station** is over there.

The difference between **wa** and **ga** is very subtle, so don't worry too much if it seems confusing at the moment. It will gradually become clear the more you hear it.

✓ Describing location

Prepositions (e.g. 'next to', 'in front of', 'inside') come after the name of the place they refer to, so the word order for describing the location of a place is rather like 'the bank's front' – **ginkó no mae**.

> Takushii wa **ginkó no mae** ni arimasu. The taxi's in front of the bank.
> [*literally* the taxi – it's at the bank's front]

ACTIVITY 8

Imagine you're describing the local area to a stranger. How would you explain where the following places are?

1 park
2 police box
3 coffee shop
4 restaurant
5 cinema

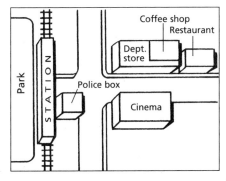

 Now do activities 9 and 10 on the recording.

Doko ni imasu ka

🔊 **ACTIVITY 11** is on the recording.

ACTIVITY 12

1 Is Ogawa san already in Meguro?
2 Does Ogawa san still have the map?
3 What two buildings can Ogawa san see?
4 What two things does Wada san ask about to confirm where she is?

DIALOGUE 3

○ Moshi moshi, Ogawa desu ga.
■ Ogawa san! Ima doko ni imasu ka.
○ Wakarimasen. Meguro ni imasu ga …
■ Wakarimasen ka. Demo chizu ga arimasu ne.
○ Ē, arimasu ga, kono chizu wa chotto …
■ Ja, sono chikaku ni nani ga arimasu ka.
○ Sō desu ne. Mukai ni, sūpā ga arimasu. Sono sūpā no tonari ni eigakan ga arimasu.
■ A, wakarimashita. Sūpā no mae ni shingo ga arimasu ne. Sore kara, eigakan no mae ni kōban ga arimasu.
○ Iie, shingo wa arimasen. Kōban mo arimasen.
■ A, sō desu ka. Ja, watashi mo wakarimasen.

VOCABULARY

imasu	be, exist [*used with people and other living things*]
chizu	map
mukai	opposite
sūpā	supermarket
sono	that [*adjective*]
shingō	traffic signals

✓ Using *imasu* with people and other living things

The verb **arimasu** ('be', 'exist') is only used to describe the location of objects. When talking about living animate things such as people, animals, or birds (but not plants), use **imasu**.

Kōen ni kodomo ga takusan imasu ne. There are a lot of children in the park, aren't there?
Neko wa imasu ka. Do you have a cat? [*literally* Is there a cat?]

✓ Describing this and that item with *kono / sono / ano*

In English we can use the words 'this' and 'that' as both pronouns ('**this** is expensive') and adjectives ('**this steak** is expensive'), but this is not the case in Japanese. You've already learned the pronouns **kore, sore, are**. The corresponding adjectives are **kono, sono, ano**. These words cannot stand alone, but must always be followed by the name of the object they're referring to.

Ano hito wa Ikeda san desu ka. Is that person Ikeda san?
Kono chikaku ni, ginkō wa arimasu ka. Is there a bank in this area?

✓ More on *ga*

Use **wa** with negatives and questions, but always use **ga** after question words, such as **nani, doko**.

Aisu kuriimu wa, **nani ga** arimasu ka. What kinds of ice cream do you have? [*literally* ice cream – what is there?]

Resutoran wa, **doko ga** ii desu ka. Where's a good restaurant?

ACTIVITY 13

Answer these questions about yourself and your home.

1 Ima doko ni imasu ka.
2 Kodomo wa imasu ka.
3 Uchi no naka ni neko wa imasu ka. Neko no namae wa nan desu ka.
4 Uchi wa doko ni arimasu ka.
5 Uchi no chikaku ni, nani ga arimasu ka. Kōen wa arimasu ka.

🎧 Now do activities 14 and 15 on the recording.

4.4 Japanese Culture
Nihon no bunka

FINDING AN ADDRESS

It can be difficult even for Japanese people to find a place just from its address, because of the confusing system of numbering buildings, and because only the major streets and thoroughfares are named. Japanese addresses are based on the area, beginning with the largest designation, and then dividing and sub-dividing this into ever-smaller areas. Houses used to be numbered in the order in which they were built, rather than in physical sequence, so even the number of a house is no guide to what might be next door to it.

People generally have to depend on maps to find a place. There are large maps of the local area outside stations and at intervals along the streets. The many small police boxes, or **kōban**, located near train stations and major intersections also have large maps of the area, and one of the main tasks of the policemen who run the **kōban** is to give directions to passers-by. Some places, such as restaurants and hotels, print maps on their business cards, so it's useful to carry these to show to your taxi driver.

Mieko Koyama
2-19-4 Minami-cho
Miyamae-ku
Kawasaki-shi
Kanagawa-ken

This address shows that Ms Koyama lives in the city (**-shi**) of Kawasaki, which is in the prefecture (**-ken**) of Kanagawa. Large cities are divided into wards (**-ku**) and these are further divided into areas given individual names, often with the suffix **-chō**. These areas are then divided into numbered areas called **chōme**, and the **chōme** are further divided into **banchi**. The address above is in 19-4 **banchi**, in the area of 2-chōme.

The nine largest cities in Japan:

Tōkyō   Kōbe
Yokohama   Kyōto
Ōsaka   Kawasaki
Nagoya   Hiroshima
Sapporo

ACTIVITY 16

The nine largest cities in Japan are marked on the map, but in kanji characters. Can you match the kanji to the city names above?

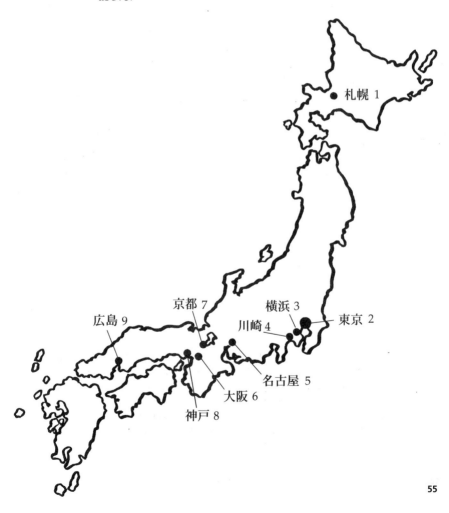

札幌 1
京都 7
横浜 3
東京 2
川崎 4
広島 9
名古屋 5
大阪 6
神戸 8

THE PICNIC CONTINUES
MIDORI-YA NO PIKUNIKKU – 2

Everyone is having a good time at the picnic, but the combination of warm sun, plentiful food, and copious amounts of drink is taking its toll. The gentle sound of snoring is apparent.

dare	who?
bakari	only, nothing but
tokorode	by the way
ki no ue	top of the tree
ki no shita	under the tree [*also* bottom of the tree]
minna	everybody [*also* everything]
yopparaimashita	is/are drunk
kaban	bag
bideo	video
shizuka	quiet, peaceful

ACTIVITY 17

Listen for these events in the dialogue, and number them in the order they occur.

a ___ Ikeda san sees someone asleep under a tree.
b ___ Harada san makes Hayashi san drink some sake.
c ___ Hayashi san joins Ikeda san and Harada san.
d ___ Hayashi san talks about what's in his bag.

ACTIVITY 18

Read these sentences, and circle the words or phrases which are different from what you hear.

1 Tokorode, masutā wa koko ni imasu ka.
2 Mō 5.30 desu yo.
3 Hayashi san, kore wa nan desu ka.
4 Kore wa Igirisu no bideo desu.

ACTIVITY 19

Which person makes the following comments, Hayashi san (the film bore), or Harada san (the bad-tempered woman)?

1 He's a very odd person.
2 It's only 5.30.
3 These are my videos.
4 This is a park. It's not a cinema.
5 Have some sake.
6 What's in the bag?
7 Is it OK (if I join you)?

STORY TRANSCRIPT

Harada	Hen-na hito desu ne.
Ikeda	Dare desu ka. Hayashi san desu ka.
Harada	Sō desu. Hayashi san. Eiga bakari desu ne.
Ikeda	Sō desu ne.
Ikeda	Tokorode, Harada san, masutā wa doko ni imasu ka.
Harada	Asoko ni imasu.
Ikeda	Doko desu ka.
Harada	Masutā wa Ikeda san no ushiro.
Ikeda	A, imasu ne. A! Saitō san wa ano ki no ue, Ogawa san wa ano ki no shita ni imasu ne.
Harada	Mada 5.30 desu yo. Minna yopparaimashita.
Hayashi	Harada san, Ikeda san, ii desu ka.
Harada	Hai, dōzo.
Hayashi	Arigatō. (yoisho!)
Ikeda	Hayashi san, sore wa nan desu ka.
Harada	Kaban no naka ni nani ga arimasu ka.
Hayashi	Kono kaban desu ka. Kore wa watashi no bideo desu.
Ikeda	Bideo desu ka.
Hayashi	Hai. Chotto matte kudasai. A, kono bideo wa ....
Harada	Hayashi san! Kyō wa pikunikku desu yo. Koko wa kōen desu. Eigakan ja arimasen.
Hayashi	Hai, demo.....
Harada	Hayashi san, o-sake, dōzo.
Hayashi	A, sake desu ka. Watashi wa, o-sake wa chotto....
Harada	Hayashi san, dōzo!
Hayashi	Hai, hai, arigatō. Kanpai. ...
Harada	Hai, mo sukoshi.
Hayashi	Hai. Kono sake wa ....
Harada/Ikeda	A, shizuka desu ne.

Test

Now it's time to test your progress in Unit 4.

1 Look at the map, and say if the statements are true or false.

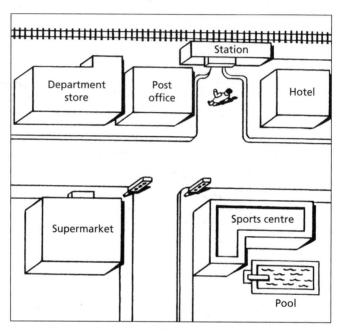

1 Sūpā wa depāto no mukai ni arimasu.   T / F
2 Eki no tonari ni, yūbinkyoku ga arimasu.   T / F
3 Supōtsu sentā wa hoteru no ushiro ni arimasu. T / F
4 Wada san wa, eki no mae ni imasu.   T / F
5 Pūru wa, supōtsu sentā no naka ni arimasu. T / F

| | 5 |

2 Look at the map again, and complete these sentences.

1 _____ _____ migi ni, yūbinkyoku ga arimasu.
2 Hoteru ____ ____ ni, eki ga arimasu.
3 Supōtsu sentā ___ ___ ___, eki to hoteru ga arimasu.
4 ___ ___, sūpā no mukai ni arimasu.

58

| | 9 |

3 Match these statements to the situations.

1 Chotto matte kudasai.
2 Mitsukoshi Depāto made onegai shimasu.
3 Wakarimasen.
4 Asoko ni arimasu.
5 Doko ni imasu ka.
6 Iie, hidari ni arimasu.
7 Wakarimashita.

a You're looking for the bank, and you've just seen it.
b You've just got in a taxi.
c You need someone to wait a moment.
d You don't understand something.
e Someone thinks the hotel is on the right, but it's not.
f You confirm that you've understood what someone said.
g You wonder where Ms Fukuda is.

▮ 7

4 Circle the appropriate word in the sentences below.

1 Neko wa uchi no naka ni (imasu / arimasu) ka.
2 (Sono / Sore) hito wa Ikeda san desu ka.
3 Yūbinkyoku wa (are / asoko) ni arimasu.
4 Shimada san no uchi wa Yokohama ni (imasu / arimasu) ka.
5 Are wa ii resutoran desu ka. (Wakarimasen. / Wakarimashita.)

▮ 5

5 Answer these questions about yourself.

1 Ima kaisha ni imasu ka. Daigaku ni imasu ka.
2 Uchi no chikaku ni kōen wa arimasu ka.
3 Uchi no naka ni kodomo wa ima imasu ka.
4 Saifu wa arimasu ka. Doko ni arimasu ka. Saifu no naka ni ikura arimasu ka.

▮ 10

TOTAL SCORE ▮ 36

If you scored less than 26, look at the Language Building sections again before completing the Summary on page 60.

Summary 4

 Now try this final test summarizing the main points covered in this unit. You can check your answers on the recording.

How would you:
1 ask a taxi driver to take you to Tokyo Station?
2 say you don't understand something?
3 say your hotel is in Nakano?
4 ask someone where Meiji Shrine is?
5 ask if there's a post office in this area?
6 say there's a park opposite your house?
7 ask where someone is right now?
8 ask someone to please wait a moment?

REVISION

Before going on to the next unit, you might find it useful to review the use of **koko / soko / asoko** (page 49), **kore / sore / are** (page 31), and **kono / sono / ano** (page 53).

To practise explanations of where things are, think of a familiar building – your home or office, for example – and describe what's around it. (Use your dictionary for any words you don't know.) If you're studying with someone else, see if they can guess which place you're describing.

5

Getting around
Tōkyō made 1-mai kudasai

OBJECTIVES

In this unit, you'll learn how to:

✓ buy train tickets

✓ make sure you're on the right train or bus

✓ talk about different kinds of transportation

And cover the following grammar and language:

✓ **-nin** to count people

✓ **ga** ('but') used to join sentences

✓ **e** ('to') to show direction

✓ verbs of movement

✓ **de** ('by') to show means of transport

✓ **ni** ('at') in time phrases

LEARNING JAPANESE 5

Practise speaking aloud, even when you're by yourself. Saying words and sentences aloud is quite a different matter from reading them silently in your head, so talk to yourself when you're in the car, or in the bath, or doing the washing up. Speaking aloud helps you think about the intonation and phrasing of what you're saying, instead of simply whether the language is correct or not. Listen to non-English speakers in radio and TV news interviews, and you'll notice that the ones who sound more fluent are not necessarily the ones with the most correct English. They're the ones whose pronunciation and intonation sound most natural.

Now start the recording for Unit 5.

5.1 Buying tickets

Yokohama made no kippu

ACTIVITY 1 is on the recording.

ACTIVITY 2

1 Where are the people going?
2 How many children are with them?
3 How many people are travelling altogether?
4 Which platform does their train leave from?

DIALOGUE 1

○ Sumimasen. Yokohama made, ikura desu ka.
■ Yokohama desu ka. Chotto matte kudasai. … ¥450 desu.
○ Dōmo arigatō. Anō … otona futari to kodomo hitori desu ga, dono botan desu ka.
■ Hai, o-kane wa koko desu. Sore kara, kono botan to kono botan desu. Hai, kippu desu. Otona ni-mai, kodomo ichi-mai desu.
○ Dōmo arigatō. Sumimasen ga, Yokohama yuki wa nan-ban sen desu ka.
■ San-ban sen desu.

VOCABULARY	
anō…	uh, um …
otona	adult
futari	two people
hitori	one person
ga	but
dono	which?
botan	button
o-kane	money
kippu	ticket
Yokohama yuki	bound for Yokohama
nan-ban	what number?
nan-ban sen	which platform? [*literally* what number line?]

✅ Counting people with -nin

People are counted with the suffix **-nin**, with the exceptions of 'one person' (**hitori**) and 'two people' (**futari**).

> Basu no naka ni, **go-nin** imasu. There are five people in the bus.
> Shain wa, **nan-nin** imasu ka. How many employees are there?

(Note that in the dialogue when the man says **Otona ni-mai, kodomo ichi-mai**, he is referring to adults' and children's tickets, not to the people.)

✅ Using *ga* to join sentences

You have already come across **ga** as a subject marker (see page 51). This **ga** is a different word meaning 'but'. It is used to connect two contrasting sentences.

> Otona no kippu wa ¥150 desu **ga**, kodomo no kippu wa ¥70 desu. An adult's ticket is ¥150, but a child's ticket is ¥70.
> Kore wa chotto takai desu **ga**, ii desu ne. This is rather expensive, but it's nice, isn't it?

✅ Use of *o-* before some words

Certain words are prefixed with **o-** in general conversation, including words associated with money: **o-kane** (money), **o-kanjo** (the bill), **o-tsuri** (change). See also 9.4 Japanese Culture.

The prefix **o-** also makes a word polite, and so it is often used to indicate that you are referring to someone else. (It is sometimes referred to as an 'honorific.')

O-namae wa Suzuki san desu ka. Is your name Suzuki san?
Iie, **namae** wa Itó desu. No, my name is Itō.

ACTIVITY 3

How would you complete this conversation at the ticket window if you wanted to buy 3 train tickets to Yokohama, for 2 adults and 1 child?

Customer	_____ kudasai.
Clerk	Otona 3-mai desu ka.
Customer	Iie, _____ to _____ desu.
Clerk	Hai. ¥3,400 desu.
Customer	_____
Clerk	3-ban sen desu.

🎧 Now do activities 4 and 5 on the recording.

Finding the right train
Nan-ban sen desu ka

ACTIVITY 6 is on the recording.

ACTIVITY 7

1	The passenger wants to go to Kyoto.	T / F
2	The Osaka train leaves from platform 3.	T / F
3	The next stop is Kyoto.	T / F
4	The train will arrive in Kyoto in forty minutes.	T / F

DIALOGUE 2

○ Sumimasen, kono densha wa Kyōto e ikimasu ka.
■ Iie, Kyōto e ikimasen. Kono densha wa Ōsaka yuki desu.
○ Sō desu ka. Kyōto yuki no densha wa nan-ban sen desu ka.
■ San-ban sen desu.
○ Arigatō.

○ Sumimasen, tsugi wa Kyōto desu ka.
■ Iie, chigaimasu. Tsugi wa Ōtsu desu. Kyōto wa sono tsugi desu. Ato 40-pun gurai kakarimasu.
○ 40-pun desu ka. Wakarimashita. Dōmo arigatō.

VOCABULARY	
densha	train
e	to, towards
ikimasu	go
ikimasen	doesn't go
tsugi	the next
sono tsugi	the one after that
ato 40-pun	in 40 minutes, after 40 minutes
gurai	about, approximately
kakarimasu	take, last

✅ Use of e ('to')

The particle **e** ('to') indicates movement towards a place, and it always comes *after* the name of the place.

Dono basu ga **Nakano** e ikimasu ka. Which bus goes to Nakano?
Jon san wa kyō **Igirisu** e kaerimasu. John is returning to England today.

The particle **ni** is sometimes used instead of **e** with the same meaning.

✅ Subject pronouns

You've probably noticed that you have hardly come across words for 'I' (**watashi**), 'you' (**anata**), 'he' (**kare**), or 'she' (**kanojo**). They are rarely used if the meaning is obvious without mentioning them.

Ashita **kaerimasu** ka. Are (you) going back tomorrow?
Iie, asatte **kaerimasu**. No, (I) am going back the day after tomorrow.

✅ More about present tense verbs

Remember that verbs (**ikimasu, arimasu, imasu**, etc.) always come at the end of the sentence.

Tōkyō kara Kōbe made, dono gurai **kakarimasu** ka. How long does it take from Tokyo to Kobe?

✅ Talking about lengths of time

You express a length of time in hours with **-jikan**.

Nan-jikan kakarimasu ka. How many hours does it take?
San-jikan han kakarimasu. It takes three and a half hours.
Ichi-jikan jup-pun kakarimasu. It takes an hour and ten minutes.

ACTIVITY 8

How long does it take on the Bullet Train?

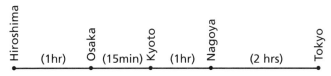

Hiroshima — (1hr) — Osaka — (15min) — Kyoto — (1hr) — Nagoya — (2 hrs) — Tokyo

Example: Kyoto to Nagoya
Kyōto kara Nagoya made, ichi-jikan kakarimasu.

1 Tokyo to Kyoto
2 Osaka to Hiroshima
3 Hiroshima to Nagoya

🎧 Now do activities 9 and 10 on the recording.

🎧 **ACTIVITY 11** is on the recording.

ACTIVITY 12

Which of these schedules gives the correct information?

1
```
Ski trip to Niigata
by car
leave tomorrow 6.00,
arrive 1.00
return day after tomorrow
```

2
```
Ski trip to Niigata
by train and bus
leave 6.00, arrive 10.00
return tomorrow
morning
```

3
```
Ski trip to Niigata
by bus
leave tomorrow 5.00,
arrive Niigata 11.00
return day after tomorrow
```

DIALOGUE 3

○ Ashita sukii ni ikimasu yo.

■ Sukii desu ka. Ii desu ne. Doko e ikimasu ka.

○ Niigata desu.

■ Sō desu ka. Densha de ikimasu ka.

○ Iie, basu de ikimasu.

■ Basu de? Nan-ji ni ikimasu ka.

○ Asa go-ji ni ikimasu. Niigata wa, 11-ji ni tsukimasu.

■ Roku-jikan desu ka. Taihen desu ne. Demo sukii wa tanoshii desu ne. Itsu made Niigata ni imasu ka.

○ Asatte kaerimasu.

■ Asatte!!??

VOCABULARY	
sukii	skiing
sukii ni ikimasu	go skiing
Niigata	*an area north of Tokyo with many ski resorts*
basu de	by bus
nan-ji ni	at what time?
tsukimasu	arrive
taihen	awful, terrible
itsu made	until when?

✅ Talking about transportation with *de*

The particle **de** ('by') is used to show the means of transportation. It comes *after* the word for the transport.

> **Shinkansen de** Ōsaka e ikimasu ka. Are you going to Osaka by Bullet Train?
> **Hikōki de** kaerimasu. I'm coming back by plane.

Other means of transportation are **chikatetsu** ('underground'), **kuruma** ('car'), and **jitensha** ('bicycle'). Note that you don't need **de** when talking about going on foot (**aruite**).

> Mainichi kaisha kara **aruite** kaerimasu. I walk home from work every day.

✅ Use of *ni* with time

The particle **ni** ('at') is used to show the time at which something happens.

> Sapporo kara no hikōki wa, **nan-ji ni** tsukimasu ka. (At) what time does the plane from Sapporo arrive?
> Ashita no gogo **san-ji han ni** kaerimasu. I'll be back at 3.30 tomorrow afternoon.

However, you don't use **ni** when you're saying what time it is.

> **Yo-ji** desu. It's 4.00.

✅ Talking about the future

The **-masu** form of verbs is used to talk about the future as well as the present. If you need to make it clearer which you mean, simply use time words such as 'tomorrow', 'next week', 'later', etc. Compare these two sentences.

> Mainichi shichi-ji han ni **kaerimasu**. I always get home at 7.30.
> Ashita ku-ji ni **kaerimasu**. Tomorrow I'll get home at 9.00.

ACTIVITY 13

Imagine that tomorrow is a holiday and you're going to visit a friend in Osaka. How would you explain your plans?

Today	holiday!
	to Osaka (Bullet Train)
	arrive 10.20
	taxi to Koyama san's house
Tomorrow	in Osaka
Next day	return to Tokyo (plane)

 Now do activities 14 and 15 on the recording.

5.4 Japanese Culture
Nihon no bunka

TRAVELLING AROUND

Japan has an excellent public transport system. The trains may be crowded, but they are punctual, frequent, clean, and safe. In the largest cities there are comprehensive train systems both above and below ground. Although most of the signs are in Japanese, it isn't difficult to use the trains, especially if you go armed with a map written in roman letters, freely available from tourist information centres and large hotels.

There are maps above the ticket machines at stations that show the fares to various destinations, but these are usually only in Japanese script, so you'll need to compare them to your romanized map. If this proves difficult, then either ask someone how much it is to your destination (people are always very willing to help), or buy the cheapest ticket and pay the extra at the other end.

In the large cities there are usually signs on the platforms that show the station name in roman letters, and also indicate the names of the previous station and the next station along the line, which is very helpful for confirming that you're going in the right direction. Another useful guide is that the colour of the trains on any particular line is the same as the colour of the line on the maps.

With long-distance trains, the cost of a ticket consists of a basic fare plus various supplements depending on whether you want a reserved seat (**shitei-seki**) or unreserved seat (**jiyu-seki**), and also on the speed with which you need to get to your destination. The **futsū** (ordinary) trains stop at every local station, the **kyūkō** (ordinary express) stops only at the larger stations, and the **tokkyū** (limited express) stops only at the largest stations. The fastest trains in Japan are the **shinkansen** or Bullet Trains. They usually have announcements in English as well as Japanese about the next stop. And it's as well to be ready and waiting at the train door with your belongings already gathered up – the **shinkansen** trains stop at each station for less than a minute.

Here are some signs you may see as you travel around on the trains. Note that the first three all contain the same kanji character. How is this kanji pronounced? Can you guess what it means?

1 入口   (iriguchi) – entrance

2 出口   (deguchi) – exit

3 改札口   (kaisatsuguchi – ticket barrier

4 切符売場   (kippu uriba) – ticket counter

5 駅   (eki) – station

6 地下鉄   (chikatetsu) – underground

7 お手洗い (otearai) – toilets

8 男   (otoko) – men

9 女   (onna) – women

THE ACCIDENT
ABUNAI!

It's the morning after the picnic, and Ikeda san is out shopping bright and early. She's very surprised to see Itō san, the owner of Midori-ya, coming along the street – jogging.

jogingu	jogging
maiasa	every morning
jogingu shimasu	go jogging
itsu kara	since when?
kinō	yesterday
ichi-jikan mo	as much as an hour
tōi	far, a long way
kaeri	return journey, round trip
tsukaremasu	get tired
... ni notte imasu	is riding ...
abunai	look out! [*literally* danger!]

ACTIVITY 17

Listen out for these verbs, and count the number of times you hear them.

jogingu shimasu _____   ikimasu _____
kakarimasu _____   kaerimasu _____
tsukaremasu _____

ACTIVITY 18

Who said the equivalent of the following sentences, and how did they say them in Japanese?

	Ikeda	Itó
1 Where are you going?		
2 It's a long way to the park.		
3 How about the return trip?		
4 It's very tiring, you know!		

ACTIVITY 19

How does Itō san travel for each part of his journey?

ACTIVITY 20

Here is a summary of the conversation in the street, but there are four mistakes. Can you find them?

Ikeda san meets Itō san, the 'master' of Midori-ya, out jogging. He said he goes jogging every morning, but it turns out he only started today. He's going to run as far as the park, and then take the bus back home. Ikeda san estimates it should take about 40 minutes to get to the park, but Itō san says it takes around an hour. They see Harada san drive by, but unfortunately when Ikeda san calls out to her, Harada san is distracted and has a crash.

STORY TRANSCRIPT

Ikeda	Masutā! Masutā! Itō san!
Itō	A, Ikeda san. Ohayō.
Ikeda	Masutā. Jogingu desu ne.
Itō	Ē, maiasa jogingu shimasu yo.
Ikeda	Maiasa desu ka. Taihen desu ne. Itsu kara desu ka.
Itō	Kinō kara desu.
Ikeda	Sō desu ka. Doko made ikimasu ka.
Itō	Kōen made.
Ikeda	Kōen made desu ka. Taihen desu ne. Dono gurai kakarimasu ka. 30-pun gurai?
Itō	Iie, ichi-jikan gurai kakarimasu yo.
Ikeda	Ichi-jikan mo kakarimasu ka.
Itō	Ē, koko kara aruite ikimasu yo.
Ikeda	Haaaa.
Itō	Kōen wa tōi desu yo. Uchi kara koko made jogingu shimasu ga, koko kara aruite ikimasu.
Ikeda	Sō desu ka. Koko kara aruite ikimasu ka. Ja, kaeri wa?
Itō	Basu de kaerimasu.
Ikeda	Basu de?
Itō	Ē. Tsukaremasu yo.
Ikeda	Haaaa. ... A, Harada san desu ne.
Itō	E? Doko desu ka.
Ikeda	Asoko desu. Jitensha ni notte imasu.
Itō	Harada san ga?! Jitensha ni notte imasu ka?!
Ikeda	E, asoko ni imasu yo. Harada san! Harada san, ohayo!
Harada	E? Nan desu ka.
Ikeda	Abunai!
Harada	Nan desu ka. CRASH!!!

Test

Now it's time to test your progress in Unit 5.

1 Match the verbs to their English equivalents.

1 ikimasu	a arrive
2 kaerimasu	b go
3 wakarimasu	c be, exist
4 tsukimasu	d take, last
5 arimasu	e return, go home
6 kakarimasu	f know, understand

6

2 Use the verbs above to complete these sentences.

Wada san wa mainichi 8.00 ni kaisha e _____. Chikatetsu de
_____. Uchi kara kaisha made 45-fun gurai _____. 8.45 ni
kaisha ni _____. Gogo 6.30 ni uchi e _____.

5

3 Imagine you need to confirm some information – how
would you ask about the following?
Example: plane – arriving at 2.00?
Hikōki wa ni-ji ni tsukimasu ka.

1 adult ticket – this button?
2 this train – bound for Osaka?
3 Tokyo train – platform 3?
4 bus ticket – ¥200?
5 Wada san – returning the day after tomorrow?

10

4 Match these questions and answers.
(Note that there's one answer too many.)

1 Meguro yuki wa dono basu desu ka.
2 Nan-nin imasu ka.
3 Kōbe made dono gurai kakarimasu ka.
4 Tsugi wa Kyōto desu ka.
5 Nani de ikimasu ka.

a Aruite ikimasu.
b 23-ban desu.
c 30-pun desu.
d Futari imasu.
e Ni-ban sen kara desu.
f Hai, sō desu.

5

5 Put the words in the right order to make a conversation.

wa / basu / ka / ikimasu / Nakano / kono / e

A _____

kono / yuki / iie / wa / basu / desu / Meguro

B _____

basu / yuki / Nakano / nan-ban / no / desu / wa / ka

A _____

B 13-ban desu.

6

6 Answer these questions about yourself.

1 Ashita doko e ikimasu ka.
2 Uchi kara eki (sūpā, kaisha, kōen) made, dono gurai kakarimasu ka.
3 Asatte wa yasumi desu ka.
4 Mainichi kaimono ni ikimasu ka.
5 Kuruma wa arimasu ka.
6 Uchi ni ima dare ga imasu ka. Zenbu de nan-nin imasu ka.
7 Nani de kaisha (daigaku, sūpā) e ikimasu ka.

14

TOTAL SCORE 46

If you scored less than 36, look at the Language Building sections again before completing the Summary on page 74.

Summary 5

Now try this final test summarizing the main points covered in this unit. You can check your answers on the recording.

How would you:
1 ask for three tickets to Kobe?
2 ask which platform the train for Tokyo leaves from?
3 say there are two adults and one child in your group?
4 ask if this train goes to Kyoto?
5 ask if the next stop is Yokohama?
6 say it takes 15 minutes from home to the station?
7 say that tomorrow you're going on the Bullet Train to Hiroshima?
8 ask about the time of arrival?

REVISION

For more practice with verbs, describe your daily schedule. Where do you go every day? What time do you go there? How do you get there? What time do you arrive? What time do you get home? How long does the journey take? Are you going there tomorrow? If you're studying with someone else, describe a place in this way and see if they can guess where you're talking about.

Day in, day out
Mainichi mainichi

OBJECTIVES

In this unit, you'll learn how to:

✓ talk about everyday activities

✓ say how often you do something

✓ describe things

And cover the following grammar and language:

✓ **o** to indicate the direct object of a verb

✓ days of the week

✓ verbs with **shimasu**

✓ adverbs of frequency

✓ adjectives ending in **-i**

LEARNING JAPANESE 6

When Japanese people pause to work out how to answer a question or think about what they're going to say next, they'll often say **Sō desu ne ...** ('Let me see ...'), or **Ēto ....'** ('um'), or **Anō ...'** ('Well ...'). Listen out for these strategies in the conversations in this unit, and try using them yourself. The use of such phrases (rather than an English-sounding 'um ...') can make your Japanese sound quite fluent even though you're simply stalling for time!

Now start the recording for Unit 6.

6.1 Talking about daily activities
Getsuyōbi kara kinyōbi made

 ACTIVITY 1 is on the recording.

ACTIVITY 2

When does each action occur?

	morning	afternoon	evening
1 watch TV			
2 drink wine			
3 go to museums			
4 read the paper			
5 study			

DIALOGUE 1

Getsuyōbi kara kinyōbi made Itariago o benkyō shimasu.
Maiasa 9.30 kara 12.30 made desu. Hiru-gohan wa ni-jikan mo
kakarimasu. Gogo wa benkyō shimasen. Hakubutsukan e
ikimasu. Totemo ii hakubutsukan desu. Yoru wa, Itaria no
terebi o mimasu ga, wakarimasen. Itaria no shinbun mo
yomimasu ga, yoku wakarimasen. Ban-gohan wa 10.00 kara
desu! Itaria no supagetti wa oishii desu yo. Wain mo oishii
desu. Minna wain o takusan nomimasu.

VOCABULARY	

getsuyōbi kara kinyōbi made	from Monday to Friday
Itariago	Italian language
-go	*indicates the language of a country*
o	*shows direct object of verb*
benkyō shimasu	to study
hiru-gohan	lunch [*literally* midday meal]
hakubutsukan	museum
totemo	very
yoru	evening
terebi o mimasu	watch television
shinbun o yomimasu	read a newspaper
yoku wakarimasen	don't understand very well
ban-gohan	dinner [*literally* evening meal]
nomimasu	drink

✓ Indicating the direct object of a verb with *o*

When **o** comes after a word or phrase, it indicates the object of the action. In other words, it shows the thing that is being eaten, watched, read, etc.

Mainichi **shinbun o** yomimasu ka. Do you read a paper every day?
Nan-ji ni **ban-gohan o** tabemasu ka. What time do you eat dinner?
Ashita **eiga o** mimasu. I'm going to see a movie tomorrow.

When **mo** ('too, also') is used, you can leave out **o**.

Ikeda san wa **Eigo o** hanashimasu. **Furansugo mo** hanashimasu. Ikeda san speaks English. She speaks French, too.

✓ Days of the week

The days of the week, starting with Monday, are:
getsuyōbi, kayōbi, suiyōbi, mokuyōbi, kinyōbi, doyōbi, nichiyōbi

Doyōbi ni kaerimasu. I'm going back on Saturday.
Kinyōbi no asa, hakubutsukan e ikimasu. I'm going to the museum on Friday morning.

Note that you don't need to use **ni** ('on') when you're specifying morning, afternoon, or evening (**asa, gogo, yoru**).

To ask 'what day?' use **nanyōbi**.

ACTIVITY 3

Answer these questions about yourself.

1 Dono shinbun o yomimasu ka.
2 Nan-ji ni asa-gohan o tabemasu ka.
3 Mainichi Nihongo o benkyō shimasu ka.
4 Furansugo o hanashimasu ka.

ACTIVITY 4

Make sentences about Wada san's schedule for the week.

Monday	–	to Osaka
Tuesday	–	return to Tokyo
Wednesday	–	day off
Thursday	–	am: French class
Friday	–	evening: film!

Now do activities 5 and 6 on the recording.

6.2 Do you do that often?
Yoku shimasu ka

 ACTIVITY 7 is on the recording.

ACTIVITY 8

How often does Suzuki san do the following?

1 take part in any sports
2 drink coffee
3 eat bacon and eggs for breakfast
4 eat fruit
5 drink beer

DIALOGUE 2

○ Suzuki san, asa-gohan wa nani o tabemasu ka.
■ Sō desu ne. Itsumo tōsuto to bēkon-eggu o tabemasu.
○ Hiru-gohan wa?
■ Tokidoki supagetti ya hanbāgā o tabemasu.
○ Ja, yasai ya kudamono o tabemasu ka.
■ Iie, amari tabemasen ne.
○ Sō desu ka. Kōhii wa?
■ Hai, kōhii o yoku nomimasu.
○ Ja, sake o nomimasu ka.
■ Yoku nomimasu. Sake mo, biiru mo.
○ Sō desu ka. Supōtsu o shimasu ka.
■ Supōtsu desu ka. Iie, zenzen shimasen.

VOCABULARY	
asa-gohan	breakfast
itsumo	always
bēkon-eggu	bacon and eggs
ya	and [*also* or]
yasai	vegetables
kudamono	fruit
amari tabemasen	don't often eat it
yoku	often [*also* well, skilfully]
... mo, ... mo	both ... and ... [*also* neither ... nor ... *with negative*]
shimasu	do, play [*with sports*]
zenzen ... masen	never, not at all

✅ How often?

Adverbs showing the frequency with which you do something (such as 'sometimes', 'often', etc.) can either come at the beginning of a sentence, or just before the verb. If it comes at the beginning, the subject is omitted.

Yoku sakana o tabemasu ka. / Sakana o **yoku** tabemasu ka. Do you often eat fish?

The most commonly used adverbs of frequency are **itsumo** ('always'), **yoku** ('often'), **tokidoki** ('sometimes'), and with the negative **amari** ('not often') and **zenzen** ('never').

Terebi o **amari** mimasen. I don't often watch television.
Kōcha o **yoku** nomimasu ga, kōhii o **zenzen** nomimasen. I often drink tea but I never drink coffee.

✅ Verbs with *shimasu*

shimasu by itself means 'do', but it is also very useful for adding on to nouns to create all sorts of other meanings. It's possible to leave out **o** with these verbs.

benkyō (o) shimasu – study
shigoto (o) shimasu – work
tenisu (o) shimasu – play tennis
kaimono (o) shimasu – do the shopping

Maiban 6.30 made **shigoto shimasu**. I work until 6.30 every evening.
Doyōbi no gogo, itsumo **tenisu o shimasu**. On Saturday afternoons I always play tennis.

ACTIVITY 9

Put a tick in the appropriate column, and then use the chart to describe how often you do the following. Try writing the responses and then refer to the table and practise saying them.

	often	sometimes	rarely	never
1 play tennis				
2 eat fish				
3 go to restaurants				
4 watch TV				
5 work on Sundays				
6 read the paper				

Now do activities 10 and 11 on the recording.

6.3 Describing things
Uchi wa ōkiku nai desu

ACTIVITY 12 is on the recording.

ACTIVITY 13

1 Akira does various sports.	T / F
2 He's not very tall.	T / F
3 He often goes to the swimming pool.	T / F
4 He goes to work by train.	T / F

DIALOGUE 3

○ Kore ga Akira desu.

■ Atarashii bōifurendo desu ka.

○ Hai, sō desu.

■ Supōtsuman desu ka.

○ Ē, yoku supōtsu o shimasu. Yakyū mo karate mo shimasu.

■ Se ga takai desu ka.

○ Amari takaku nai desu ga, o-kane ga arimasu. Uchi wa ōkiku nai desu ga, pūru ga arimasu. Sore kara, Bentsu de kaisha e ikimasu.

■ Akira san wa kyōdai ga imasu ka.

VOCABULARY

atarashii	new
bōifurendo	boyfriend
supōtsuman	sporty type
yakyū	baseball
se ga takai	tall [*of a person*]
takaku nai	not tall
ōkiku nai	not big
Bentsu	Mercedes-Benz
kyōdai	brothers and sisters

✅ Describing something with *-i* adjectives

You have already come across a number of adjectives ending in -**i**, e.g.

atsui	hot	**tanoshii**	enjoyable
hayai	fast	**atarashii**	new
takai	high, expensive	**yasui**	cheap
ōkii	big	**chiisai**	small

To describe what something isn't, change the final -**i desu** to -**ku nai desu**. (You may also come across the ending -**ku arimasen** which means the same thing.)

Tōkyō wa ima atsui desu ga, Sapporo wa **atsuku nai desu**. Tokyo is hot right now, but Sapporo isn't (hot).
O-sake wa takai desu ka. Is sake expensive?
Iie, amari **takaku nai desu**. No, it isn't very expensive.
Kaisha wa **ōkiku nai desu**. The company isn't very big.

The negative of **ii** ('good, fine') is **yoku nai**.

Tenki wa **yoku nai** desu ne. The weather's not good, is it?

When an -**i** adjective comes before the thing it's describing, rather than by itself at the end of the sentence, it doesn't change its form.

Atarashii kuruma desu ka. Is it a new car?
Iie, **atarashii kuruma** ja arimasen. No, it isn't a new car.

ACTIVITY 14

How would you complain about the following?
Example: this train – not very fast
Kono densha wa amari hayaku nai desu ne.

1 this fish – doesn't taste very good
2 this restaurant – not cheap
3 the station – not close by
4 this hotel – not big
5 this spaghetti – not hot
6 picnic – not fun

🎧 Now do activities 15 and 16 on the recording.

Nihon no bunka

CULTURE

THE OLD AND THE NEW IN EVERYDAY LIFE

In Japan, the conveniences of modern life are in evidence everywhere – in new and efficient transportation systems, domestic appliances, communication systems, construction, and technology. In the cities especially, the pace of life seems hectic, but the traditional arts are still common features of everyday life.

This can be seen in the continued popularity of classes teaching the tea ceremony (**sadō**, or **cha no yū**), flower arranging (**ikebana**), and calligraphy (**shodō**). Such classes can often be found among those offered after hours at the workplace, alongside the ever-popular English language classes.

Kimono are rarely seen in the cities these days except on ceremonial occasions such as weddings and at New Year festivities. They are complicated to put on, expensive, and too restrictive for today's busy lifestyles. However, at summer festivals you will often see both men and women in **yukata**, a kind of simple cotton **kimono**. You will also find **yukata** provided if you stay in a **ryokan**, or traditional Japanese inn, and these **yukata** can be worn for relaxing, going out for a walk, and for sleeping in.

On television, the traditional sport of **sumō**, with all its splendid ceremony and ancient symbolism, is as popular as baseball (**yakyū**). And at school, clubs for **karate** and **kendō** (Japanese fencing) and other traditional martial arts thrive.

Nō and **kabuki** are two styles of Japanese theatre which, although centuries old, very stylized, and sometimes difficult to understand, are still popular today. For the foreign visitor, a synopsis of the story is usually available in English.

ACTIVITY 17

Can you remember the meaning of the following Japanese words? Try to match them to their English meanings without looking back at the reading.

1	shodō	a	a theatre style
2	kendō	b	a simple cotton kimono
3	kabuki	c	calligraphy
4	sumō	d	flower arranging
5	yukata	e	traditional wrestling
6	ikebana	f	traditional fencing

ACTIVITY 18

Look at this diary page, and work out which day of the week each kanji character represents. Then, using the hiragana chart on page viii, work out which three activities have been marked in the diary.

月曜日	いけばな
火曜日	
水曜日	からて
木曜日	
金曜日	
土曜日	かいもの
日曜日	

6.5　Midori-ya

VISITING TIME AT THE HOSPITAL
BYŌIN DE

Harada san is in hospital, recovering from her bicycle
accident. Itō san, Hayashi san, and Ikeda san come to visit her
one day.

byōin	hospital
o-genki desu ka	how are you? [*literally* are you well?]
genki	well, healthy
gomen nasai	I beg your pardon, sorry
atama	head
itai	hurting, painful
ashi	leg [*also* foot]
itai!	ouch!
sawaranaide kudasai	please don't touch
shokuji	meal

ACTIVITY 19

Listen for these topics of conversation in the dialogue, and
number them in the order they occur.

1　Hayashi san hurting Harada san's leg
2　the hospital food
3　Harada san's headache
4　how long Harada san will be in hospital

ACTIVITY 20

Listen again, and say if these statements are true, false, or you
don't know because the information isn't in the conversation.

1　Harada san doesn't have much of a headache,
　but her leg hurts.　　　　　　　　　　　T / F / DK
2　Hayashi san sits on Harada san's leg.　　　T / F / DK
3　Harada san will be coming out of hospital
　on Friday.　　　　　　　　　　　　　　T / F/ DK
4　She passes the time by watching films on TV.　T / F/ DK
5　The hospital food is horrible.　　　　　　T / F/ DK

ACTIVITY 21

Circle the words or phrases which are different from what you hear, and write in any words which are missing.

1 Hayashi: Harada san! Watashi wa imasu yo.
2 Hayashi: A, sō desu ne, zenzen genki ja arimasen ne.
3 Ikeda: Tokorode, Harada san, itsu made koko ni imasu ka.
4 Itō: Shokuji wa oishii desu ka.

STORY TRANSCRIPT

Itō	Harada san wa doko ni imasu ka.
Ikeda	A, asoko ni imasu! Harada san! Ohayō gozaimasu.
Harada	Ikeda san? Ohayō gozaimasu. A, Itō san mo imasu ka.
Itō	Hai, ohayō.
Hayashi	Harada san! Watashi mo imasu yo
Harada	A, Hayashi san desu ne.
Hayashi	Hai, sō desu. O-genki desu ka. A, sō desu ne, amari genki ja arimasen ne. Gomen nasai.
Ikeda	Mada atama ga itai desu ka.
Harada	Atama wa amari itaku nai desu ga, ashi ga totemo itai desu. AAA! Itai! Hayashi san! Itai!
Hayashi	Nan desu ka.
Harada	Watashi no ashi desu yo! Sawaranaide kudasai.
Hayashi	A, gomen nasai.
Ikeda	Tokorode, Harada san, itsu made byōin ni imasu ka.
Harada	Kinyōbi made desu.
Hayashi	Ii desu ne. Terebi no eiga o takusan mimasu ne.
All	Hayashi san!
Hayashi	Hai.
Harada	Taihen desu yo. Asa-gohan o tabemasu. Shinbun o yomimasu. Sore kara terebi o mimasu. Sono tsugi wa hiru-gohan desu. Sore kara mata shinbun o yomimasu. Mata terebi o mimasu. Ban-gohan o tabemasu...
Itō	Shokuji wa dō desu ka.
Harada	Zenzen oishiku nai!
Itō	Shhhhhh!

Test

Now it is time to test your progress in Unit 6.

1 Choose the ending that best completes each sentence.

1	Watashi wa supōtsu o amari	a	hanashimasu.
2	Itsumo chikatetsu de kaisha e	b	nomimasen.
3	Nan-ji ni ban-gohan o	c	shimasu.
4	Maiasa 8.30 kara shigoto o	d	yomimasu ka.
5	Takahashi san wa amari se ga	e	shimasen.
6	Kōhii o zenzen	f	takaku nai desu.
7	Eigo o sukoshi	g	tabemasu ka.
8	'Mainichi Shinbun' o	h	ikimasu ka.

8

2 Complete these sentences with **ni, wa** or **o**.

1 Yasumi ___ nichiyōbi desu ka.
2 Dono eiga ___ mimasu ka.
3 Kono hoteru ___ amari ōkiku nai desu ne.
4 Itsumo 12.00 ___ hiru-gohan o tabemasu ka.
5 Ikeda san wa eigo ___ hanashimasu ka.
6 Doyōbi ni nani ___ shimasu ka.

6

3 Look at this schedule, and then answer the questions.

Mon	6.00-8.00 Italian class	
Tue	–	
Wed	7.30 restaurant	
Thur	6.45 film	
Fri	am to Yokohama	
Sat	am shopping	2.30 tennis
Sun	pm museum	

1 Getsuyōbi no yoru, nani o benkyō shimasu ka.
2 Suiyōbi no yoru, doko e ikimasu ka.
3 Nanyōbi ni Yokohama e ikimasu ka.
4 Mokuyōbi no yoru, nani o shimasu ka.
5 Kayōbi ni hakubutsukan ni ikimasu ka.
6 Itsu kaimono o shimasu ka.

12

4 Re-order these sentences to make a conversation.

1 ___ Chiisai desu ne. Doyōbi mo shigoto desu ka.
2 ___ Iie, ōkiku nai desu. Shain wa, 55-nin imasu.
3 ___ Amari yoku nai desu. Maiban 8.00 made kaisha ni imasu.
4 ___ Atarashii shigoto wa dō desu ka.
5 ___ Iie, doyōbi mo nichiyōbi mo yasumi desu.
6 ___ Taihen desu ne. Ōkii kaisha desu ka.

6

5 Make up some appropriate questions to go with these answers.

1 A _____
  B Itsumo 7.30 ni tabemasu.

2 A _____
  B Kinyōbi ni ikimasu.

3 A _____
  B Iie, amari ōkiku nai desu.

4 A _____
  B Iie, zenzen hanashimasen.

5 A _____
  B Tōsuto to bēkon-eggu o tabemasu.

6 A _____
  B Hai, tenisu o shimasu.

12

6 Answer these questions about yourself. Be truthful!

1 Yoku wain o nomimasu ka.
2 Mainichi Nihongo o sukoshi benkyō shimasu ka.
3 Furansugo ya Itariago o hanashimasu ka.
4 Nan-ji ni ban-gohan o tabemasu ka.
5 Tokidoki eiga o mimasu ka. Nanyōbi ni?
6 Yoku supōtsu o shimasu ka. Dono supōtsu?

12

TOTAL SCORE **56**

If you scored less than 46, look at the Language Building sections again before completing the Summary on page 88.

Summary 6

 Now try this final test summarizing the main points covered in this unit. You can check your answers on the recording.

How would you:
1 say the days of the week?
2 ask someone if she often visits Osaka?
3 ask someone if he works on Saturdays?
4 say the weather isn't good, is it?
5 ask someone what he eats for breakfast?
6 say you never eat fish?
7 ask someone what newspaper she reads?
8 say you sometimes watch Japanese television?
9 say you study every day?
10 ask someone what he is doing tomorrow?

REVISION

Before you go on to Unit 7, why not review the different uses of **o** and **wa**? You'll find information on these on pages 17 and 51.

Practise using **wa** and **o** in your own sentences by describing what you do every day. (Use your dictionary for any vocabulary you don't know.) For example, compare what time you eat breakfast on a weekday with what time you eat breakfast at the weekend. When do you go shopping? Do you ever go out to see a film? Do you watch sport on television?, etc.

Playtime
Umi e ikimasen ka

OBJECTIVES

In this unit, you'll learn how to:

- ✓ express your likes and dislikes
- ✓ talk about where activities take place
- ✓ give and accept invitations
- ✓ make suggestions

And cover the following grammar and language:

- ✓ **de** ('in, at') with location
- ✓ the verb ending **-masen ka** for invitations
- ✓ the verb ending **-mashō ka** for suggestions

LEARNING JAPANESE 7

Try recording your voice when you speak Japanese. You'll probably feel self-conscious at first, but it's very useful for pronunciation practice. You may find that you sound different from the way you think you sound, or the way you should sound. Listening to the way you speak will help you pinpoint the areas you need to concentrate on and improve.

Now start the recording for Unit 7.

7.1 Talking about likes and dislikes
Suki desu ka

ACTIVITY 1 is on the recording.

ACTIVITY 2

Note what each person likes or doesn't like.

	Man	Woman
classical music rock music wrestling golf		

DIALOGUE 1

○ Ongaku wa suki desu ka.

■ Hai, kurashikku ga suki desu.

○ Sō desu ka. Watashi wa kurashikku wa amari suki ja arimasen. Rokku ga dai-suki desu. Yoku konsāto ni ikimasu.

■ Sō desu ka. Shumi wa supōtsu desu ne. Donna supōtsu desu ka.

○ Puro resu ga dai-suki desu.

■ Sō desu ka. Watashi wa gorufu ga suki desu ga, gorufu o shimasu ka.

○ Iie, zenzen shimasen.

VOCABULARY

ongaku	music
suki desu	like
kurashikku	classical music
amari suki ja arimasen	don't like very much
rokku	rock music
dai-suki desu	like very much
konsāto	concert
shumi	interests, hobbies
donna	what kind of?
puro resu	wrestling
gorufu o shimasu	play golf

✅ Likes and dislikes

To ask if someone likes something, use **... wa suki desu ka** ('Do you like ...?'). Possible responses are:

... ga dai-suki desu	I love ...
... ga suki desu	I like ...
... wa mā-mā desu	I don't mind ... /It's OK
... wa amari suki ja arimasen	I don't really like ...
... ga kirai desu	I dislike ...
... ga dai-kirai desu	I hate ...

Note that **wa** is generally used with questions and negative answers, and **ga** is used with positive answers.

Ryōri wa suki desu ka. Do you like cooking?
Haikingu ga suki desu ga, jogingu wa amari suki ja arimasen.
I like hiking, but I don't really like jogging.
Hayashi san wa **eiga ga** suki desu ne. Hayashi san likes films, doesn't he?

kirai and **dai-kirai** are rather strong, so it's probably best to use **amari suki ja arimasen** when you're talking about something you don't like.

ACTIVITY 3

Make sentences about the various likes and dislikes of these three people using the cues provided.

	Tanaka san	Saitō san	Fukuda san
hiking	likes a lot	likes	not really
films	likes a lot	not really	likes a lot
kabuki	not really	likes	not really

Example: (Tanaka, Fukuda – hiking)
Tanaka san wa, haikingu ga dai-suki desu ga, Fukuda san wa amari suki ja arimasen.

1 Saitō, Fukuda – kabuki
2 Tanaka, Saitō – films
3 Tanaka – hiking, films
4 Fukuda – hiking, kabuki

🎧 Now do activities 4 and 5 on the recording.

7.2 Saying where something happens
Doko de shimasu ka

ACTIVITY 6 is on the recording.

ACTIVITY 7

1 When will the group go shopping in Harrods?
2 Where will they have lunch?
3 What will they do in the afternoon, and where?
4 Where will they eat dinner?
5 Why will they have an early dinner?

DIALOGUE 2

Mina san, ohayō gozaimasu. Kyō wa ii tenki desu ne. Dewa, kyō no sukejūru desu. Asa, Harodzu depāto de kaimono o shimasu. Hiru-gohan wa, pabu de tabemasu. Totemo furui pabu desu.

Gogo wa, Winburudon de tenisu o mimasu. Tenisu wa 2.00 kara desu. Chotto hayai desu ga, 6.00 ni Soho no resutoran de Indo ryōri o tabemasu. Sore kara Pikaderi Gekijo de, myūjikaru o mimasu. Tanoshii myūjikaru desu yo.

Sore ja, mina san, ikimashō.

VOCABULARY	
dewa	well... [*formal equivalent of* ja]
sukejūru	schedule
Harodzu	Harrods
de	in, at
pabu	pub, bar
furui	old
Winburudon	Wimbledon
Indo ryōri	Indian cooking, Indian food
Pikaderi Gekijo	Piccadilly Theatre
myūjikaru	a musical

⊘ Using *de* to show the place where an action occurs

You've already come across **ni** to indicate the place where something exists, e.g. Kaisha wa **Tōkyō ni** arimasu. It is generally used with the verbs **imasu** and **arimasu**. However, when you're talking about an action taking place somewhere (e.g. eating, watching, working), use the particle **de** to show where it's happening.

Watashi wa yoku **sono resutoran de** hiru-gohan **o** tabemasu. I often eat lunch at that restaurant.

Asoko no kippu uriba de kippu o kaimasu. You buy the tickets at that ticket window over there.

Daigaku de Nihongo o benkyō shimasu. I study Japanese at university.

ACTIVITY 8

Answer these questions by naming the places where you can do these various activities. Choose from the following.

> eigakan   eki
> gekijo   supōtsu sentā
> kaisha   kissaten   daigaku
> ginkō   yūbinkyoku

1 Doko de kitte o kaimasu ka.
2 Doko de badominton o shimasu ka.
3 Doko de shigoto o shimasu ka.
4 Doko de eiga o mimasu ka.
5 Doko de myūjikaru o mimasu ka.
6 Doko de kóhii o nomimasu ka.

Now do activities 9 and 10 on the recording.

Nani o shimashō ka

ACTIVITY 11 is on the recording.

ACTIVITY 12

1	The two friends are going to the sea tomorrow.	T / F
2	There are hot springs in Atami.	T / F
3	They're going by car.	T / F
4	The beer is good in Atami, but the fish isn't too good.	T / F
5	They're going to meet in front of the station.	T / F

DIALOGUE 3

○ Ashita nani o shimashō ka.
■ Umi e ikimasen ka.
○ Ii desu ne. Atami wa dō desu ka. Atami no sakana wa oishii desu. Biiru mo oishii desu yo. Onsen mo arimasu ne.
■ Onsen wa, suki desu ne. Un, onsen ni mo hairimashō. Watashi no kuruma de ikimasen ka.
○ Densha de ikimashō.
■ Densha de ikimashō. Nan-ji desu ka.
○ 7.00 ni eki no mae de aimashō.
■ Hai, sō shimashō.

VOCABULARY

nani o shimashō ka	what shall we do?
umi	the sea
... e ikimasen ka	why don't we go to ...?
Atami	*popular resort on Izu peninsula*
onsen	hot springs
hairimashō	let's go in
ikimashō	let's go
aimashō	let's meet
sō shimashō	let's do that

✓ Invitations with -*masen ka*

To invite someone to do something, use the verb ending -**masen ka**, which is rather like the English 'Why don't we...?'

> Konban eiga o **mimasen ka**. Why don't we see a film this evening?
> Issho ni ban-gohan o **tabemasen ka**. Would you like to have dinner together?

✓ Making suggestions with -*mashō*

If you want to suggest doing something, then change the verb ending from -**masu** to -**mashō** ('Let's ...' or 'Let me ...'), or -**mashō ka** ('Shall we /I ...?').

> Takushii de **kaerimashō**. Let's go home by taxi.
> Watashi ga ryōri **shimashō ka**. Shall I do the cooking?
> Issho ni badominton o **shimashō**. Let's play badminton together.
> Ano atarashii resutoran de **tabemashō ka**. Shall we eat at that new restaurant?

ACTIVITY 13

Here are some of the things you've been invited to do this week. What did your friends say when they invited you?
Example: Wednesday evening, study French with Ogawa san
Suiyōbi no yoru, issho ni Furansugo o benkyō shimasen ka.

1 Thursday evening, badminton at sports centre
2 Friday evening, film with Wada san
3 Saturday morning, shopping in Yokohama with Ogawa san
4 Saturday afternoon, picnic in the park

ACTIVITY 14

How would you suggest:

1 meeting at 7.30 at the sports centre?
2 that you will buy the drinks for the picnic?

Now do activities 15 and 16 on the recording.

Japanese Culture
Nihon no bunka

LEISURE TIME

Until recently, the tradition of working long hours in Japanese companies meant limited leisure time, especially for office workers. Children also had much of their free time taken up with after-school clubs and extra lessons to help them through their all-important exams, and this trend continues. The only group able to concentrate on having a good time are university students, relaxing in the pressure-free space between studying hard at school to pass university entrance exams, and working hard for a company after graduation. Traditional student pastimes include playing mah jong, reading comic books, and drinking.

However, things are gradually changing as government, businesses and individuals begin to put a higher value on leisure time, and the opportunity to relax with friends and family. The six-day working week is no longer common, and more and more people are able to get away at the weekend.

Skiing is very popular in the winter, as are tennis and baseball in the summer. Golf, too, is a national passion, even though space for golf courses in this mountainous country is at a premium and club fees are sky-high. Most people content themselves with practising their swings at the many practice ranges in the city – look out for the green nets against the skyline, some even on the top of office buildings and department stores. It's also common to see people absent-mindedly practising while waiting for trains on station platforms – usually with a rolled umbrella or newspaper.

It's not all sport. Walk down any shopping street and sooner or later you will hear the noise of tens of thousands of steel balls whizzing around rows and rows of upright pinball machines. You will be outside a **pachinko** parlour, where people stop on their way home from the office, or shopping, to play for a while on the **pachinko** machines. Other games such as **mājan** (mah jong) and **shōgi** (a kind of chess) need a lot more mental agility and concentration, but are also very popular.

ACTIVITY 17

Here are eight leisure activities that are popular in Japan. First, simply look at the words, and see if you can recognize from the shape of the characters if they are written in hiragana or katakana. Circle H or K as appropriate.

1	ゴルフ	H / K
2	スキー	H / K
3	やきゅう	H / K
4	いけばな	H / K
5	テニス	H / K
6	えいが	H / K
7	からて	H / K
8	しょうぎ	H / K

ACTIVITY 18

Now look at the list again and work out what the activities are. Use the hiragana and katakana charts on page viii to help you.

🎧 TIME FOR A CHANGE?
MIDORI-YA WA FURUI MISE DESU

Business is falling off a little at Midori-ya, and Itō san is wondering if it's time to modernize the place a little. He talks over his ideas one evening with some of the customers.

yakitori	small pieces of barbecued chicken on a stick
jitsu wa	the fact is
mise	shop, store; premises
sore ni	and also, and on top of that
sukunai	few
deshō	right? isn't it? [*asking for listener's agreement*]
karaoke o okimashō	let's put in karaoke
minna de	altogether
utaimashō	let's sing
kōhii mo dashimashō	let's serve coffee, too
urusai	noisy
ii kangae	a good idea [*literally* a good thought]
dame desu ka	is it a bad idea? [*literally* is it no good? is it useless?]
kochira e	come this way, come over here [*polite*]
kono mama de	the same as it is now

ACTIVITY 19

Listen to the conversation in Midori-ya, and count how many words you hear ending in **-mashō** (meaning 'let's'). (Be careful not to confuse the **-mashō** ending with **-masu yo**.)

ACTIVITY 20

Listen to the conversation in Midori-ya, and say if these statements are true, false, or you don't know because the information isn't mentioned.

1 One of Itō san's ideas is to install a karaoke machine.   T / F / DK
2 Ikeda san agrees that karaoke would be a good idea as Midori-ya is small.   T / F / DK
3 Ikeda san often drinks coffee in the evenings.   T / F / DK

4 Hayashi san suggests installing a television.   T / F / DK
5 Harada san comes in and orders beer.   T / F / DK
6 Harada san came straight from the hospital
to Midori-ya.   T / F / DK
7 Harada san agrees that there should be some
changes.   T / F / DK

ACTIVITY 21

Who said the Japanese equivalent of these sentences, Itō san (the owner), Ikeda san (the customer), or Hayashi san (the film bore)?

1 Karaoke is noisy.

3 This place is old.

2 I've got a good idea.

4 It isn't a coffee shop!

STORY TRANSCRIPT

Ikeda	Masutā, biiru o kudasai. Sore kara, yakitori mo.
Itō	Hai. Biiru to yakitori desu ne.
Ikeda	Ē.
Itō	Jitsu wa, Midori-ya wa furui mise desu. Sore ni, o-kyaku san ga sukunai deshō.
Ikeda	Sō desu ne.
Itō	Ikeda san wa karaoke ga suki desu ne.
Ikeda	Ē, suki desu ga ...
Itō	Koko ni, karaoke o okimashō. Minna de utaimashō.
Ikeda	Ha...?
Itō	Sore kara, Ikeda san wa kōhii ga suki desu ne.
Ikeda	Ē, suki desu ga...
Itō	Kōhii mo dashimashō yo.
Ikeda	Koko desu ka? Midori-ya ni? Iie, kono mise wa chiisai deshō. Karaoke wa urusai desu yo. Sore ni, Midori-ya wa kissaten ja nai desu yo.
Hayashi	Masutā? Ii kangae ga arimasu yo.
Itō	Nan desu ka, Hayashi san?
Hayashi	Bideo wa dō desu ka. Asoko ni terebi ga arimasu ne. Sono shita ni bideo o ...
Itō/Ikeda	Hayashi san!!
Hayashi	Dame desu ka.
Harada	Masutā, biiru o kudasai.
Ito	Irasshaimase. A! Harada san desu! Irasshai! Mina san, Harada san desu yo.
Ikeda	Harada san, dōzo, kochira e.
Harada	Arigatō.
Itō	Biiru o dōzo. Harada san, kanpai.
All	Kanpai!
Harada	Byōin wa iya desu ne.
Ikeda	Anō... Masutā wa ima, Midori-ya ni, karaoke ya, bideo ya, kōhii o...
Harada	Dame desu. Masutā, Midori-ya wa kono mama de ii desu yo.
Itō	Hai.

99

Test

Now it's time to test your progress in Unit 7.

1 Number these phrases in order from liking very much to not liking at all.

___ kirai desu   ___ dai-suki desu

___ dai-kirai desu ___ amari suki ja arimasen

___ suki desu   ___ mā-mā suki desu

`6`

2 Circle the appropriate word within the brackets to complete the sentences.

1 Gekijō wa doko (**ni** / **de**) arimasu ka.
2 Kono wain wa amari suki (**desu** / **ja arimasen**).
3 (**Donna** / **Dō**) eiga ga suki desu ka.
4 Yoku kono depāto de kaimono o (**shimasu** / **kaimasu**).
5 Watashi ga kaimono o (**shimashó** / **shimasen**) ka.
6 Doko (**de** / **ni**) eigo o benkyō shimasu ka.

`6`

3 Match the questions to the appropriate responses.

1 Doko de aimashō ka.
  a Eigakan no mae de.
  b Eigakan wa koko desu.
2 Konban nani o shimashō ka.
  a Hai, sō shimashō.
  b Eiga wa dō desu ka.
3 Wain wa suki desu ka.
  a Hai, kirai desu.
  b Mā-mā desu.
4 Yoku konsāto e ikimasu ne.
  a Sō desu ka.
  b Hai, kurashikku ga dai-suki desu.
5 Ashita tenisu o shimasen ka.
  a Ii desu ne.
  b Hai, sō desu.

`5`

4 Cross out the word in each sentence which isn't necessary.

1 Sukii wa suki ja arimasen ga, haikingu to tenisu ga amari suki desu.

2 Ban-gohan wa doko de ni tabemashō ka.

3 Doyōbi ni onsen e ikimasu ga, issho ni to ikimasen ka.

4 Tenki wa yoku nai desu arimasu ne. Dō shimashō ka.

5 Ashita Yokohama de atarashii jitensha o doko kaimasu.

6 Gekijō wa eigakan no chikaku ni de arimasu ka.

_____ | **6**

5 Complete these sentences suggesting various things to do this weekend, using the **-mashō** form.

1 Gekijō de myūjikaru o _____.

2 Furansu ryōri o _____.

3 Nihongo no benkyō o _____.

4 Densha de umi e _____.

5 Oishii wain o _____.

_____ | **5**

6 Answer these questions about yourself.

1 Donna ongaku ga suki desu ka.

2 Tokidoki umi e ikimasu ka.

3 Doko de shigoto shimasu ka./Doko de benkyō shimasu ka.

4 Yoku resutoran de tabemasu ka.

5 Myūjikaru wa suki desu ka.

6 Shumi wa nan desu ka.

7 Mainichi ryōri o shimasu ka.

_____ | **14**

TOTAL SCORE | **42**

If you scored less than 32, look at the Language Building sections again before completing the Summary on page 102.

Summary 7

Now try this final test summarizing the main points covered in this unit. You can check your answers on the recording.

How would you:
1 invite someone to go to a concert with you tonight?
2 say you really like Japanese food?
3 suggest going home by taxi?
4 ask someone if she likes sumo?
5 ask someone where he's going shopping tomorrow afternoon?
6 suggest meeting at 7.30?
7 ask someone what kind of music she likes?
8 say you study Japanese at university?

REVISION

The next section is a review of Units 1–7, so perhaps this is a good time to go back and revise the areas you're still not sure about. It's also a good idea to listen once again to the three main dialogues from the previous units. Try this without looking at the text, and see how much you can now understand compared with when you first heard them.

What are your hobbies and interests? If you don't know the vocabulary, look the words up in a dictionary. Imagine someone has asked you what you like to do in your free time (and where, when, who with, how much it costs, etc.), and think about how you would tell them about your interests.

Review 2

VOCABULARY

1 Number these activities in the order you do them every day.

___ asa-gohan o tabemasu

___ hiru-gohan o tabemasu

___ kōhii ya kōcha o nomimasu

___ uchi e kaerimasu

___ shinbun o yomimasu

___ terebi o mimasu

___ kaisha e ikimasu

___ Nihongo o benkyō shimasu

2 Put the words from the box into the appropriate categories.

> dare   ikebana   chikatetsu   sūpā   uchi   ryōri
> itsu   hikōki   ryokan   sukii   nanyōbi   donna
> yakyū   densha   depāto   eki   kuruma   doko
> jitensha   eigakan

hobbies/interests: _____

buildings: _____

transport: _____

question words: _____

3 Match the words and phrases to appropriate verbs.

1	shigoto o	a	nomimasu
2	shinbun o	b	kakarimasu
3	eigakan no mae de	c	tabemasu
4	Nihongo o	d	shimasu
5	uchi e	e	yomimasu
6	2-jikan	f	hanashimasu
7	jūsu o	g	aimasu
8	supagetti o	h	kaerimasu

4 Complete these sentences with one of the following: **o, wa, de, ni, e**.

1 Yamada san ___ yoku sono pabu ____ nomimasu ne.
2 Sumimasen ga, Puraza Hoteru __ kono chikaku __ arimasu ka.
3 Ashita no yoru, eiga ___ mimasen ka.
4 Osoi desu ne. Takushii de uchi ___ kaerimashō.
5 Nan-ji ___ ban-gohan ___ tabemashō ka.
6 Watashi no kuruma ___ umi ___ ikimasen ka.

5 Make up some suitable questions to go with these answers.

1 Q _____
  A Iie, amari takaku nai desu.
2 Q _____
  A Ichi-jikan gurai kakarimasu.
3 Q _____
  A Asoko ni imasu.
4 Q _____
  A Kurashikku ga suki desu.
5 Q _____
  A Iie, aruite kaerimasu.
6 Q _____
  A Iie, totemo samui desu.

6 Make sentences by joining the phrases 1–6 with the phrases a–f.

1 Kono hoteru wa takai desu ga,
2 Kyō wa nichiyōbi desu ga,
3 Kōhii o yoku nomimasu ga,
4 Kono kuruma wa furui desu ga,
5 Jogingu wa taihen desu ga,
6 Tokidoki Furansu no eiga o mimasu ga,

a kaisha e ikimasu.
b tanoshii desu.
c amari yoku nai desu.
d yoku wakarimasen.
e kōcha wa amari suki ja arimasen.
f totemo hayai desu.

7 Listen to Koyama san talking about some of the things she usually does during the week, and write them in her diary.

Mon:
Tue: work at: _____
         evening: _____
Wed: evening: _____
Thur:
Fri: evening: _____
Sat:
Sun: aft: _____ with _____
        sometimes: _____

8 Listen to the message on Koyama san's answerphone, and answer the questions.

1 What time does Shimada san call?
2 When does she suggest going for a meal?
3 Where is the restaurant?
4 What kind of restaurant is it, and what is especially good there?
5 Where and when does she suggest meeting for the meal?

9 Imagine you've arranged to go hiking for a couple of days, and now you're telling a friend about it. After you've practised this dialogue several times, listen to the recording and try to do it without referring to the book.

Friend	Doko e ikimasu ka.
You	(You're going to Nagano.)

1 _____

Friend	Ii desu ne. Densha de ikimasu ka.
You	(No – by car.)

2 _____

Friend	Sō desu ka. Nagano made dono gurai kakarimasu ka.
You	(About four hours.)

3 _____

Friend	Itsu ikimasu ka.
You	(Saturday morning. You'll be there until Monday afternoon.)

4 _____

Friend	Sō desu ka.
You	(Ask if he likes hiking.)

5 _____

Friend	Watashi desu ka. Hai, dai-suki desu.
You	(Perhaps he'd like to come too – ask him.)

6 _____

Friend	Ii desu ne. Demo doyōbi mo nichiyōbi mo shigoto desu.

10 You'll hear some questions on the recording. See if you can answer them in the pauses without stopping the recording. The questions will be about the following topics, but in a different order. You'll be asked about:

- your interests
- eating out
- likes and dislikes

Use this list to prepare what you're going to say, then use the recording to test yourself.

All in the past
Itsu deshita ka

OBJECTIVES

In this unit, you'll learn how to:

✓ describe past experiences

✓ give personal information

✓ talk about your background

✓ say when something happened

And cover the following grammar and language:

✓ verbs in the past tense

✓ dates

✓ giving reasons using **kara** ('because', 'so')

✓ saying your age

✓ **toki** ('the time when …')

LEARNING JAPANESE 8

Look through the TV listings for Japanese films or programmes about Japan. Foreign films are usually shown in their original language with subtitles, so it will give you a chance to hear colloquial Japanese being spoken at speed. Though it's unlikely you'll understand very much at this stage, you will be able to recognize some words, and, with the help of the subtitles, will also find that you pick up some new vocabulary. Keep a dictionary handy, and look up any words that you notice occurring regularly.

Now start the recording for Unit 8.

Describing events in the past

Nani o kaimashita ka

ACTIVITY 1 is on the recording.

ACTIVITY 2

Correct the statements which are false.

1	Koyama san called her friend last week.	T / F
2	Her friend got back from Europe this morning.	T / F
3	She travelled alone.	T / F
4	She didn't buy anything in Paris because it was so expensive.	T / F
5	She bought some shoes in Rome.	T / F

DIALOGUE 1

○ Senshū denwa shimashita ga, imasen deshita ne.

■ Senshū? Sō desu yo. Yōroppa ni imashita. Kinō no asa kaerimashita. Tomodachi no Kimura san to issho ni ikimashita.

○ Kaimono wa? Takusan kaimashita ka.

■ Pari wa totemo takai desu yo. Pari de wa nani mo kaimasen deshita ga, Roma de wa iroiro kaimashita.

○ Nani o kaimashita ka.

■ Sō desu ne. Kutsu to, jaketto to, kaban o kaimashita.

○ Ii desu ne.

VOCABULARY

senshū	last week
denwa shimashita	I called, I phoned
imasen deshita	you weren't there
Yōroppa	Europe
hitori de	alone, by yourself
tomodachi no Kimura san	a friend, Kimura san
nani mo kaimasen deshita	I didn't buy anything
kutsu	shoes
jaketto	jacket

✓ The past tense

To talk about things that happened in the past, simply change the verb ending -**masu** to -**mashita**.

> Maishū no doyōbi umi e **ikimasu**. We go to the sea every Saturday.
> Senshū no doyōbi umi e **ikimashita**. We went to the sea last Saturday.
> Kyonen Nihon e **kimashita**. I came to Japan last year.
> Natsu yasumi wa dō **deshita** ka. How was your summer holiday?

To say that something didn't happen in the past, change the ending to -**masen deshita**.

> Zenzen **wakarimasen deshita**. I didn't understand it at all!
> Kinō no ban, nani mo **shimasen deshita**. I didn't do anything yesterday evening.

✓ Short questions

When you ask several questions about the same topic, it's not always necessary to repeat the full question form. You can simply state the topic with **wa**, and leave the rest of the question to be understood.

> Q Tenki wa dō deshita ka. How was the weather?
> A Totemo ii tenki deshita. It was excellent weather.
> Q **Tabemono** wa? And the food?

ACTIVITY 3

Here's a list of the things Koyama san planned to do yesterday on her day off. Make sentences about what she did and didn't manage to do.

> watch TV ✗ — Terebi o mimasen deshita.
> go to park ✓ — Koen e ikimashita.
>
> 1 buy new shoes   ✓
> 2 go to bank   ✗
> 3 buy concert tickets   ✗
> 4 study English   ✓
> 5 tennis with Fukuda san   ✓
> 6 jogging in evening   ✗

(4♪) Now do activities 4 and 5 on the recording.

8.2 Giving personal information

Sapporo de umaremashita

 ACTIVITY 6 is on the recording.

ACTIVITY 7

Fill in this form with Tamura san's details.

Family name:	Tamura
Place of birth:	_____
Age:	_____
Marital status:	Single / Married
Current occupation:	_____
Previous occupation:	_____

DIALOGUE 2

Namae wa Tamura Yukio desu. San-jū-roku-sai desu. Sapporo de umaremashita. 1986-nen ni, kōkō o sotsugyō shimashita. Sapporo no resutoran de hatarakimashita. 1992-nen ni, kekkon shimashita. Ni-jū-ni-sai deshita. Ni-jū-roku-sai no toki, Tōkyō ni kimashita. Takushii no untenshu ni narimashita. Ototoi, o-kyaku ga, takushii no naka ni, ¥50,000,000 (go-sen man en) o wasuremashita. Kinō, kūkō ni takushii ga arimashita ga, Tamura mo okusan mo imasen deshita.

VOCABULARY

san-jū-roku-sai	36 years old
Sapporo de umaremashita	he was born in Sapporo
kōkō	senior high school
sotsugyō shimashita	graduated
hatarakimashita	worked
kekkon shimashita	got married
ni-jū-roku-sai no toki	when he was 26
takushii no untenshu	taxi driver
... ni narimashita	became a
ototoi	the day before yesterday
wasuremashita	left behind
kūkō	airport
okusan	his wife

⊘ Giving your age

To give your age, add **-sai** to the number. There are pronunciation changes in three cases: **is-sai** (1 year old), **has-sai** (8 years old), and **jus-sai** (10 years old). Note that 20 years old, the age at which people legally become adults, is irregular – **hatachi**.

To ask how old someone is, use **Ikutsu desu ka** or, more politely, **O-ikutsu desu ka**. When speaking to children, **Nan-sai desu ka** is often used.

⊘ Saying your name

Japanese people give their family name first, followed by their 'first' names. However, when speaking or writing in English, they tend to reverse this order to conform with English-speaking conventions. You should give your name in the English order, even when speaking Japanese.

⊘ *toki* — time, period

toki ('time') is used to describe a period of time.

Kodomo no toki, supōtsu ga dai-suki deshita. When I was a child, I loved sports.

Kare wa **26-sai no toki**, eigo no sensei ni narimashita. When he was 26, he became an English teacher.

Kanojo wa, **daigakusei no toki**, kekkon shimashita. She got married when she was a university student.

ACTIVITY 8

Look at Fukuda san's personal profile and complete the description of him.

> Name: Toshio Fukuda
> Place of birth: Kobe, Japan
> Education: Graduated Kyoto University (1985)
> Marital status: Married 1995
> Work: 1987–92 Toyota (Nagoya)
>   1992–98 Japanese teacher (New York)
>   1999–: Japanese teacher (Kyoto International University)

Fukuda san wa Kōbe de _____. 1987 ni Kyōto Daigaku o _____ shimashita. 1992 made Toyota de _____ ga, 26-sai no _____, Amerika e ikimashita. Nihongo no sensei ni _____. 1995 ni _____ shimashita. 1999 ni Fukuda san to okusan wa Nihon e _____.

🎧 Now do activities 9 and 10 on the recording.

Giving dates

Nan-gatsu nan-nichi desu ka

🎧 **ACTIVITY 11** is on the recording.

ACTIVITY 12

1 What day of the week is Ishii san's birthday?
2 What present did the woman give Ishii san last year, and what happened to them?
3 Why is a lighter of no use to Ishii san?
4 Why is a cake not suitable as a present?

DIALOGUE 3

○ Ishii san no tanjōbi no purezento o mō kaimashita ka.
■ Tanjōbi? Itsu desu ka.
○ Jū-gatsu futsuka desu yo. Raishū no doyōbi desu.
■ Sō desu ka. Ja, iyaringu wa dō desu ka.
○ Kyonen iyaringu o agemashita ga, Ishii san wa sugu nakushimashita.
■ Sō desu ka. Ja, raitā wa?
○ Iie, sengetsu tabako o yamemashita kara, irimasen.
■ Ja, Ishii san wa kēki ga suki desu kara, kēki o tsukurimashō.
○ Demo kanojo wa ima daietto-chū desu kara …

VOCABULARY	
tanjōbi no purezento	birthday present
jū-gatsu futsuka	2 October
raishū	next week
agemashita	gave
sugu nakushimashita	she soon lost (them)
raitā	lighter
sengetsu	last month
tabako o yamemashita kara	because she gave up smoking
irimasen	she doesn't need (one)
tsukurimashō	let's make
daietto-chū desu kara	because she's on a diet

⊘ The months and dates

To give the month, simply add **-gatsu** to the number of the month, e.g.
January: **ichi-gatsu**, August: **hachi-gatsu**. Use the **shi-** and **shichi-**
alternatives for April and July.
The dates are rather more complicated.

1st **tsuitachi**	4th **yokka**	7th **nanoka**	10th **tōka**
2nd **futsuka**	5th **itsuka**	8th **yōka**	
3rd **mikka**	6th **muika**	9th **kokonoka**	

After the 10th, things get a little easier. Add **-nichi** to the number (e.g.
18th, **jū-hachi-nichi**) with these exceptions:

14th **jū-yokka**   24th **ni-jū-yokka**   20th **hatsuka**

When giving the full date, say the month first.

Kyō wa ku-gatsu tōka desu. Today is September 10.

⊘ Giving reasons using *kara*

Use **kara** ('because', 'so') to explain the reason for something. Note that
kara always comes at the end of the clause which gives the reason. This
clause usually comes before the main clause.

Tanjōbi deshita **kara**, pātii o shimashita. It was my birthday, so we had
a party.
Tomodachi ga kimashita **kara**, kēki o tsukurimashita. A friend came, so
I made a cake.
Q Dō shite kōban e ikimashita ka. Why did you go to the police box?
A Saifu o nakushimashita **kara**. Because I lost my purse.

ACTIVITY 13

How would you give the dates of:

1 Christmas Day?   3 Valentine's Day?
2 April Fool's Day?   4 your birthday?

ACTIVITY 14

Join the sentence halves with **kara**.

1 Kinō wa yasumi deshita   hanbāgā o yamemashita.
2 Daietto-chū desu   o-kane ga arimasen.
3 O-sake ga kirai desu | **kara** | umi e ikimashita.
4 Saifu o nakushimashita   nomimasen.

🎧 Now do activities 15 and 16 on the recording.

113

Nihon no bunka

WEATHER AND WHEN TO VISIT JAPAN

Japan is made up of four main islands (**Honshū**, the largest, **Kyūshū**, **Hokkaido**, and **Shikoku**) and numerous smaller ones, and stretches for almost 3000 km from north to south. Being such a long country, there are wide variations in climate from region to region, but most of Japan enjoys a temperate climate.

Spring (**haru**) is warm and dry, and late March or early April is the time when the famous cherry trees (**sakura**) are in bloom. The blossoms are spectacularly beautiful, as indicated by the huge numbers of people who turn out to picnic under the trees in the parks, but the flowers are only on the trees for a few days, and can easily be spoiled by a few days of wind or rain.

There is a rainy season (**tsuyu**) from mid-June to mid-July, when the weather is hot, humid, and wet. Summer (**natsu**) continues hot and unpleasantly humid across much of the Pacific coast of Honshú, where most of the major cities are, although it is much pleasanter in the mountains and in the north of the country. This muggy weather lasts until mid-September when the air begins to clear and temperatures fall to a comfortable warmth. This pleasant weather continues through October and into November. Autumn (**aki**) is a good time to travel around the country, especially as there is the added bonus of spectacular colours as the leaves change. However, southern parts of the country may be hit by typhoons in September, causing widespread wind and flood damage.

The winter (**fuyu**) is cold, with heavy snow in the mountains and northern regions, but it is dry and clear, with many pleasant days of bright sunshine and blue skies.

COUNTING YEARS

Although the Western way of counting years is used widely in Japan, especially in business, the years are also known by the name of the era. Each era begins when a new emperor comes to the throne. The **Heisei** era began in 1989 when Emperor Akihito succeeded his father, Emperor Hirohito. 1990 is therefore equivalent to Heisei 2, 1991 is Heisei 3, and so on.

ACTIVITY 17

Given that the kanji 月 means month or moon, and 日 means day or sun, can you read the dates for the Japanese national holidays?

1 月 1 日	New Year's Day (Ganjitsu)
1 月 15 日	Coming-of-Age Day (Seijin no hi)
2 月 11 日	National Foundation Day (Kenkoku kinenbi)
3 月 21 日 [*varies*]	Spring Equinox (Shunbun no hi)
4 月 29 日	Greenery Day (Midori no hi)
5 月 3 日	Constitution Day (Kenpō kinenbi)
5 月 4 日	designated National Holiday
5 月 5 日	Children's Day (Kodomo no hi)
7 月 20 日	Marine Day (Umi no hi)
9 月 15 日	Respect for the Aged Day (Keirō no hi)
9 月 23 日 [*varies*]	Autumn Equinox (Shūbun no hi)
10 月 10 日	Sports Day (Taiiku no hi)
11 月 3 日	Culture Day (Bunka no hi)
11 月 23 日	Labour Thanksgiving Day (Kinrō kansha no hi)
12 月 23 日	Emperor's Birthday (Tennō tanjōbi)

PART 8: THE POSTCARD FROM AMERICA
AMERIKA KARA NO HAGAKI

It's Saturday evening and Ikeda san has just arrived at Midori-ya with a friend.

yoroshiku	pleased to meet you [*informal*]
kesa	this morning
A, sō da	oh, yes, right! [*informal*]
yonde kudasai	please read it
Hariuddo	Hollywood
eiga no naka no hoteru no heya	a hotel room in a film
... to onaji	similar to, like ...
bā	bar
saigo no hi	the last day
haka	grave
hana	flower
sayōnara	goodbye
ji	characters, handwriting
yappari!	so it is!
kurasu	class

ACTIVITY 18

Listen for these topics of conversation and number them in the order they occur.

1 ___ somebody reads a postcard
2 ___ two people order drinks
3 ___ somebody recognizes the handwriting on the postcard
4 ___ somebody notices there aren't many customers
5 ___ a man is introduced

ACTIVITY 19

Circle any differences between this postcard and the one Hayashi san wrote. (There are six differences.)

13 June

To everyone at Midori-ya,
How is everyone? Hollywood is hot! Arrived on Monday. Hotel is very large, but it's like a hotel room in a film. Saw Chuck Strong the day before yesterday with girlfriend in front of the hotel. Yesterday morning, saw Barbara Anderson in the hotel bar. She's 58, but still beautiful! She was with Brad Brown, 35. Today's the last day, so going to put flowers on Jack Hopper's grave. Bye.

Hayashi Ichiro

STORY TRANSCRIPT

Itō	Ikeda san, irasshaimase.
Ikeda	Konbanwa. Masutā, kochira wa tomodachi no Nishimura san desu. Tenisu kurabu no tomodachi desu.
Nishimura	Yoroshiku. Nishimura desu.
Itō	Irasshaimase. Biiru desu ka.
Ikeda	Hai, onegai shimasu.
Itō	Nishimura san wa?
Nishimura	Hai, watashi mo biiru o kudasai.
Ikeda	O-kyaku san ga sukunai desu ne.
Itō	Sō desu yo… A, sō da. Ikeda san wa kono hagaki o mō yomimashita ka.
Ikeda	Dare kara desu ka.
Itō	Wakarimasen. Kesa kimashita. Dōzo, yonde kudasai.
Ikeda	Hai.
	'Midori-ya no mina san e.
	O-genki desu ka. Hariuddo wa atsui desu. Mokuyōbi no yoru tsukimashita. Hoteru wa totemo takai desu ga, eiga no naka no hoteru no heya to onaji desu. Ototoi, hoteru no mae de Chakku Sutorongu to gārufurendo o mimashita. Kinō no yoru, hoteru no bā de Babara Andason o mimashita. Kanojo wa 58-sai desu ga, mada kirei desu. 25-sai no Buraddo Buraun to issho ni imashita. Ashita wa saigo no hi desu kara, Jakku Hoppa no haka ni, hana o agemasu.
	Dewa, sayōnara. 6-gatsu 23-nichi.'
	Namae ga wakarimasen ga, Hayashi san kara ja arimasen ka.
Nishimura	Kono ji wa Hayashi san desu ne.
Itō	Aaaa, yappari. Ē? Nishimura san wa dō shite kono ji ga wakarimasu ka.
Nishimura	Daigaku no toki, onaji kurasu deshita. Ano eiga no Hayashi san desu ne.

Test

Now it's time to test your progress in Unit 8.

1 How would you say these dates in Japanese?

    1 26 September   4 20 June
    2 6 April   5 16 March
    3 1 November   6 14 August

| | 6 |

2 Match the questions to the responses.

    1 Dō shite nani mo kaimasen deshita ka.
    2 Eiga wa dō deshita ka.
    3 Nan-nen ni daigaku o sotsugyō shimashita ka.
    4 Tanjōbi wa itsu desu ka.
    5 Kanojo wa dō shite kaisha o yamemashita ka.
    6 Kinō nani o shimashita ka.

    a Yoku wakarimasen deshita.
    b San-gatsu jū-hachi-nichi desu.
    c O-kane ga arimasen deshita kara.
    d 1980-nen desu.
    e Sono shigoto ga kirai deshita kara.
    f Nani mo shimasen deshita.

| | 6 |

3 Complete this description of Matsumoto san's week by referring to the diary entries.

Mon July 29	went to Kyoto
Tue July 30	evening – back from Kyoto
Wed July 31	shopping with Ishii san (didn't buy anything!)
Thur Aug 1	saw French film (didn't understand it at all!)
Fri Aug 2	made dinner (friends came)
Sat Aug 3	Ishii san's birthday (party at Italian restaurant)
Sun Aug 4	didn't do anything!

Getsuyōbi ni, Kyōto ___ _____. Kayōbi no yoru, Kyōto
____ _____. Suiyōbi ni, Ishii san to issho ni _____
_____ ga, nani mo _____ _____. Mokuyōbi wa
hachigatsu ____ deshita. Furansu-go no eiga ____ _____
ga, zenzen _____ _____. Kinyōbi ni, tomodachi ga
uchi e _____ _____, ban-gohan o _____. Hachi-gatsu
_____ wa Ishii san no tanjōbi deshita kara, _____ _____
no resutoran de, pātii o _____.

☐ **12**

4 Complete these sentences with **kara** or **ga**.

1 Kurasshiku ongaku ga suki desu _____, yoku konsāto e
  ikimasu.
2 Furansu ryōri wa oishii desu ____, totemo takai desu.
3 Kinō wa nichiyōbi deshita _____, hatarakimashita.
4 Ototoi wa yasumi deshita ____, kaisha e ikimasen
  deshita.
5 Kono jaketto wa chotto furui desu ____, mada suki desu.
6 Tanjōbi desu ____, purezento o agemasu.

☐ **6**

5 Make up some questions to go with these answers.

1 Iie, tomodachi no Yamada san to issho ni ikimashita.
2 Kyonen no 3-gatsu ni kimashita.
3 Nani mo kaimasen deshita.
4 Hatachi desu.
5 Umi e ikimashita.

☐ **10**

6 Answer these questions about yourself.
1 Doko de umaremashita ka.
2 Nan-sai desu ka.
3 Kodomo no toki, shumi wa nan deshita ka.
4 Tanjōbi wa itsu desu ka.
5 Kyonen no natsu yasumi, doko e ikimashita ka.
6 Senshū no doyōbi, nani o shimashita ka.

☐ **12**

TOTAL SCORE ☐ **52**

If you scored less than 42, look at the Language Building
sections again before completing the Summary on page 120.

Summary 8

Now try this final test summarizing the main points covered in this unit. You can check your answers on the recording.

How would you:
1 say you went to Europe last year?
2 say you came to Japan alone?
3 say that someone got married when she was 23 years old?
4 say someone's birthday is 24 May?
5 ask someone when he graduated from university?
6 ask someone where he studied English?
7 say you went to Spain in 1997?
8 say you don't eat cake, because you're on a diet?
9 say that someone was born in London?
10 say you didn't go to the bank today?

REVISION

Before you move on to Unit 9, make sure you can talk about things that happened in the past. Can you form statements, both positive and negative? Ask questions about past events? If you're still not quite sure, review the information on pages 108–113.

How much can you say about yourself now? Where were you born? Where did you go to school? When did you leave school or university? Where have you worked, and when? How old were you when … ?, and so on. As well as being useful practice, this will help you prepare how to introduce yourself in Japan.

People
Donata desu ka

OBJECTIVES

In this unit, you'll learn how to:

✓ talk about your family and friends

✓ describe people

And cover the following grammar and language:

✓ vocabulary for family members

✓ **ni** to indicate the indirect object

✓ adjectives used with **-na**

✓ colours

LEARNING JAPANESE 9

The best way for you to learn and remember vocabulary will depend on the kind of learner you are. If you have a good visual memory, try writing new words on cards or in a small notebook and go through them when you have a spare moment. If, on the other hand, you are better at remembering things you hear, use a cassette to record vocabulary lists and play it whenever you can.

Now start the recording for Unit 9.

Kazoku–1

(🔊) **ACTIVITY 1** is on the recording.

ACTIVITY 2

Correct the statements which are false.

1 The woman's father and younger sister are
together in one photo.   T / F
2 Her younger sister doesn't like shopping.   T / F
3 They all played golf together every day.   T / F
4 Her mother didn't go with them.   T / F

DIALOGUE 1

○ Hawaii wa dō deshita ka. Shashin o torimashita ka.

■ Ē, takusan torimashita yo. Koko ni arimasu. Dōzo.

○ Umi ga kirei desu ne! Kono kata wa donata desu ka.

■ Imōto desu.

○ Imōtosan desu ka. Kirei desu ne.

■ Imōto wa kaimono ga dai-suki desu kara, mada Hawaii ni
imasu.

○ Ushiro no kata wa otōsan desu ka.

■ Hai, chichi desu. Demo chichi wa kono hi dake issho ni
imashita. Hoka no hi wa gorufu deshita.

○ Okāsan mo issho ni irasshaimashita ka.

■ Iie, haha wa ikimasen deshita.

VOCABULARY

kazoku	family
shashin o torimashita	took photos
kirei	pretty, beautiful, clear
kono kata	this person [*polite*]
donata	who? [*polite*]
imōto	my younger sister
imōtosan	your younger sister
otōsan	your father
chichi	my father
kono hi dake	only this day
hoka no hi	other days
okāsan	your mother
irasshaimashita ka	did she go? [*polite*]
haha	my mother

⊘ Family relationships

Words to describe family relationships differ depending on the situation. Formal terms are used when talking about someone else's family and more familiar terms are used to describe one's own family, much as we may refer to our own 'mum and dad' but to someone else's 'mother and father'. (See also *Japanese Culture* on page 128.)

Relation	My family	Someone else's family
family	**kazoku**	**go-kazoku**
mother	**haha**	**okāsan**
father	**chichi**	**otōsan**
older sister	**ane**	**onēsan**
older brother	**ani**	**oniisan**
younger sister	**imōto**	**imōtosan**
younger brother	**otōto**	**otōtosan**
brothers and sisters	**kyōdai**	**go-kyōdai**

Chichi wa enjinia desu. My father's an engineer.
Onēsan wa o-ikutsu desu ka. How old is your older sister?

⊘ Other forms of polite address

Different words are sometimes used to indicate the degree of politeness when speaking to or referring to someone older or more senior in status, or when you don't know someone well. Examples used in this section are:

Polite	Familiar	English
donata	**dare**	who?
kata	**hito**	person
o-ikutsu	**ikutsu, nan-sai**	how old?
irasshaimasu	**ikimasu, kimasu, imasu**	go, come, be

Compare these two sentences.

Oniisan wa mada Pari ni **irasshaimasu** ka. Is your older brother still in Paris?
Ani wa mada Pari ni **imasu**. My older brother is still in Paris.

ACTIVITY 3

How would you …

1 … say your younger sister is a university student?
2 … say your father was an English teacher?
3 … say your mother loves Italian food?
4 … ask if someone's mother and father are in Tokyo?
5 … ask how old someone's younger brother and sister are?

⊙ Now do activities 4 and 5 on the recording.

🎧 **ACTIVITY 6** is on the recording.

ACTIVITY 7

1 When did Yamaguchi san get married?
2 What nationality is her new husband?
3 How many children does he have?
4 What is his job, and who does he work for?

DIALOGUE 2

○ Ohayō gozaimasu. Hisashiburi desu ne. O-genki desu ka.
■ Ē, okage sama de. Okusan wa o-genki desu ka.
○ Hai, genki desu. Saikin, Yamaguchi san ni aimashita ka.
■ Ē, sengetsu kekkon shimashita yo.
○ Ē? Kekkon shimashita ka. Dare to?
■ Go-shujin wa Amerika-jin desu. Kodomo ga futari mo imasu.
○ Sō desu ka. Go-shujin no shigoto wa nan desu ka.
■ Repōtā desu. Amerika no shinbun no repōtā desu.

VOCABULARY	
hisashiburi desu ne	it's been a long time!
o-genki desu ka	how are you? [*literally* are you well?]
ē, okage sama de	fine, thank you [*literally* thanks to you]
okusan	your wife
saikin	recently
dare to?	who to?
go-shujin	her husband
Amerika-jin	American (person)
-jin	*indicates nationality*
repōtā	reporter

✓ More on the family

These are the words you need for referring to husbands, wives, and children.

Relation	My family	Someone else's family
husband	**shujin**	**go-shujin**
wife	**kanai**	**okusan**
daughter	**musume**	**musumesan**
son	**musuko**	**musukosan**

Q **Go-shujin** wa issho ni irasshaimashita ka. Did your husband go with you?

A Hai, **shujin** mo **musuko** mo issho ni ikimashita. Yes, both my husband and my son went with me.

✓ *ni* to show indirect object

The indirect object (which in English is often shown by a preposition – 'write *to them*', 'give *to him*') is indicated in Japanese by the use of **ni**: this appears after the noun or pronoun which is the indirect object. It is commonly used with verbs such as **denwa shimasu** (phone), **hanashimasu** (speak), **aimasu** (meet), **agemasu** (give), and **kakimasu** (write).

Kinō **Katō san ni** denwa shimashita. I called Kato san yesterday.
Okāsan ni hagaki o kakimashita ka. Have you written a postcard to your mother?

✓ Sentence structure

Remember that the small words such as **o**, **wa**, **ni**, known as particles, come after the words or phrases to which they refer. If you need to pause in the middle of a sentence, pause after a particle.

Watashi wa / sensei ni / ringo o / agemashita.
(I / to the teacher / an apple / gave.)
I gave an apple to the teacher.

ACTIVITY 8

Imagine this is your *Things To Do* list and write down what you did and didn't do yesterday.

> 1 call mother ✓
> 2 meet Kato san and husband at station ✓
> 3 give birthday present to Yamada san's son ✓
> 4 write letter to Ikeda san ✗
> 5 give photos to the teacher ✗

🔊 Now do activities 9 and 10 on the recording.

9.3 Describing people
Donna hito desu ka

ACTIVITY 11 is on the recording.

ACTIVITY 12

Circle the characteristics which best describe the real Saito san.

1 Looks: handsome / plain
2 Weight: thin / fat
3 Height: short / tall
4 Clothes sense: good / bad

DIALOGUE 3

○ O-miai wa dō deshita ka. Saitō san wa hansamu-na hito deshō.

■ Iie, shashin to zenzen chigaimasu. Hansamu ja arimasen.

○ Sō desu ka. Demo sumāto-na hito deshō.

■ Sumāto?! Hyaku kiro gurai arimasu. Se ga takaku nai desu. Sore ni, shiroi sūtsu to akai sokkusu deshita.

○ Demo o-kanemochi deshō.

■ E? Resutoran de watashi ga haraimashita yo.

○ Sō desu ka. Wakarimashita. Dewa, kono hito wa dō desu ka. Namae wa Hashimoto san desu.

VOCABULARY

o-miai	meeting with a view to marriage
hansamu-na	handsome
deshō	isn't he? don't you think? [*asking for confirmation*]
... to zenzen chigaimasu	completely different from ...
sumāto-na hito	slim, stylish
kiro	kilogram
shiroi	white
sūtsu	suit
akai	red
sokkusu	socks
o-kanemochi	rich person
watashi ga haraimashita	I paid

✓ -na adjectives

You have already come across -i adjectives (e.g. **takai, atsui**, etc., see page 81). Japanese also has **-na** adjectives, so-called because they need the addition of **-na** when followed by the noun they are describing.

shinsetsu-na	kind	**iya-na**	horrible
hansamu-na	handsome	**yūmei-na**	famous
kirei-na	pretty, clean	**hen-na**	odd, strange
taihen-na	serious, tough	**benri-na**	handy, useful

Kanojo wa **hen-na hito** desu ne. She's strange, isn't she!
Kirei-na shashin desu ne. What beautiful photos!

These adjectives don't need **-na** when they stand alone (i.e. not next to the noun they are describing) or are used in a negative context.

Kono konpyūtā wa amari **benri** ja arimasen. This computer isn't very useful.

Chichi no kaisha wa **yūmei** desu yo. My father's company is famous.

✓ Colours – *iro*

Some words for colours are -i adjectives.

akai	red	**kuroi**	black	**shiroi**	white
chairoi	brown	**kiiroi**	yellow	**aoi**	blue/green

Akai kutsu wa kirei desu. The red shoes are pretty.
Sono **kuroi** sutsu wa ikura desu ka. How much is that black suit?

These colour words also have a noun form: the final **-i** is dropped.

Suki-na iro wa **aka** desu. The colour I like is red.

Other colour words have only noun forms, especially those borrowed from English. This means they must be followed by **no** when joining them to the word they are describing.

midori	green	**orenji**	orange	**pinku**	pink
murasaki	purple	**gurē**	grey	**burū**	blue

Ano **gurē no kuruma** wa dare no desu ka. Whose is the grey car?
Kono **burū no T-shatsu** wa takai desu. This blue T-shirt is expensive.

ACTIVITY 13

How would you compliment/commiserate someone on the following, using **desu ne**:

1 a pretty daughter?   2 a handsome boyfriend?
3 a handy camera?   4 horrible weather?   5 a tough job?

Now do activities 14 and 15 on the recording.

9.4 Japanese Culture
Nihon no bunka

INSIDERS AND OUTSIDERS

A key concept in Japanese society and therefore in its language is that of **uchi** ('inside') and **soto** ('outside'). **uchi** can be applied to the close world of one's family, home, and work colleagues, while **soto** refers to the rest of the world outside. The differences between these are clearly reflected in the language chosen to describe them. The use of **haha**, **chichi**, **imōto** ('my mother', 'my father', 'my younger sister') makes it clear that the speaker is referring to his own family, whereas the corresponding honorific terms **okāsan**, **otōsan**, and **imōtosan** would be used to refer to the members of someone else's family, outside the speaker's own circle.

As honorifics such as those with the prefix **o-** or **go-** are used when talking about people outside your group, and humble forms are only used to refer to those in your own group, it isn't necessary to use words for 'my' or 'your' as this meaning is implicit. **o-namae** and **o-genki** are only used when asking about someone else's name or health. When responding to such a question with information about yourself, use **namae** and **genki**.

Although humble forms are used when talking to an outsider about your family, the honorific terms are used when actually addressing an older member of your own family, such as parents or grandparents, to show respect. Older brothers and sisters call the younger ones by name.

Another way of showing the degree of intimacy is the use or non-use of **san** after a name, and this can change depending on the circumstances. For example, when addressing someone of similar rank at work, you would use **san** with her name. However, when introducing her to people from a different company, you would refer to her without **san** to show that she is part of your in-group.

The word **uchi** is also sometimes used to refer to someone within one's own group, e.g. **uchi no Yamada san** ('our Mr Yamada') or **uchi no shachō** ('our company president'). In contrast, **o-taku**, a polite word for 'house, home, in-group' is used when showing respect to a person in someone else's in-group, so **o-taku no shachō** would mean 'your president'.

ARRANGED MEETINGS

Today about a quarter of all marriages in Japan come about through **o-miai**, or arranged meetings between prospective marriage partners. The **o-miai** is a way of bringing together young people who for one reason or another do not have the opportunity to meet suitable marriage partners, fulfilling a similar role to a dating agency or marriage bureau. The **nakōdo**, or go-between, is usually someone known personally to one of the families involved, perhaps someone of influence in the neighbourhood or in the company. At the first meeting, often in the coffee lounge of a large hotel, the parents of the couple may also attend, but after this, if the two young people want to continue meeting, they do so on a more social level as friends until they decide whether or not they are suited as marriage partners.

ACTIVITY 16

Which of the words and phrases 1–10 refer to one's own in-group, and which are honorific, referring to someone else's group?

1	uchi no kuruma	a	おなまえ
2	otaku no neko	b	うちのむすこ
3	go-shujin	c	おくさんのかいしゃ
4	o-namae	d	おたくのねこ
5	chichi	e	このかた
6	uchi no musuko	f	ごしゅじん
7	otaku no musumesan	g	うちのかいしゃ
8	uchi no kaisha	h	うちのくるま
9	okusan no kaisha	i	ちち
10	kono kata	j	おたくのむすめさん

ACTIVITY 17

Now look at the list again and match the phrases to their hiragana equivalents.

HAYASHI SAN'S BACK IN TOWN
HAYASHI SAN WA KAERIMASHITA

It's another evening at Midori-ya. It's raining and Ikeda san has just arrived to have something to eat and see her friends.

ame	rain
kasa	umbrella
o-kaeri nasai	welcome back
bōshi	hat
omoshiroi	interesting
kaubōi	cowboy
konna	such as this, like this
būtsu	boots
shatsu	shirt
dō itashimashite	you're welcome; think nothing of it
chotto shitsurei shimasu	excuse me a moment
toire	toilet
sama	*polite form of* **san**
kōra de ii desu	cola is fine
o-kyaku no koto	it's about a customer
apāto	flat, apartment
motte kimashita	brought

ACTIVITY 18

Listen to the conversation and find the words for:

1 a colour   3 three items of clothing
2 two drinks   4 three family members

ACTIVITY 19

Which two events do not occur in the dialogue?

1 Ikeda san comes in with an umbrella.   ☐
2 Hayashi san comes in wearing a cowboy hat.   ☐
3 Hayashi san orders beer.   ☐
4 Itō san asks what colour the boots are.   ☐
5 Hayashi san gives Itō san a present from America.   ☐
6 Two customers come in asking about Hayashi san.   ☐
7 Hayashi san's parents have just been to his flat.   ☐
8 His mother sent him a letter.   ☐

ACTIVITY 20

Who …

1 … got back today?
2 … doesn't need an umbrella?
3 … gets a present?
4 … wants a cola?
5 … is 32 years old?

STORY TRANSCRIPT

Itō	A, Ikeda san, irasshaimase.
Ikeda	Konbanwa. Iya-na tenki desu ne. Mainichi mainichi ame desu ne.
Itō	Un, yappari tsuyu desu ne. Kasa wa asoko desu.
Hayashi	Mina san, konbanwa.
Itō	Hayashi san desu ka.
Hayashi	Sō desu yo.
Ikeda	O-kaeri nasai. …. Anō… sono bōshi wa … omoshiroi desu ne. Kaubōi no bōshi desu ka.
Hayashi	Ē, sō desu. Amerika de kaimashita. Konna iya-na tenki ni wa, totemo benri desu yo. Kasa wa irimasen.
Itō	Sō desu ka. Hayashi san, sono būtsu mo Amerika de kaimashita ka.
Hayashi	Ē, kaubōi būtsu desu yo.
Itō	Demo shiroi desu yo! Shiroi kaubōi būtsu?
Hayashi	Masutā, dōzo. Amerika no o-miyage desu.
Itō	E? Arigatō. Nan deshō… A … kore … kaubōi shatsu … Dōmo arigatō.
Hayashi	Iie, dō itashimashite. Chotto shitsurei shimasu. Toire…
Itō	Irasshaimase. O-futari sama desu ka. Dōzo, kochira e.
Mother	Watashi wa kōra de ii desu. Anata wa biiru desu ne.
Itō	Hai.
Mother	Masutā, kono mise no o-kyaku no koto desu ga.
Itō	Hai, dare deshō.
Mother	Namae wa Hayashi Ichiro desu. 32-sai desu. Se ga amari takaku nai desu. Uchi no musuko desu ga. Ima Ichiro no apāto e ikimashita ga, imasen deshita. Yoku koko e kimasu ne.
Itō	Hayashi san desu ka. Hai, asoko ni imasu yo.
Mother	Ichiro?
Hayashi	E? E?! Okāsan? Otōsan? Dō shite… koko e kimashita ka.
Mother	O-miai no shashin o motte kimashita yo. Watashi no tegami o yomimasen deshita ka.

Now it's time to test your progress in Unit 9.

1 Choose the ending that best completes each sentence.

1 Kono kata wa	a sakura wa kirei desu ne.
2 Go-shujin wa	b shinsetsu ja arimasen.
3 Ototoi Yamada san ni	c go-shujin desu ka.
4 Kare wa hansamu-na	d o-genki desu ka.
5 Yoyogi Kōen no	e hito desu ne.
6 Atarashii sensei wa amari	f aimashita yo.

6

2 Fill in the boxes on the family tree with the appropriate terms.

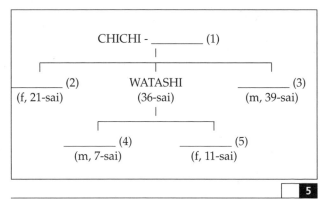

```
            CHICHI - _____ (1)
                        |
     ┌──────────────────┼──────────────────┐
  _____ (2)     WATASHI         _____ (3)
  (f, 21-sai)        (36-sai)        (m, 39-sai)
                        |
             ┌──────────┴──────────┐
        _____ (4)        _____ (5)
        (m, 7-sai)           (f, 11-sai)
```

5

3 How would you answer these questions if the family tree above were yours?

1 Go-kyōdai wa nan-nin irasshaimasu ka.
2 Imōtosan wa o-ikutsu desu ka.
3 Musukosan wa o-ikutsu desu ka.

3

4 Choose the correct words from the box to complete these sentences.

| chichi hito irasshaimashita donata |
| shinsetsu-na benri dore o-ikutsu |

1 Otōsan mo okāsan mo issho ni Hawaii e _____ ka.
2 Haha mo _____ mo kōkō no sensei desu.
3 Sono _____ wa Tanaka san no otōto-san desu.
4 Imōtosan wa _____ desu ka.
5 Yamada san wa _____ hito desu ne.
6 Kono kata wa _____ desu ka.

6

5 Complete this dialogue between two people who haven't seen each other for a while.

A Hisashiburi _____ ne.
B Sō _____ ne. Mina san _____ desu ka.
A Hai, _____ de. Hayashi san wa?
B Hai, _____ desu yo.

5

6 Answer these questions about yourself.

1 Kuruma wa arimasu ka. Nani iro desu ka.
2 Go-kyōdai wa irasshaimasu ka. O-ikutsu desu ka.
3 Saikin tegami ya hagaki o kakimashita ka. Dare ni kakimashita ka.
4 Nani iro ga suki desu ka.
5 Nan-kiro arimasu ka.
6 Kamera wa arimasu ka. Benri-na kamera desu ka. Shashin o yoku torimasu ka.

12

TOTAL SCORE **37**

If you scored less than 27, look at the Language Building sections again before completing the Summary on page 134.

Now try this final test summarizing the main points covered in this unit. You can check your answers on the recording.

How would you:
1 ask someone if his mother and father are in Tokyo?
2 ask someone how old her younger brother is?
3 say your older brother is a high school teacher?
4 comment on someone's beautiful photos?
5 say you like that red car?
6 say your new computer is really useful?
7 say you met Ishii san and his wife yesterday?
8 say your Japanese teacher's husband is English?
9 greet someone you haven't seen for a long time?
10 respond to someone who asks if you're well?

REVISION

Before going on to the next unit, make sure that you can remember all the various words for members of the family. Think about your own family, or friends and neighbours and their families. What can you say about them? What are their names and where do they all live? What are their various jobs? Do they have children? What are they like? What do they like doing? See how long you can keep talking about them!

Eating out
Resutoran de

OBJECTIVES

In this unit, you'll learn how to:

- ✓ order food and drink
- ✓ answer questions often asked of foreigners
- ✓ describe things in the past

And cover the following grammar and language:

- ✓ **to iimasu** to ask for a translation
- ✓ non-specific counters **hitotsu**, **futatsu**, etc.
- ✓ the counter **-hon** for long thin objects
- ✓ past tense of adjectives

LEARNING JAPANESE 10

As your confidence in speaking Japanese grows, consider learning how to read and write Japanese. There is a little reading practice in each unit of this course, which will get you started. Learning hiragana and katakana may take some time, but these scripts are not difficult, and a knowledge of them will certainly widen your understanding of Japanese. Kanji characters are more difficult, but the study of them is fascinating, and knowing even just a few will help. You can find books to help you learn the various Japanese scripts in most large bookshops.

Now start the recording for Unit 10.

🔊 **ACTIVITY 1** is on the recording.

ACTIVITY 2

Correct the statements which are false.

1	The restaurant has various set dishes on the menu today.	T / F
2	Yaki-zakana is a fish dish.	T / F
3	The two people both order tempura.	T / F
4	They're going to drink beer.	T / F

DIALOGUE 1

○ Jonson san wa nani ni shimasu ka. Kyō no teishoku wa, tenpura teishoku, sukiyaki teishoku, tonkatsu teishoku …
■ Yaki-zakana wa nan desu ka.
○ Sakana desu. Eigo de 'grilled fish' to iimasu.
■ Ja, yaki-zakana wa 'grilled fish' desu. Sore ni shimasu.
○ Hai. Watashi wa tenpura teishoku ni shimasu. Sumimasen!
▼ O-kimari desu ka.
○ Hai. Yaki-zakana teishoku o hitotsu, tenpura teishoku o hitotsu, sore kara biiru o nihon kudasai.
▼ Hai, kashikomarimashita.

VOCABULARY	
… ni shimasu	I'll have …
teishoku	*set meal, usually including rice and miso soup*
tenpura	tempura [*deep-fried fish and vegetables in batter*]
sukiyaki	pieces of beef and vegetables in soy sauce
tonkatsu	pork cutlet
yaki-zakana	grilled fish
sakana	fish
eigo de	in English
… to iimasu	it's called …
o-kimari desu ka	have you decided?
hitotsu	one (object)
nihon	two (bottles)
kashikomarimashita	certainly, of course [*polite*]

✅ Asking for a translation

To ask how to say something in English or Japanese, use the phrase
… **nan to iimasu ka** ('How do you say …?')

Yaki-zakana wa eigo de **nan to iimasu ka**. How do you say 'yaki-zakana' in English?
'Meat' wa nihongo de **nan to iimasu ka**. How do you say 'meat' in Japanese?

✅ Counting objects with *hitotsu*, *futatsu* and *ip-pon*, *ni-hon*

You have already come across different ways of counting depending on the type of object, e.g. **-mai** for flat things and **-nin** for people. To count long, thin objects such as bottles, pens, or barbecued food on sticks, use **-hon**. In some cases, the variants **-pon** or **-bon** are used. To ask 'how many?', use **nan-bon**

1	ip-pon	3	san-bon	5	go-hon	7	nana-hon	9	kyū-hon
2	ni-hon	4	yon-hon	6	rop-pon	8	hap-pon	10	jup-pon

Yakitori o **rop-pon** kudasai. Six sticks of yakitori, please.
Banana wa **ip-pon** ikura desu ka. How much is one banana?

Some objects have no specific counter: in such cases the following set of numbers is used. (After ten, it reverts back to **jū-ichi**, **jū-ni**, **jū-san**, and so on.) To ask 'how many?', use **ikutsu**.

1	hitotsu	3	mittsu	5	itsutsu	7	nanatsu	9	kokonotsu
2	futatsu	4	yottsu	6	muttsu	8	yattsu	10	tō

how many? **ikutsu**

Kore o **mittsu** kudasai. Three of these, please.
Ringo o **ikutsu** kaimashō ka. How many apples shall we buy?

(You can also use these numbers if you can't remember the specific counter for a particular group of objects!)

ACTIVITY 3

What did the customers say to order these items?

1 two coffees and one glass of coke
2 three tempura set meals and three bottles of beer
3 two hamburgers and one bottle of beer

🎧 Now do activities 4 and 5 on the recording.

🎧 **ACTIVITY 6** is on the recording.

ACTIVITY 7

1 Why is Mr Johnson used to eating with chopsticks?
2 Where has he eaten sushi and sashimi before?
3 What does he think about the Japanese language?

ACTIVITY 8

Answer these questions about yourself.

1 Hashi o yoku tsukaimasu ka.
2 Doko no ryōri ga suki desu ka.
3 Hashi wa eigo de nan to iimasu ka.

DIALOGUE 2

○ Kore wa oishi-sō desu ne. Itadakimasu.
■ Itadakimasu. Jonson san, hashi ga jōzu desu ne.
○ Arigatō. Watashi wa nihon ryōri to chūka ryōri ga suki desu kara, yoku Amerika de mo hashi o tsukaimasu yo.
■ Sō desu ka. Nihon ryōri wa ikaga desu ka. Sushi ya sashimi wa suki desu ka.
○ Hai, dai-suki desu. Nyū Yōku de wa Nihon ryōri no resutoran ga takusan arimasu kara, yoku tabemasu.
■ Sō desu ka. Tokorode, Jonson san wa, Nihongo ga jōzu desu ne. Muzukashii desu ka.
○ Sō desu ne. Kanji wa muzukashii desu ne.

VOCABULARY	
oishi-sō	looks delicious
itadakimasu	*set phrase said before eating*
hashi	chopsticks
... ga jōzu desu	be good at ...
chūka ryōri	Chinese food
tsukaimasu	use
ikaga	how about? [*polite equivalent of* **dō**]
sashimi	raw fish
muzukashii	difficult

✓ Set phrases at mealtimes

The phrase **itadakimasu** (somewhat similar to 'Bon appétit' in French) is always said before eating, especially if you are a guest at a meal. After finishing the meal, use the phrase **Go-chisō sama deshita** as an expression of thanks. This phrase is often repeated as you leave the restaurant or someone's home.

✓ Typical questions asked of foreigners

Although Western visitors are now a common sight in Japan, people still find it worthy of comment when they come across foreigners using chopsticks, eating sashimi and sushi, and speaking Japanese, so you will often hear comments like the following.

Nihongo ga o-jōzu desu ne. You're good at Japanese, aren't you!
O-hashi ga o-jōzu desu ne. You're good at using chopsticks, aren't you!

It's best to give a modest response such as **Iie, mada heta desu** ('No, I'm still no good.').

Other common topics of small talk to foreigners are:

O-kuni wa dochira desu ka. Which country are you from?
Nihon ni, dono gurai irasshaimasu ka. How long have you been in Japan?
Kekkon shite irasshaimasu ka. Are you married?
O-ko-san wa irasshaimasu ka. Do you have any children?
Nihon wa ikaga desu ka. What do you think of Japan?

ACTIVITY 9

Match the questions and comments with appropriate responses.

1 Nihongo ga o-jōzu desu ne.
2 Kekkon shite irasshaimasu ka.
3 O-kuni wa dochira desu ka.
4 Tōkyō wa ikaga desu ka.
5 Kanji wa muzukashii desu ka.
6 O-ko-san wa irasshaimasu ka.

a Muzukashii desu ga, omoshiroi desu.
b Hai, futari imasu.
c Iie, mada heta desu.
d Ōkii desu ne!
e Igirisu desu.
f Iie, mada dokushin ('single') desu.

 Now do activities 10 and 11 on the recording.

10.3 Describing things in the past
Oishikatta desu

 ACTIVITY 12 is on the recording.

ACTIVITY 13

Number the topics in the order you hear them mentioned.
Which of the topics is not mentioned at all?

a a comment on the prices
b a comment on the freshness of the fish
c a suggestion to order some more beer
d an amount of money
e the time
f a comment on the size of the restaurant

DIALOGUE 3

○ Biiru o mo ip-pon dō desu ka.
■ Jū-ichi-ji desu kara, mō kekkō desu.
○ Sō desu ne. Soro soro kaerimashō. Sumimasen, o-kanjō,
onegai shimasu.
▼ Hai, kashikomarimashita. ¥29,500 de gozaimasu. ... Hai,
arigatō gozaimashita.
○ Go-chisō sama deshita.

○ Takakatta desu ne!
■ Sō desu ne. Hontō ni takakatta desu ne. Sashimi teishoku
wa dō deshita ka. Oishikatta desu ka.
○ Sashimi wa chiisakatta desu. Sore ni, amari shinsen ja
nakatta desu yo.
■ Kono mise wa dō shite yūmei deshō ka.
○ Wakarimasen ne.

VOCABULARY	
kekkō desu	I've had enough
soro soro	it's about time
takakatta desu	was expensive
hontō ni	really, very
oishikatta	was delicious
chiisakatta desu	was small
shinsen ja nakatta desu	wasn't fresh
dō shite ... deshō ka	I wonder why ...?

✓ Past tense of adjectives

Unlike English, some Japanese adjectives have a different form if they are used to describe something in the past. To make the past-tense form of **-i** adjectives, the final **-i desu** changes to **-katta desu**.

> Kinō no pikunikku wa hontō ni **tanoshikatta desu.** The picnic yesterday was really fun.
> Sapporo wa **samukatta desu.** Sapporo was cold.

Ii ('good', 'nice') has the alternative form **yoi**, and it's this form that is used for the past tense.

> Resutoran wa **yokatta** desu ga, takakatta desu. The restaurant was good, but it was expensive.

To form the negative, change the present tense ending **-ku nai desu** to **-ku nakatta desu.** (You may also hear **-ku arimasen deshita** – it's slightly more formal.)

> Eiga wa amari **omoshiroku nakatta desu.** The film wasn't very interesting.

-na adjectives don't change form when referring to the past: only the verb changes to the past tense.

> Hoteru wa kirei deshita ga, amari benri **ja arimasen deshita.** The hotel was nice, but it wasn't very convenient.

(The negative ending **ja nakatta desu** is often used instead of **ja arimasen deshita.**)

✓ Use of *deshó*

deshō is often used at the end of a sentence to show probability, or in a question to ask for confirmation.

> Ano hito wa Yamashita san **deshō**? That's Yamashita san, isn't it?

However, when followed by **ka**, it means 'I wonder …'

> Kore wa ikura **deshō ka**. I wonder how much this is.
> Furansugo wa muzukashii **deshō ka**. I wonder if French is difficult.

ACTIVITY 14

Say what went wrong for this tourist yesterday.

1 hotel rooms weren't very clean
2 weather was cold
3 had a headache
4 TV wasn't interesting
5 restaurant was expensive
6 fish wasn't fresh

 Now do activities 15 and 16 on the recording.

(10.4) Japanese Culture
Nihon no bunka

EATING OUT IN JAPAN

There is amazing variety in Japanese food, with something to suit every taste. While it is possible to spend a small fortune on a traditional meal, beautifully presented in exquisite tableware chosen to harmonize with the food and the season, you can also find a huge number of cheap restaurants where fresh and tasty meals are available. Even the stand-up noodle bars serve fresh, delicious, and nutritious food.

A typical meal of meat or fish will always be accompanied by rice (**gohan**), miso soup (**miso shiru** – soup made with fermented soya beans), and some pickled vegetables. Each item of food is presented in a separate small dish, and one setting may include half a dozen dishes of varying shape, size, and colour, so the presentation will delight the eye as much as the tastes please the palate. Natural flavours and fresh ingredients are very important, and seasonings tend to be light, intended only to enhance the subtle flavours of the food.

Inside the restaurant, you will be shown to a seat and given a glass of water or cup of green tea, and an **oshibori** (hand towel) with which to wipe your hands while you decide what to order. Don't forget, if you are having difficulties with the menu, many restaurants have a display window with incredibly realistic wax models of the food, along with the prices. Don't be embarrassed to take the waiter outside and point to what you want. Disposable chopsticks come joined together at the top, so simply pull them apart before you begin to eat. Western-style meals, however, are eaten with a knife and fork.

If you're drinking beer or **sake** with your meal, remember that it is courteous always to keep your eye on your companions' glasses, and refill them when necessary. Don't worry about your own drink - your companions will make sure that your glass is always full.

Although there is a small consumption tax, there is no tipping in Japan.

ACTIVITY 17

Here are 12 things to eat in Japan. Use the hiragana chart on page viii to find out what these typical food items are.

1	てんぷら	small pieces of food deep-fried in a light batter, and served with a dipping sauce
2	すし	bite-sized pieces of raw fish on rice
3	さしみ	raw fish
4	やきざかな	grilled fish
5	みそしる	soup made with miso
6	ごはん	rice
7	そば, うどん	different kinds of noodles
8	おでん	small pieces of tofu, vegetables, pressed fish cakes, etc., boiled in fish-based stock
9	やきとり	pieces of chicken barbecued over charcoal
10	おべんとう	boxed lunches sold at stations or in local shops, or prepared at home with loving care by wives and mothers
11	すきやき	thin slices of beef and vegetables cooked at the table
12	おこのみやき	do-it-yourself thick savoury pancakes with pieces of meat, seafood, or vegetables

**GOSSIP IN THE STREET
MICHI DE**

It's a Saturday morning and Ikeda san is shopping. She
bumps into Harada san by a fruit and vegetable stall.

michi	street
konde imasu	be crowded
dake	only
isogashii	busy
painappuru	pineapple
ryōshin	parents
o-tsuri	change
hazukashi-sō	look embarrassed
aite	partner
iya da sō desu	is apparently reluctant
ganbatte kudasai	good luck!; go for it!

ACTIVITY 18

Write down the six numbers that are mentioned in the
conversation.

ACTIVITY 19

Say if the following statements are true or false, or you don't
know because the information isn't in the dialogue. Correct
those that are false.

1 Harada san gives the storekeeper the exact
  money.   T / F / DK
2 The two women see Hayashi san with his
  mother.   T / F / DK
3 Hayashi san is embarrassed to see the women. T / F / DK
4 His parents have arranged an o-miai for
  tomorrow.   T / F / DK
5 The o-miai will be in a restaurant.   T / F / DK
6 The woman is from Kyushu, she's 25 years
  old, and pretty.   T / F / DK
7 Harada san wishes him luck with tomorrow's
  o-miai.   T / F / DK

ACTIVITY 20

Here is a summary of the conversation in the street, but there are four mistakes. Can you find them?

Ikeda san and Harada san meet in the street on a busy Saturday afternoon. Harada san buys some apples, bananas, and a pineapple, and they continue chatting. They see Hayashi san with his parents, and Ikeda san says they're visiting from Kyushu to show him some o-miai photos. She tells Harada san that he was embarrassed when Itō san, the owner of Midori-ya, had a look at the photos too. Tomorrow Hayashi san is supposed to be meeting a prospective partner who's travelling from Kyushu, but he's unhappy about the arrangement because Sunday is usually his day for going to see old films.

STORY TRANSCRIPT

Ikeda	Harada san! Ohayō gozaimasu. O-kaimono desu ka.
Harada	Sō desu. Konde imasu ne!
Ikeda	Sō desu ne. Doyōbi desu kara ne.
Stallholder	Hai, tsugi no o-kyaku san.
Harada	Watashi desu. Anō… sono akai ringo o mittsu to …
Stallholder	Ringo o mittsu desu ne. Hai.
Harada	Sore kara, banana ….
Stallholder	Nan-bon desu ka.
Harada	Rop-pon, onegai shimasu.
Stallholder	Banana o rop-pon… Hai. Painappuru mo oishii desu yo. Shinsen desu yo. Hitotsu ¥650. Kyō wa yasui desu yo.
Harada	Iie, ringo to banana dake de ii desu.
Stallholder	¥710 desu. Hai, ¥290 no o-tsuri desu.
Harada	Arigatō. Are wa Hayashi san ja nai desu ka.
Ikeda	Doko desu ka. A sō desu ne. Go-ryōshin to issho desu ne.
Harada	Go-ryōshin desu ka. Dō shite wakarimasu ka. Mō aimashita ka.
Ikeda	Senshū Midori-ya e kimashita.
Harada	Ē? Dō shite? Hayashi san wa Kyūshū deshō.
Ikeda	E, ryōshin wa Kyūshū kara kimashita. O-miai no shashin o motte kimashita. Midori-ya no o-kyaku-san minna o-miai no shashin o mimashita. Hayashi san wa hontō ni hazukashi-sō deshita
Harada	Sō desu ka. Sore kara?
Ikeda	Ashita Kyūshū kara o-miai no aite ga kimasu.
Harada	Ē? Kyūshū kara?
Ikeda	Sō desu. Kanojo wa 26-sai desu.
Harada	Shashin o mimashita ka.
Ikeda	Un, kirei desu yo. Demo Hayashi san wa iya da sō desu.
Harada	Dō shite desu ka.
Ikeda	Ashita wa nichiyobi desu kara ne. Hayashi san wa itsumo nichiyōbi ni atarashii eiga o mimasu ne.
Harada	Yappari sō desu ne. Hayashi san! Hayashi san!
Hayashi	A, Harada san desu ka. Ohayō gozaimasu.
Harada	Hayashi san, ashita ganbatte kudasai ne!

Test

Now it's time to test your progress in Unit 10.

1 Number these phrases in the order they're likely to occur when someone eats in a restaurant.

   a O-kanjo, onegai shimasu.
   b Go-chisō sama deshita.
   c Tenpura teishoku o kudasai.
   d O-kimari desu ka.
   e Itadakimasu.
   f Oishi-sō desu ne.

| | 6 |

2 How would someone with a group of friends order the following items in a restaurant or coffee shop?

1
2 tonkatsu
   set meals,
1 hamburger
   set meal,
3 beers
	2
	3 coffees,
	1 orange juice,
	4 mixed
	  sandwiches
		3
		8 sticks of
		  yakitori,
		2 tempura,
		4 beers

| | 12 |

3 Put these words in the correct order to make sentences.

   1 wa / shimasu / watashi / ni / supagetti
   2 jōzu / Jonson san / nihongo / wa / ga / desu
   3 nakatta / konsāto / amari / desu / wa / yoku
   4 hito / ka / deshō / ano / wa / dare
   5 wa / sashimi / desu / ni / oishikatta / hontō
   6 ja / sakana / shinsen / desu / wa / amari / nakatta

| | 12 |

4 Choose the most appropriate responses.

   1 Nihon ni, dono gurai irasshaimasu ka.
      a Ashita kimasu.   b Sengetsu kara desu.
   2 O-kimari desu ka.
      a Iie, mada desu.   b Hai, sō desu.

3 Biiru mō ip-pon, ikaga desu ka.
   a Iie, kekkō desu.   b Dai-suki desu.
4 'Itadakimasu' wa, eigo de nan to iimasu ka.
   a Go-chisō sama deshita.   b Wakarimasen.
5 Chūka ryōri no resutoran wa dō deshita ka.
   a Hai, ikimashita.   b Amari oishiku nakatta desu.
6 Hashi ga jōzu desu ne.
   a Arigatō.   b Sō desu.

| | 6 |

5 Put 1–7 below in the correct order to make a conversation
   between a Japanese person and a foreign tourist.

   A Shitsurei desu ga, dono gurai Nihon ni irasshaimasu ka.
   B _____
   A _____
   B _____
   A _____
   B _____
   A _____
   B _____

   1 Sō desu ne. Chotto muzukashii desu ne.
   2 Igirisu desu ka. Nihongo ga o-jōzu desu ne. Igirisu de
      nihongo o benkyō shimashita ka.
   3 Ē, sō desu. Daigaku de benkyō shimashita.
   4 Sō desu ka. O-kuni wa dochira desu ka. Amerika desu ka.
   5 Iie, Igirisu desu.
   6 1998-nen kara desu.
   7 Muzukashii desu ka.

| | 6 |

6 How would you say the following in Japanese?

   1 The fish wasn't very fresh, so I didn't eat it.
   2 I wonder if that restaurant is expensive.
   3 No, thank you.
   4 Another beer, please.
   5 I'm no good at cooking.
   6 Tokyo was fun, but it was expensive.

| | 12 |

TOTAL SCORE | 54 |

If you scored less than 44, look at the Language Building
sections again before completing the Summary on page 148.

Summary 10

 Now try this final test summarizing the main points covered in this unit. You can check your answers on the recording.

How would you:
1 count pens or bottles of beer up to ten?
2 count other objects (without a specific counter) up to ten?
3 ask how to say 'fish' in Japanese?
4 respond to someone who compliments you on your Japanese?
5 say the set phrase used before a meal?
6 say the set phrase of thanks after a meal?
7 ask someone if he's married?
8 say you've had enough if someone offers you more food or drink?
9 say the fish was delicious?

REVISION

When you eat out, whether it's a quick sandwich in a coffee shop or a three-course meal in an expensive restaurant, think about how you would order it in Japanese. What would you say to the waiter? How would you ask about something you're not sure of? How would you ask for the bill? How much does it all cost? What's your favourite kind of food?

The next section is a review of all the units so far, with emphasis on Units 8–10, so this is a good time to go back and revise the areas you're still not sure about. Try listening to the three main dialogues from the previous units without looking at the text to see how much you can understand.

Review 3

VOCABULARY

1 Number these words in the order of furthest in the future to furthest in the past.

asatte   ashita   kesa   senshū

kinō   kyonen   ototoi   sengetsu

2 Which are the odd ones out in the following groups?

1 akai / kuroi / kirei / shiroi / aoi
2 hatsuka / mikka / kokonoka / tsuitachi / futatsu
3 ani / imōto / otōto / chichi / haha / onna
4 mittsu / kokonotsu / hitotsu / shatsu / muttsu
5 shinsen / tenpura / yaki-zakana / tonkatsu / butaniku

3 Match the words and phrases 1–8 to appropriate situations a–h.

1 Itadakimasu.
2 O-kaeri nasai.
3 Hisashiburi desu ne.
4 Go-chisō sama deshita.
5 Hai, o-kage sama de.
6 Wakarimashita.
7 O-genki desu ka.
8 Dō itashimashite.

a said in response to 'thank you'
b said before a meal
c said to someone who has just returned from somewhere
d said to someone you haven't seen for a while
e said after a meal
f said to ask about someone's health
g said when you've understood something
h said when someone asks how you've been

4 Look at the details about Takahashi san, and make
   sentences in Japanese about the information.

> **Personal details:**
> 1 **Name:**   Ichiro Takahashi
> 2 **Nationality:**   Japanese
> 3 **Date of birth:** 10 April, 1964
> 4 **Place of birth:** Osaka
> 5 **Education:**   Kyoto University, graduated 1986
> 6 **Occupation:**   reporter
> 7 **Marital status:** married in 1991

1 Namae wa Takahashi Ichiro desu.
2 Takahashi san wa _____
3 Shi-gatsu _____
4 Ōsaka _____
5 _____
6 _____
7 _____

5 Choose the best response.

1 O-cha o dōzo.
   a Itadakimasu.
   b Go-chisō sama deshita.
2 'Hisashiburi' wa eigo de nan to iimasu ka.
   a Wakarimasen.
   b Sō desu ne. Hisashiburi desu ne.
3 Atarashii sūtsu wa nani iro desu ka.
   a Gurē ga ii desu.
   b Burū desu.
4 Takahashi san wa donna hito desu ka.
   a Totemo shinsetsu-na hito desu yo.
   b Hai, Takahashi san desu.
5 Tanjōbi wa raishū deshō.
   a Nani o agemashita ka.
   b Watashi no tanjōbi desu ka. Iie, 23-nichi deshita.
6 Dō shite umi e ikimasen deshita ka.
   a Hai, umi wa totemo kirei desu kara.
   b Samukatta kara desu.

6 Choose the best word or phrase to complete the sentences.

   1 Sūtsu wa totemo takakatta desu (kara / ga), kaimasen
     deshita.
   2 (Imōto / Imōtosan) mo issho ni Hawai ni
     irasshaimashita ka.
   3 Ano (burū / burū no) kuruma wa dare no desu ka.
   4 Kinō wa taihen (atsukatta desu / atsui deshita) ne.
   5 Tōkyō ni wa, daigaku ga (ikutsu / nan-bon) arimasu ka.
   6 Kono kata wa (dare / donata) desu ka.

🎧 LISTENING

7 Listen to someone describing his best friend, Tatsuo Ishii,
  and answer the questions below.

   1 Where did the two friends meet?
   2 What interests did they share?
   3 Why did Tatsuo improve his English while he was at
     university?
   4 Which year did they graduate?
   5 Why don't the two friends meet often now?
   6 When did Tatsuo get married?

8 Listen to Yamada san as she shows her friend a family
  photo, and draw a picture of where everyone is standing.
  Then answer the questions below.

   1 How many people in the photo are mentioned?
   2 Who took the photo?
   3 When did Yamada san's sister get married?

🎧 SPEAKING

9 Imagine you sent a lot of postcards like the one on page 152
  when you were on vacation recently. Now one of your
  Japanese friends is asking about your holiday. Use the
  information on the postcard to help with your side of the
  conversation.

15 July
In Rome last week. Very hot!
Hotel expensive but really
beautiful. Food wonderful! Drank
lots of wine. Arrived in Paris
yesterday. Expensive, so haven't
bought anything. Back on 21st.
See you then.
Pat

MS S YAMADA, 4-26-28
SAKURAGICHO,
SETAGAYA KU 156,
TOKYO,
JAPAN

Friend	Doko e ikimashita ka.
You	1 _____
Friend	Ii desu ne. Tenki wa dō deshita ka?
You	2 _____
Friend	Yokatta desu ne. Hoteru wa?
You	3 _____
Friend	Sō desu ka. Ryōri wa dō deshita ka. Oishikatta deshō.
You	4 _____
Friend	Itaria no wain mo yūmei desu ne.
You	5 _____
Friend	Pari de kaimono o shimashita ka.
You	6 _____
Friend	Sō desu ka. Itsu kaerimashita ka.
You	7 _____

After you've practised this dialogue several times, listen to the recording and try to take part without referring to the book.

10 You'll hear some questions on the recording. See if you can answer them in the pauses without stopping the recording. The questions will be about the following topics, but in a different order. You'll be asked:

– when your birthday is
– if you have any children
– where you were born
– what you did yesterday
– where you're from

What's happening?
Nani o shite imasu ka

OBJECTIVES

In this unit, you'll learn how to:

✓ describe what's happening now

✓ say where you live and work

✓ describe what someone is wearing

And cover the following grammar and language:

✓ the **-te imasu** ('-ing') form of verbs

✓ negative questions

✓ verbs used with clothing

LEARNING JAPANESE 11

If you find it's getting more difficult to work through the
units, don't give up. It may simply be that you've forgotten
the good study habits you started out with. Keep reminding
yourself that you will learn better if you are relaxed. Perhaps
you're getting impatient and are trying to do too much in each
session. You are more likely to remember new language if you
study little and often. Are you still setting yourself goals for
each week? Do you still practise speaking Japanese aloud as
much as possible? Do you go back and review previous units
now and then? Are you keeping your vocabulary notebook up
to date? Take a short rest if you need it – but make sure you
come back again!

Now start the recording for Unit 11.

11.1 Saying what's happening now
Ima eiga o mite imasu

 ACTIVITY 1 is on the recording.

ACTIVITY 2

Match the people to the activities they were doing when Terada san called.

1 Saito san	a	playing games with a friend
2 Saito san's daughter	b	making a cake
3 Saito san's wife	c	playing tennis
	d	watching TV
	e	cleaning the next room

DIALOGUE 1

○ Moshi moshi, Saitō desu.

■ Saitō san, dōmo. Terada desu. Ashita no tenisu no koto desu ga … Are wa nan desu ka. Daijōbu desu ka.

○ Hai, terebi desu yo. Ima eiga o mite imasu. Chotto matte kudasai … Sumimasen. Tenisu no koto desu ne.

■ Hai. Nan-ji ni kurabu ni ikimashō ka. … Dō shimashita ka. Daijōbu desu ka.

○ Hai, kodomo desu. Emiko ga tonari no heya de tomodachi to asonde imasu yo. Sore dake desu. Chotto matte. … Ja, ashita no tenisu desu ne. … Sumimasen ne. Kanai ga ima ryōri o shite imasu. Kēki o tsukutte imasu. Chotto matte kudasai.

■ Iie, kekkō desu. Ashita mata denwa shimasu. Shitsurei shimasu.

VOCABULARY	
kurabu	club
dō shimashita ka	what happened?
Emiko	[*girl's name*]
asonde imasu	is playing [*from* **asobimasu**]
sore dake desu	that's all, it's only that
ryōri o shite imasu	is cooking [*from* **shimasu**]
kēki	cake
tsukutte imasu	is making [*from* **tsukurimasu**]
kekkō desu	it's alright

✓ Saying what's happening now with -te imasu

The -**masu** form of a verb is used to talk about events or activities that occur regularly, such as what you watch on TV every evening.
To describe something that is happening at the moment (e.g. 'She's watching TV now'), use the -**te** form of the verb, plus **imasu**. The rules for forming the -**te** (or sometimes -**de**) form are regular, but complicated. You'll find an explanation of these rules in the Grammar Summary on page 226–7, but you may find it easier simply to learn the -**te** forms by heart.

The -**te** form has many uses. When combined with **imasu** to describe what's going on now, it's similar to the '-ing' form in English.

-masu form	-te form	English
tabemasu	**tabete imasu**	am/is/are eating
mimasu	**mite imasu**	am/is/are seeing, looking
nemasu	**nete imasu**	am/is/are sleeping
shimasu	**shite imasu**	am/is/are doing
yomimasu	**yonde imasu**	am/is/are reading
nomimasu	**nonde imasu**	am/is/are drinking
kikimasu	**kiite imasu**	am/is/are listening
asobimasu	**asonde imasu**	am/is/are playing

Nani o **mite imasu ka**. What are you looking at?
Konpyūtā de **asonde imasen** yo. Benkyō o **shite imasu**. I'm not playing on the computer, I'm studying!
Ikeda san wa dono hon o **yonde imasu** ka. What book is Ikeda san reading?

ACTIVITY 3

Which of these activities are you doing now?

terebi o mite imasu   benkyō o shite imasu
ongaku o kiite imasu   sandoitchi o tabete imasu
kōhii o nonde imasu   ryōri o shite imasu

ACTIVITY 4

Explain these people's reasons for staying in this evening.
e.g.: older brother: watching video (loves films)
Ani wa, eiga ga suki desu kara, bideo o mite imasu.

1 my younger sister: sleeping (has a headache)
2 Yoshida san: studying English (going to US next week)
3 Kimura san: making a cake (loves cooking)

 Now do activities 5 and 6 on the recording.

11.2 Actions that continue over time

Tōkyō ni sunde imasu

ACTIVITY 7 is on the recording.

ACTIVITY 8

Correct the statements which are false.

1 Matsuda san is standing inside the department store. T / F
2 Matsuda san doesn't live in Tokyo any more. T / F
3 She and her husband moved three months ago. T / F
4 The woman didn't know Matsuda san was married. T / F
5 They moved because she got a new job in Kyoto. T / F

DIALOGUE 2

○ Ano hito wa Matsuda san ja nai desu ka. Depāto no iriguchi no mae ni tatte imasu ne.

■ Iie, Matsuda san wa mō Tōkyō ni sunde imasen yo.

○ Sō desu ka.

■ Ē, ima Kyōto ni sunde imasu. Shirimasen deshita ka. Mō san-kagetsu mae ni Kyōto e hikkoshi shimashita. Go-shujin ga Kyōto shisha ni tsutomete imasu kara.

○ Go-shujin?! Matsuda san wa kekkon shite imasu ka.

■ Ē, kekkon shite imasu yo. Shirimasen deshita ka.

○ Hai, shirimasen deshita.

▼ Katō san? Katō san desu ka. Hisashiburi desu ne.

○ Yappari, Matsuda san deshita.

VOCABULARY

ja nai desu ka	isn't it …? [alternative to ja arimasen ka]
iriguchi	entrance
tatte imasu	is standing [from tachimasu]
ni sunde imasen	isn't living in [from sumimasu]
shirimasen deshita ka	didn't you know?
san-kagetsu mae	three months ago
hikkoshi shimashita	moved house
shisha	branch office
tsutomete imasu	works, is employed [from tsutomemasu]
kekkon shite imasu	is married

LANGUAGE BUILDING

✓ More on the *-te* verb form

In some cases, the **-te imasu** form is used where an action continues over
a long period of time (e.g. living or working in a certain place), or where
the action has resulted in a state of being (e.g. being married, as a result
of getting married). Verbs commonly used in the **-te imasu** form are:

-masu form	-te form	English
sumimasu	**sunde imasu**	be living (in a place)
kekkon shimasu	**kekkon shite imasu**	be married
tsutomemasu	**tsutomete imasu**	be employed
oshiemasu	**oshiete imasu**	be teaching
shirimasu	**shitte imasu**	know (something)

Note that the negative 'I don't know' is **shirimasen**

> Ikeda san no denwa bangō o **shitte imasu** ka. Do you know Ikeda san's
> phone number?
> Kanojo wa Amerika de Nihongo o **oshiete imasu**. She's teaching
> Japanese in America.

✓ *hai* and *iie* with negative questions

Take care when answering negative questions, such as 'Don't you like it?'
in Japanese. The answers **hai** and **iie** refer to whether or not you think
the questioner's supposition is correct, rather like 'Yes, you're right. I
don't like it.' or 'No, you're wrong. I do like it.'

> O-sake ga suki ja nai desu ka. Don't you like sake?
> **Hai**, amari suki ja nai desu. No, I don't really like it. [*literally* yes,
> (you're right), I don't really like it.]

ACTIVITY 9

Imagine you need some information about someone. What
questions would you ask to complete this form?

> 1 Current address:...
> 2 Marital status: ....
> 3 Place of work: ....

ACTIVITY 10

How would you answer these questions?

1 Amerika-jin ja arimasen ka.
2 Nihongo wa muzukashiku nai desu ka.
3 Daigakusei ja arimasen ka.

 Now do activities 11 and 12 on the recording.

157

11.3 Describing what someone's wearing
Sumāto-na sūtsu o kite imasu

ACTIVITY 13 is on the recording.

ACTIVITY 14

Say which of the two candidates:

	Ishii	Katō
1 ... studies economics.		
2 ... was dressed smartly.		
3 ... was wearing sunglasses.		
4 ... has experience of the job.		
5 ... seems intelligent.		
6 ... seems energetic.		

DIALOGUE 3

○ Ishii san wa ii hito deshita ne.

■ Sō desu ne. Kare wa daigakusei deshō?

○ Hai, sō desu. Keizai o benkyō shite imasu. Atama ga ii deshō.

■ Un, ii gakusei desu ne.

○ Ii sūtsu o kite imashita ne.

■ Ja, Ishii san ni kimemashō. Tsugi wa Katō san desu ga.

○ Katō san wa jiinzu o haite imashita yo. Sangurasu mo kakete imashita. Sore kara, kami wa orenji desu.

■ Sō desu ga, totemo genki-na hito deshō. Sore ni, keiken mo arimasu ne. Sengetsu made Yokohama no sūpā ni tsutomete imashita ne.

VOCABULARY	
keizai	economics
atama ga ii	clever
kite imashita	was wearing
... ni kimemashō	let's decide on ...
jiinzu o haite imashita	was wearing jeans
sangurasu mo kakete imashita	was wearing sunglasses too
kami	hair
genki-na	lively, energetic
keiken	experience
tsutomete imashita	was employed

✅ Continuous actions in the past

To describe an action continuing over a long period in the past, simply use the **-te** form with the past tense of **imasu**.

> **Nete imashita** kara, nani mo kikimasen deshita. I was sleeping, so I didn't hear anything.
> Sono toki kekkon **shite imasen deshita**. I wasn't married then.
> Kyonen no 3-gatsu made ginkō ni **tsutomete imashita**. I worked in a bank until last March.

✅ Verbs used with items of clothing

There is no single word for 'wear,' as the verb varies depending on the item of clothing.

hakimasu (haite imasu) for clothes which are worn on the lower half of the body, e.g. shoes, socks, jeans, skirts

kimasu (kite imasu) for clothes worn on the upper half of the body such as shirts, jackets, coats

kaburimasu (kabutte imasu) for hats

kakemasu (kakete imasu) for glasses

shimasu (shite imasu) for accessories such as jewellery, gloves, neckties, scarves, belts

> Dō shite kyō nekutai o **shite imasen** ka. Why aren't you wearing a tie today?
> 2-nen mae kara megane o **kakete imasu**. I've been wearing glasses for two years (*literally* since two years ago).

ACTIVITY 15

Can you describe exactly what you're wearing now?

ACTIVITY 16

Answer these questions about yourself.

1 5-nen mae ni, doko ni sunde imashita ka.
2 Kinō, nani iro no kutsu o haite imashita ka.
3 Ima kekkon shite imasu ka. 10-nen mae wa kekkon shite imashita ka.
4 Kesa 7.30 ni nete imashita ka.

Now do activities 17 and 18 on the recording.

Nihon no bunka

THE JAPANESE PEOPLE

The origins of the Japanese people are a matter for dispute, although it is probable that long ago groups of people arrived from the areas of modern-day Korea, China, and Siberia on the Asian mainland. Certainly there is a variety of facial features, body shape, and skin colour, although perhaps there is less diversity than in other developed nations. Most people have black hair and eyes but there are also shades of dark brown, and hair may be fine and wavy as well as thick and straight.

The Japanese body shape is changing very rapidly, and the average young Japanese man is now around six inches taller than his pre-war counterpart. This is commonly attributed to radical changes in diet since the end of World War II, and the increasingly westernized lifestyle. Women too are filling out, so the smooth lines of the **kimono** now have a different fit.

Kimono are rarely seen in the cities nowadays except on formal occasions such as weddings, funerals, or New Year celebrations, although they may still be worn by the older generation in country areas. A woman's **kimono** in particular is complex to put on and very restrictive. Young women often attend classes to learn how to put on the various layers involved and how to move elegantly when wearing a **kimono**. They are made only in approximate sizes, and it needs skill and experience to adjust the fit to the individual as it is put on.

The cotton **yukata** is an informal, cotton **kimono** generally worn at home in the summer or after a bath. They are also commonly seen at summer festivals when they make a cool alternative to western wear in the hot, sticky weather.

Western clothing was first seen in Japan around the end of the last century and adaptations of the English names for clothing were also imported.

ACTIVITY 19

12 items of clothing

Read the hiragana and katakana to find out the names of these items of clothing, then match them to their English equivalents. (If you don't know a word, try guessing it, especially if it's a katakana word. As a last resort, check the Glossary.)

1	ずぼん	a	socks
2	ぼうし	b	skirt
3	くつ	c	trousers
4	セーター	d	yukata
5	くつした	e	dress
6	ネクタイ	f	sweater
7	ゆかた	g	suit
8	ブラウス	h	hat
9	スカート	i	kimono
10	ワンピース	j	tie
11	スーツ	k	shoes
12	きもの	l	blouse

FIRST MEETINGS WITH MORITA SAN
O-MIAI NO MORITA SAN

It's early evening and Harada san comes into Midori-ya with the news that she has just met Hayashi san and his **o-miai** partner.

chekku	check design
handobaggu	handbag
taka-sō	looks expensive
Dioru	Dior
suteki	great, wonderful
Kyūshū	*the southernmost of the four main Japanese islands*
Kita-Kyūshū	*one of the main cities in Kyushu*
chūgakkō	middle school, junior high school
ni-nen-kan	two years
tokui	good at
machi	town, city
shumi	hobby, interest
sore de?	so what?
eiga o yamemashō	let's not (go to see) a movie

ACTIVITY 20

What five items of clothing or accessories are mentioned in the conversation?

ACTIVITY 21

Listen to the story and then check all the pieces of information which you know to be true about Morita san. Correct those that are false.

1 She's from Kyushu.
2 She's wearing a checked suit today.
3 She's wearing black shoes.
4 She teaches in a middle school in Kita-Kyushu.
5 She often visits Tokyo.
6 She lived in London at one time.
7 She wants to see a movie tonight.
8 She's going back to Kyushu tomorrow.

STORY TRANSCRIPT

Itō	Irasshaimase. A, Harada san, konbanwa.
Harada	Konbanwa. Ima kanojo ni aimashita yo.
Harada	Hayashi san to issho ni kaimono o shite imashita.
Itō	A, Hayashi san no o-miai no aite desu ka. Donna hito desu ka.
Harada	Ii hito desu yo. Namae wa Morita san desu. Kyūshū no hito desu.
Itō	Sō desu ka. Kirei desu ka.
Harada	Un, wakaku nai desu ga, kirei-na hito desu yo. Sore kara, kirei-na chekku no sūtsu o kite imasu. Handobaggu mo taka-sō desu. Dioru desu.
Itō	Sō desu ka.
Harada	Sore kara kuroi bōshi o kabutte imasu. Chiisai bōshi desu. Suteki desu yo. Futari wa ato de Midori-ya e kimasu yo.
Itō	A, Hayashi san, irasshaimase.
Hayashi	Konbanwa. Mina san, kochira wa Morita san desu.
Morita	Morita desu. Dōzo yoroshiku.
Itō	Itō desu. Yoroshiku onegai shimasu. O-nomimono wa?
Morita	Biiru onegai shimasu.
Itō	Hai, biiru desu ne. Morita san wa Kyūshū kara desu ne.
Morita	Hai, Kita-Kyūshū desu.
Hayashi	Morita san wa Kita-Kyūshū no chūgakkō no sensei desu. Eigo o oshiete imasu.
Itō	Eigo no sensei desu ka.
Morita	Hai, 2-nen-kan Rondon ni sunde imashita kara, eigo wa tokui desu.
Harada	Watashi mo Igirisu e ikimashita yo.
Morita	A, Harada san mo ikimashita ka. Rondon wa ii machi deshō.
Harada	Sō desu ne. Morita san, sono sūtsu o Rondon de kaimashita ka.
Morita	Hai, sō desu. Handobaggu mo, kutsu mo.
Harada	Yappari. Ii kutsu desu ne.
Morita	Chotto itai desu ga, ii deshō. Watashi wa kaimono ga shumi desu kara, takusan kaimashita.
Hayashi	Morita san, mō 7.00 desu ga …
Morita	Sore de?
Hayashi	Eiga wa 7.30 kara desu ga….
Morita	Mata eiga desu ka. Ima Harada san to hanashi o shite imasu yo. Eiga wa yamemashō. Harada san wa itsu Rondon ni imashita ka.
Harada	Kyonen no aki deshita. Kono kōto o Rondon de kaimashita.
Morita	Yappari. Ii kōto desu ne. Orenji iro wa watashi mo suki desu. Doko de …..

Now it's time to test your progress in Unit 11.

1 Complete this table with the appropriate **-te** or **-masu** forms.

play	asobimasu	(a) _____
eat	tabemasu	(b) _____
drink	(c) _____	nonde
make	tsukurimasu	(d) _____
watch	(e) _____	mite
sleep	nemasu	(f) _____
listen	(g) _____	kiite
read	yomimasu	(h) _____
stand	tachimasu	(i) _____
do	shimasu	(j) _____

10

2 Choose an appropriate verb to complete these sentences.

1 Kirei-na iyaringu o _____ ne. Purezento desu ka.
2 Atarashii jiinzu o _____ ne. Doko de kaimashita ka.
3 Kinō wa samukatta desu kara, minna bōshi o _____ ne.
4 Kōto o _____ ne. Samuku nai desu ka.
5 Itsu kara megane o _____ ka.

5

3 Match the sentence halves from the two sets below.

1 Atarashii kutsu o haite imasu kara ...
2 Ashita wa haha no tanjōbi desu kara ...
3 Kyō wa ii tenki desu kara ...
4 Kinō no ban 12.00 made nonde imashita kara ...
5 Kare wa eigo ga jōzu desu kara ...
6 Kanojo wa ima Nyū Yōku no shisha ni tsutomete imasu kara ...

a ... eigo ga totemo jōzu ni narimashita.
b ... kyō wa atama ga itai desu!
c ... ashi ga itai desu.
d ... kodomo wa kōen de asonde imasu.
e ... Igirisu no kaisha ni tsumote imasu.
f ... kēki o tsukutte imasu.

6

4 Put the words in order to make suitable questions to go with the answers.

1 Q imasen / ni / mō / Tōkyō / ka / sunde
   A Hai. Ima Nagoya ni sunde imasu.
2 Q shitte / gakkō / ka / imasu / jūsho / no / o
   A Iie, shirimasen.
3 Q e / Kōbe / shimashita / ka / dō shite / hikkoshi
   A Shujin wa Kōbe no kaisha ni tsutomete imasu kara.
4 Q shite / daigaku / nani / imasu / de / o / benkyō / ka
   A Keizai desu.
5 Q kiite / ongaku / ka / donna / imasu / o
   A Supein no ongaku desu.

[10]

5 How would this young woman describe what she and her family were doing yesterday when her friend came by?

1 father: playing tennis with Kato san
2 older brother: playing on the computer
3 mother: shopping in Yokohama
4 younger brother: watching a video at home
5 older sister: listening to music at friend's house
6 me: not doing anything!

[12]

6 Answer these questions about yourself.

1 Ima nani iro no kutsu o haite imasu ka.
2 Doko ni sunde imasu ka.
3 Kinō no asa 10.00 ni nani o shite imashita ka.
4 Yoku bōshi o kaburimasu ka.
5 Ima nani o shite imasu ka.
6 Sengetsu Rondon ni ikimasen deshita ka.

[12]

TOTAL SCORE [55]

If you scored less than 45, look at the Language Building sections again before completing the Summary on page 166.

Now try this final test summarizing the main points covered in this unit. You can check your answers on the recording.

How would you:
1 say you live in London now?
2 ask if Ishii san is married?
3 ask someone where he is studying English?
4 say you moved to Tokyo four months ago?
5 comment on the nice suit someone is wearing?
6 say you're employed at a Japanese company?
7 ask someone what book he is reading?
8 ask if someone knows Terada san's office phone number?
9 say you were watching a video at a friend's house yesterday?
10 say you're not wearing your glasses today?

REVISION

Before you go on to the next lesson, make sure you are confident of answering if someone asks you a question about what you're doing currently, or where you're living now, or where you're working. Think about everything you're doing at this very moment – what you're reading, or writing, or listening to, or looking at, or wearing, or eating … can you describe it all? Use the list of verbs in the Grammar Summary on page 224 if you need help with vocabulary and **-te** forms.

Going to work
Kaisha de

OBJECTIVES

In this unit, you'll learn how to:

- ✓ make polite requests
- ✓ use job titles and other office vocabulary
- ✓ make comparisons
- ✓ say what's biggest and best

And cover the following grammar and language:

- ✓ **-te kudasai** for making requests
- ✓ **no hō** for making comparisons
- ✓ **yori** for making comparisons
- ✓ **shi** as a conjunction
- ✓ **ichiban** in superlatives

LEARNING JAPANESE 12

Most people study a language because they want to speak it, so make sure that you do. Take the recordings when you are on a long car journey and speak aloud along with the dialogues. If you're studying alone and feel that you need more speaking practice, find out if there are any evening classes in your area. Contact the local colleges and universities to see what they have on offer.

🎧 Now start the recording for Unit 12.

Sugu okutte kudasai

ACTIVITY 1 is on the recording.

ACTIVITY 2

1 Where should Morita san fax the report?
2 What is she asked to do with the documents?
3 What else does the kachō ask her to do?
4 What is Morita san doing at the moment?

DIALOGUE 1

○ Morita san, chotto kite kudasai.
■ Hai, kachō.
○ Ōsaka shisha ni fakkusu o okurimashita ka.
■ Repōto desu ka. Sumimasen, mada desu.
○ Ja, sugu okutte kudasai.
■ Hai, wakarimashita.
○ Sore kara, kono shorui desu ga, buchō no hanko o moratte kudasai.
■ Hai, buchō desu ne.
○ A, o-cha o irete kudasai ne.
■ Kachō, ima e-mēru o okutte imasu kara, o-hiru gohan no ato de ii desu ka.
○ A, hai …

VOCABULARY	
chotto kite kudasai	could you come here a moment, please?
kachō	section manager
fakkusu	fax
okurimashita	sent
repōto	report
sugu	soon, immediately
okutte kudasai	please send
shorui	papers, documents
buchō	departmental manager
hanko	name stamp
moratte kudasai	get, obtain [*from* **moraimasu**]
o-cha o irete kudasai	please make some green tea [*from* **iremasu** put in]
e-mēru o okutte imasu	send an e-mail
o-hiru gohan no ato de	after lunch

✅ Making requests with -te kudasai

The -te form of a verb followed by **kudasai** is used when making requests, so it is similar to 'Please could you …?' (You've already come across this pattern in the phrase **Chotto matte kudasai** – 'Please wait a moment'.)

> Kono shorui o kopii **shite kudasai. Please make** a copy of this document.
> 7.30 ni **kite kudasai**. Please come at 7.30.
> Namae o koko ni **kaite kudasai**. Write your name here, please.
> Kaigi no repōto o **motte kite kudasai**. Please bring the meeting report.

To make the request softer and less like an order, it is also possible to use **kudasaimasu ka**.

> Megane o wasuremashita ga, kore o **yonde kudasaimasu** ka. I've forgotten my glasses – could you read this for me, please?

✅ Use of job titles at work

People in more senior positions at work are generally addressed by their job title, or name and job title if there is more than one person at the same rank. The most common job titles are:

shachō company president
fuku-shachō vice-president
buchō department manager
kachō section manager
kakarichō assistant manager

> **Fukuda buchō**, o-denwa desu. Department manager Fukuda, there's a call for you.
> **Shachō** no naisen bangō o oshiete kudasai. Could you tell me the president's extension number?

ACTIVITY 3

Here are some of the things the **buchō** needs to ask his staff to do today. How does he ask them?

1 Ikeda – send these documents to the Kobe office
2 Kato – write report of meeting
3 Yamada – get president's name stamp on this document
4 Ishii – book Kobe hotel for me
5 Everyone – tell me your new extension numbers

🎧 Now do activities 4 and 5 on the recording.

Dochira no hō ga ii desu ka

🎧 **ACTIVITY 6** is on the recording.

ACTIVITY 7

Correct the statements which are false.

1 The man is going to Tokyo next week on business.   T / F
2 He'll stay until Wednesday.   T / F
3 He thinks the Prince Hotel is better than the New
   Ginza Hotel.   T / F
4 The Prince Hotel is closer to the office than the
   New Ginza Hotel.   T / F
5 He'll go to Tokyo by plane.   T / F

DIALOGUE 2

○ Fujimoto san, raishū Tōkyō e shutchō shimasu kara, hoteru
   o yoyaku shite kudasai.
■ Hai, itsu kara itsu made desu ka.
○ Suiyōbi kara ni-haku onegai shimasu.
■ Ni-haku desu ne. Hai. Purinsu Hoteru to Nyū Ginza
   Hoteru to, dochira no hō ga ii desu ka.
○ Sō desu ne. Purinsu Hoteru no hō ga ii desu ne.
■ Demo Nyū Ginza Hoteru no hō ga, honsha ni chikai desu
   yo.
○ Sō desu ne. Ja, Nyū Ginza Hoteru ni shimasu.
■ Wakarimashita. Hikōki desu ka. Shinkansen desu ka.
○ Shinkansen no hō ga benri desu. Eki no chikaku ni sunde
   imasu kara.

VOCABULARY	
shutchō shimasu	go on a business trip
yoyaku shite kudasai	please make a reservation
ni-haku	two nights' stay
dochira no hō	which one (of the two)?
... no hō ga ii desu	is the better of the two
honsha	head office
chikai	close
shinkansen	Bullet Train

✓ Use of *hō* in comparatives

When comparing two things, imagine them as being one on each side (**hō**) of you, and then ask which side is bigger, smaller, more expensive, etc.

Tōkyō to Rondon to, **dochira no hō** ga takai desu ka. Which is more expensive, Tokyo or London?

Hikōki to shinkansen to, **dochira no hō** ga hayai desu ka. Which is quicker, plane or shinkansen?

To answer the question, simply say which 'side' is bigger or smaller, etc.

Ima wa **Rondon no hō** ga takai desu. At the moment, London is more expensive.

Hikōki no hō ga hayai desu. The plane is quicker.

Use **motto** (more) when you don't mention what you're comparing something with.

Motto yukkuri hanashite kudasai. Please speak more slowly.

Kono heya wa **motto hiroi** desu. This room is more spacious.

ACTIVITY 8

Complete this conversation between two people who are choosing a venue for their office party.

Papillon

price per person
¥9,500

capacity
40

distance from station
2 min

type of food
French

Pasta Land

price per person
¥7,900

capacity
60

distance from station
10 min

type of food
Italian

A Papiyon to Pasutarando to, _____ ii desu ka.

B Sō desu ne. _____ takai desu ga, _____ hiroi desu.

A Papiyon mo Pasutarando mo Shinjuku ni arimasu ne.

B Ē, demo _____ eki ni chikai desu. Tokorode,
   Furansu ryōri to _____ to, _____ suki desu ka.

A Watashi wa Furansu ryōri _____ desu ne.

🎧 Now do activities 9 and 10 on the recording.

Saying what's biggest and best
Ichiban takai biru desu

ACTIVITY 11 is on the recording.

ACTIVITY 12

Choose which statement best describes the new head office building.

1 It's the tallest building in the area, with large rooms, but not a very good dining room.
2 The building in Mitaka is bigger than the previous one, with a large, bright dining room.
3 It's a wonderful building with bright offices and a much better dining room.

DIALOGUE 3

○ Atarashii honsha biru wa dō deshita ka.
■ Rippa desu ne. Mae no biru yori zutto ōkii desu yo. Mitaka-shi de ichiban takai biru desu.
○ Sō desu ka. Biru no naka wa dō desu ka.
■ Heya wa hiroi shi, akarui shi, shokuji mo sugoku oishii desu. Shokudō wa ni-jú-ni-kai ni arimasu.
○ Mae no shokudō yori, oishii desu ka. Ii desu ne.
■ Un, karē raisu ga ichiban oishii desu yo.
○ Sō desu ka. A, tokorode, kaigi wa dō deshita ka.
■ Sō desu ne. Sengetsu no kaigi yori, yokatta desu. Umaku ikimashita yo.

VOCABULARY	
biru	building
rippa	wonderful, superb
mae no biru yori	than the previous building
zutto	by far, a great deal
Mitaka-shi	Mitaka City [*a suburb of Tokyo*]
ichiban takai	the tallest
shi	and what's more; moreover
akarui	bright, light
sugoku	extremely
mae no shokudō	the previous dining room
karē raisu	curry with rice
umaku ikimashita	it went well; it was successful

✓ More on comparatives

When describing someone or something in comparison to another person or thing, use **yori** ('than').

> Buchō wa, **okusan yori** zutto wakai desu. The buchō is far younger than his wife.
> Kono hoteru wa, **Purinsu Hoteru yori** benri desu. This hotel is more convenient than the Prince Hotel.

You can also use the following pattern to give the same information.

> **Okusan yori**, buchō no hō ga zutto wakai desu.
> **Purinsu Hoteru yori**, kono hoteru no hō ga benri desu.

✓ Use of *shi* to connect sentences

Use **shi** to join sentences in the sense of 'what's more' / 'and in addition to that' to emphasize the extra information. When **shi** comes after an -i adjective, you can omit **desu**.

> Tōkyō wa **atsui shi**, takai desu. Not only is it hot in Tokyo, it's expensive, too.
> Atarashii shigoto wa **omoshiroi shi**, kyūryō mo ii desu. My new job's interesting, and the salary's good, too.

✓ Use of *ichiban* with superlatives

ichiban is used in superlative constructions. Think of **ichiban** as 'most' or more literally 'number one' to say that something is biggest, etc.

> Sekai de **ichiban takai** yama wa Eberesuto desu. The highest mountain in the world is Mt Everest.
> Eigo no kurasu no naka de, dare ga **ichiban jōzu** desu ka. Who's the best in the English class?

ACTIVITY 13

Compare the following in as many ways as you can!
1 wain, biiru   2 Tōkyō, Pari   3 kinō, kyō

ACTIVITY 14

Answer these general knowledge questions about Japan.

1 Ichiban takai yama wa nan desu ka.
2 Ichiban ōkii machi wa doko desu ka.
3 Ichiban hayai densha wa nan desu ka.
4 Honshú to Kyúshú to Hokkaido to Shikoku no naka de, doko ga ichiban ōkii desu ka.

🎧 Now do activities 15 and 16 on the recording.   **173**

(12.4) Japanese Culture
Nihon no bunka

USE OF NAME STAMPS (*HANKO*)

In Japan it is much more common to use a seal, or **hanko**, to show identity than to sign one's name. A **hanko** is necessary in situations such as receiving registered mail, withdrawing cash across the counter at a bank, or completing a contract. Ready-made **hanko** with the most common family names are available in stationery shops, along with small carrying cases containing a tiny red inkpad. These are fine for everyday use, but for more official documents where it is important to be able to prove one's identity, most people have individually-made **hanko** engraved with their name. The stamp can be registered at the local government office and a certificate issued to prove its authenticity.

The **hanko** is very important in the decision-making process in Japanese companies. This process is characterized by its collective nature, with everyone concerned having the opportunity to provide input at a series of meetings at ever-higher levels. This lengthy decision-making process is known as the **ringi** system.

When a proposal is made, agreement is first obtained from immediate superiors in informal meetings where suggestions are made for modifications and improvements. Once there is consensus, the head of the section or department stamps his **hanko** on the revised document to show his approval, and the document is passed up to the next level of management for more scrutiny and revision. Because of the lengthy process of input and evaluation, by the time the proposal reaches the top, it is likely to be in a form readily acceptable to all. Once the **hanko** of the senior management has been stamped on the document alongside all the others, then the proposal can be quickly implemented.

Kanji commonly used in family names

kanji	*reading*	*meaning*
山	yama	mountain
川	kawa (gawa)	river
中	naka	in, inside
田	ta (da)	rice field
村	mura	village
北	kita	north
西	nishi	west
本	moto	source, origin
木	ki (gi)	tree

ACTIVITY 17

Can you read the family names in the following list? (When a kanji appears in the second position in a name, the alternative reading given in brackets above is generally used.)

1	山中 恵子	Yamanaka Keiko
2	田中 秀作	Tanaka Shusaku
3	川本 順子	Kawamoto Junko
4	木田 文子	Kida Fumiko
5	川村 理恵	Kawamura Rie
6	北川 恵美子	Kitagawa Emiko
7	木村 孝	Kimura Takashi
8	北山 秀男	Kitayama Hideo
9	西村 恵	Nishimura Megumi
10	西山 裕二	Nishiyama Yuji
11	山本 安子	Yamamoto Yasuko

CHANGES AT MIDORI-YA
ATARASHII MIDORI-YA

Yesterday Midori-ya was closed for redecoration. Today it's also closed so that Itō san can take delivery of some new furnishings. The delivery truck has just arrived.

gomen kudasai	excuse me – anyone there?
Yamamoto Unyu	Yamamoto Transporters
tēburu	table
gokurō sama desu	sorry you've had so much trouble
kakunin shite kudasai	please confirm
isu	chair
doko ni okimashō ka	where shall we put (it)?
oite kudasai	please put
tana	shelf
dō shita n' desu ka	what's happened?
arimashita	got it; here it is

ACTIVITY 18

Listen to the dialogue and check which new items Ito san has ordered for Midori-ya.

1	bar stools	5	clock
2	tables	6	plates and glasses
3	chairs	7	TV
4	karaoke machine	8	telephone

ACTIVITY 19

Listen again and answer these questions by giving the name of the appropriate person: Itō san, Ikeda san, Harada san.

Who ….
1 … checks the delivery people's paperwork?
2 … sent a report by e-mail?
3 … chose the colour of the new furniture?
4 … hasn't met Morita san yet?

Put a cross by the incidents below which do not occur in the dialogue.

1 The delivery man hands over some documents.
2 The delivery man puts the television up on a shelf.
3 Itō san offers the delivery man some tea.
4 Itō san explains that Midori-ya isn't open this evening.
5 Ikeda san's boss says that something has happened to the new computers.
6 Ikeda san tells her boss what time she will be at the office tomorrow morning.
7 Ikeda san meets Harada san and explains that she's just seen the new furniture at Midori-ya.
8 Harada san invites Ikeda san for a coffee.

STORY TRANSCRIPT

Delivery man	Gomen kudasai. Yamamoto Unyu desu ga, atarashii tēburu o motte kimashita. Kore wa shorui desu ga, dōzo kakunin shite kudasai.
Itō	Hai. Tēburu - muttsu, isu - 20, tokei - hitotsu, terebi - hai.
Delivery man	Tēburu wa doko ni okimashō ka.
Itō	Soko ni oite kudasai.
Delivery man	Hai. Ii desu ka.
Itō	Hai.
Delivery man	Terebi wa?
Itō	Terebi wa sono tana no ue ni oite kudasai.
Ikeda	Masutā, do shita n' desu ka.
Itō	A, Ikeda san, konbanwa. Sumimasen ga, konban, Midori-ya wa yasumi desu yo.
Ikeda	Sō desu ka. Shirimasen deshita.
Itō	Ikeda san, sumimasen ga…
Ikeda	Hai, shitsurei shimashita. Mata ashita kimasu. … Denwa wa doko ni … a, arimashita. A, buchō …. hai, ima kaerimashita. …. Kaigi no repōto o mō E-mēru de okurimashita. …. Hai, umaku ikimashita. … E? Dono konpyūtā? Ichiban atarashii konpyūtā desu ka. … Hai, wakarimashita. Shitsurei shimasu.
Harada	Ikeda san?
Ikeda	A, Harada san, konbanwa. Ima Midori-ya e ikimashita ga, atarashii tēburu to isu o iremashita yo.
Harada	Sō desu ne. Dō deshita ka.
Ikeda	Mae no tēburu yori ii desu ga, iro wa chotto …
Harada	Ii iro deshō? Morita san to watashi ga kimemashita.
Ikeda	Aaaa…. Sō desu ka. Morita san? Morita san wa dare desu ka.
Harada	Sō desu ne. Ikeda san wa shutchō deshita kara, Morita san ni aimasen deshita ne. Totemo ii hito desu yo.

Test

Now it's time to test your progress in Unit 12.

1 Rearrange these job titles in order of seniority.
kachō   fuku-shachō
kakarichō   shachō
buchō

| | 5 |

2 Complete this conversation with appropriate forms of the verbs provided.

A Koyama san, watashi no shutchō no repōto o kopii (shimasu) (a)_____ kudasai.

B Ima kopii (shimasu) (b)_____.

A Sō desu ka. Arigatō. Sore kara, Yokohama shisha ni fakkusu de (okurimasu) (c)_____ kudasai ne.

B Hai, (wakarimasu) (d)_____.

A Nyū Yōku shisha ni, mō denwa (shimasu) (e)_____ ka.

B Iie, mada desu.

A Ja, sugu denwa (shimasu) (f)_____ kudasai ne. Eigo de (hanashimasu) (g)_____ ne!

| | 7 |

3 Are these sentences true or false?

1 Nihon de, ichi-gatsu wa go-gatsu yori atsui desu.   T / F
2 Jitensha yori, densha no hō ga hayai desu.   T / F
3 Nihon-jin wa, Igirisu-jin yori, sakana o takusan
  tabemasu.   T / F
4 Ōsaka to Nagoya to Kōbe no naka de, Nagoya
  ga ichiban ōkii desu.   T / F
5 Nihon de, Fuji-san ga ichiban takai yama ja
  arimasen.   T / F
6 Hiragana yori, kanji no hō ga muzukashii desu.   T / F

| | 6 |

4 Choose the most suitable response to these questions.
1 O-cha o iremashō ka.
  a Hai, onegai shimasu.
  b Nonde kudasai.

2 O-namae to go-jūsho o kochira ni kaite kudasai.
  a Hai, kaimashō.
  b Koko desu ka.
3 Kaigi wa umaku ikimashita ka.
  a Senshū no kaigi yori zutto yokatta desu.
  b Ōsaka shisha ni ikimashita.
4 Ano kaisha no kyūryo wa amari yoku nai desu ne.
  a Ē, kyūryo wa yoku nai shi, eki kara zutto tōi desu.
  b Hai, kachō wa amari shinsetsu ja arimasen.
5 Dochira no hoteru o yoyaku shimashita ka.
  a Hai, yoyaku shimasen deshita.
  b Ichiban takai hoteru o yoyaku shimashita yo!
6 Buchō no naisen bangō wa nan-ban desu ka.
  a Wakarimasen.
  b Hai, oshiete kudasaimasu ka.

[6]

5 Here's a hotel questionnaire filled in by one of the guests. How would she describe the hotel in Japanese?

Example: Hotel building: large, wonderful!
Hoteru no biru wa, ōkii shi, rippa desu.

1 Restaurant: bright, attractive
2 Bar: small, noisy
3 Rooms: large, with stereo and video
4 General comment: hotel is close to theatres, close to shops – very convenient!

[8]

6 Answer these questions about yourself.

1 Ichiban suki-na tabemono wa nan desu ka.
2 Go-kazoku no naka de, ichiban se ga takai kata wa donata desu ka.
3 Tokidoki shutchō shimasu ka. Dochira e?
4 Yama to umi to, dochira no hō ga suki desu ka.
5 E-mēru to fakkusu to, dochira no hō o yoku tsukaimasu ka.
6 Machi no naka no ichiban takai biru wa nan desu ka.

[12]

TOTAL SCORE [44]

If you scored less than 34, look at the Language Building sections again before completing the Summary on page 180.

Summary 12

 Now try this final test summarizing the main points covered in this unit. You can check your answers on the recording.

How would you:
1 ask someone to tell you the company's address?
2 say the president is going on a business trip to New York tomorrow?
3 ask someone to send these documents to the head office?
4 ask which is quicker, train or car?
5 say the new building is far better than the previous one?
6 say you'll call the London office after lunch?
7 ask what the tallest building in Tokyo is?
8 ask someone to write her name and address here?
9 ask someone to wait a moment?
10 say that your new job is interesting, and also the salary is good?

REVISION

Think of all the things you ask people to do throughout the day – carry this, read that, close the door, open the window, put on your coat, take off your shoes, post this letter. How would you ask them to do these things in Japanese? Use the verb list in the Grammar summary to help you.

Choose two unconnected objects and think of as many ways as possible to compare them in Japanese. For example a hat and a cat: a hat is more (or less) expensive than a cat; a cat is more fun than a hat; a cat is noisier than a hat; a hat is more useful than a cat, etc.

13

Fit and healthy
Shū ni nan-kai undō shimasu ka

OBJECTIVES

In this unit, you'll learn how to:

- ✓ say what you think
- ✓ give advice
- ✓ say how often you do something
- ✓ say what sports and other activities you do
- ✓ say what you can and can't do

And cover the following grammar and language:

- ✓ plain forms of verbs
- ✓ **to omoimasu** ('I think')
- ✓ phrases of frequency
- ✓ **dekimasu** ('can', 'be able to')
- ✓ **hō ga ii** to give advice

LEARNING JAPANESE 13

Don't forget to go back and revise previous units. Read through the dialogues of some earlier units, listen to the recordings as often as you can, and look again at the Test sections. You'll probably be pleasantly surprised at how much you can remember. Make a note of what you still find difficult and try to brush up on these areas. It takes time and a great deal of perseverance to learn a language: practice makes perfect!

🎧 Now start the recording for Unit 13.

Saying what you think
Kaze da to omoimasu

ACTIVITY 1 is on the recording.

ACTIVITY 2

1　The woman's daughter-in-law is overweight because …
2　The woman's not feeling well because …
3　The other woman's leg is hurting because …

DIALOGUE 1

○　O-yome san wa o-genki desu ka.
■　Hai, o-kage sama de. Yoku tabemasu kara, futotte imasu.
○　Sō desu ka. Tokorode, kao iro ga warui desu ne.
■　Ē, atama ga itai shi, kibun ga warui desu. Kaze da to
　omoimasu. … Ashi wa dō shimashita ka.
○　Eki no kaidan de korobimashita.
■　Sō desu ka.
▼　Sugu naoru to omoimasu. O-daiji ni. Tsugi no kata, dōzo.
　A, mata Yamaguchi san desu ka. Kyō wa dō shimashita ka.

VOCABULARY	
o-yome san	your new daughter-in-law [*literally* the bride]
futotte imasu	has become fat; is fat [*from* **futorimasu**]
kao	face
warui	bad
kao iro ga warui	look unwell
kibun ga warui	feel unwell
kaze	a cold
da	is [*plain form of* **desu**]
to omoimasu	I think
ashi	foot, leg
kaidan de korobimashita	fell down the steps
naoru	get better; recover
o-daiji ni	please take care of yourself

✓ Plain forms of verbs

So far you have come across verbs in the polite form ending in **-masu**, or derivations of **-masu** (**-mashita**, **-masen**, etc.). However, there is another form called the plain form. It is the most basic form of the verb, and the one from which all other forms are constructed. It is also the form under which verbs are listed in dictionaries.

Some verbs drop **-ru** and some drop **-u** from the plain forms to make other verb forms. You will find more information on this in the Grammar Summary on page 224, but you may find it easier at this point simply to learn the plain forms as you come across them. Here are some examples.

Plain form	-masu form	English
taberu	**tabe**masu	eat
miru	**mi**masu	see, watch
aru	**ari**masu	exist, have
naoru	**naori**masu	get better, recover
iku	**iki**masu	go
kaeru	**kaeri**masu	return

There are only two irregular forms: **kuru** (from **kimasu**, 'come') and **suru** (from **shimasu**, 'do'). The plain form of **desu** is **da**.

The plain form of a verb has exactly the same meaning as the polite form, but the tone is very informal. However, it is the final verb which determines the level of politeness of a sentence, so as long as this is in the polite **-masu** form, any verb in the middle of a long sentence can be in the plain form without affecting the overall tone.

One use of the plain form is with **to omoimasu** ('I think') to give your opinion about something. (You can omit **desu/da** after an **-i** adjective.)

Ashi wa ashita made ni **naoru to omoimasu ka**. **Do you think** my leg will be better by tomorrow?
Ano hito wa Ikeda san **da to omoimasu**. That's Ikeda san, I think.
Chotto **takai to omoimasu**. I think it's a bit expensive.

ACTIVITY 3

How would you tell someone ...

1 ... you think you have a cold?
2 ... you think you'll go home at 3.00?
3 ... you think e-mail is convenient?
4 ... you think Ishii san is going to Nagoya tomorrow?
5 ... you think that's the buchó's wife?

🎧 Now do activities 4 and 5 on the recording.

13.2 Saying how often you do something
Shū ni nan-kai desu ka

(🎧) **ACTIVITY 6** is on the recording.

ACTIVITY 7

Complete the health check with the appropriate numbers.

Weight: ___ kgs
Height: ___ cms
Alcohol: ____ bottles of ____ per day/week
Cigarettes: _____ per day/week

DIALOGUE 2

○ Taijū wa kyū-jū-go kiro, shinchō wa hyaku nana-jū-go senchi desu ne.
■ Hai.
○ Kore kara, shitsumon shimasu. Shū ni nan-kai undō shimasu ka.
■ Undō wa shimasen.
○ Sō desu ka. O-sake o nomimasu ka.
■ Hai, nomimasu. Biiru go-hon gurai nomimasu.
○ Shū ni go-hon desu ne.
■ Iie, ichi nichi ni go-hon desu.
○ Hai …. tabako wa suimasu ka.
■ Hai, ichi nichi ni, ni-jūp-pon gurai suu to omoimasu. … Anō … ik-kagetsu ni, jū kiro yaseru to omoimasu ka.
○ Hai, dekiru to omoimasu. Demo ….

VOCABULARY

taijū	weight [*of a person*]
shinchō	height [*of a person*]
senchi	centimetre
shitsumon	question
shū	week
nan-kai	how many times?
undō shimasu	do exercise
ichi nichi	one day
suimasu	smoke; inhale [*from* **suu**]
yaseru	get thin; lose weight
dekiru	can, be able to

✓ Phrases to describe frequency

The counter for the number of times you do something is **-kai**. Use **nan-kai** ('how many times', 'how often') to ask about frequency.

Shū ni nan-kai jimu e ikimasu ka. How many times a week do you go to the gym?
Tsuki ni san-kai gurai tenisu o shimasu. I play tennis about three times a month.
Nen ni ni-kai gaikoku e shutchō shimasu. I go on business trips abroad twice a year.

Other useful phrases to describe frequency are **maiasa** ('every morning'), **maiban** ('every evening'), **maishū** ('every week'), **maitsuki** ('every month'), and **mainen** ('every year').

✓ Saying what you can and can't do

Use the verb **dekimasu** ('can', 'be able to') to talk about skills. You can use **dekimasu** with any activity where the verb **shimasu** is generally used, e.g. **gorufu o shimasu, tenisu o shimasu, ryōri o shimasu,** or where the verb is obvious from the context. Note that the particle **ga** is generally used to show what skill you are talking about, although **wa** is sometimes used with a negative.

Unten ga **dekimasu** ka. Can you drive?
Nihongo ga sukoshi **dekimasu**. I can speak a little Japanese.
Ryōri wa amari **dekimasen**. I can't cook very well.
Sukii wa zenzen **dekimasen**. I can't ski at all.

ACTIVITY 8

How often do you:

1 write letters?	2 do exercise?
3 eat Japanese food?	4 go abroad?
5 read the paper?	6 study Japanese?

ACTIVITY 9

Talk about which of the following you can do. (Use **sukoshi**, **amari**, **zenzen** where appropriate.)
e.g. badminton: Watashi wa badominton ga amari dekimasen.

1 cook	2 speak French
3 play golf	4 ski
5 play tennis	6 drive

🎧 Now do activities 10 and 11 on the recording.

Nomanai hō ga ii desu

ACTIVITY 12 is on the recording.

ACTIVITY 13

Correct the statements which are false.

1 The instructor doesn't think Watanabe san has lost much weight.   T / F
2 Watanabe san hasn't drunk any beer this month.   T / F
3 The instructor advises him not to drink any alcohol.   T / F
4 It's OK for Watanabe san to eat spaghetti, but not hamburgers.   T / F
5 Watanabe san doesn't think he'll be able to increase the amount of exercise he does.   T / F

DIALOGUE 3

○ Watanabe san, sengetsu kara no dēta desu ga. Sengetsu wa kyū-jū-go kiro deshita ga, kongetsu wa kyū-jū-ni kiro desu. Amari kawatte imasen ne.
■ Sō desu ka.
○ Watanabe san wa mada biiru o nonde imasu ka.
■ Anō .... hai.
○ Arukōru o nomanai hō ga ii desu yo.
■ Hai.
○ Sore kara, hanbāgā ya supagetti mo tabenai hō ga ii desu.
■ Supagetti mo desu ka.
○ Mochiron desu. Sore kara, motto undō shite kudasai.
■ Sonna koto dekinai to omoimasu.

VOCABULARY	
dēta	data
kongetsu	this month
kawatte imasen	isn't changed [*from* **kawarimasu**]
arukōru	alcohol
nomanai	don't drink [*plain form of* **nomimasen**]
hō ga ii	it's best (not) to
tabenai	don't eat [*plain form of* **tabemasen**]
mochiron	of course
dekinai	can't [*plain form of* **dekimasen**]

✓ Plain form of negative verbs

There are plain verb forms in the negative as well as the positive, and these too can occur in the middle of a sentence as long as the final verb is in the -masu form. With verbs that drop -ru from the plain form, add -nai.

taberu	**tabe**masen	**tabe**nai	don't eat
iru	**i**masen	**i**nai	isn't in
dekiru	**deki**masen	**deki**nai	can't

With verbs that drop -u, add -anai (or -wanai if the stem of the verb ends in a vowel) to form the negative.

kaeru	**kaer**imasen	**kaer**anai	don't return
nomu	**nom**imasen	**nom**anai	don't drink
iku	**ik**imasen	**ik**anai	don't go
kau	**ka**imasen	**kaw**anai	don't buy

Irregular forms are:

kuru	**konai**	doesn't come
suru	**shinai**	doesn't do
aru	**nai**	there isn't
da	**ja nai**	isn't

Ikanai to omoimasu. I don't think I'll go. (I think I won't go.)
Takai kara, **kawanai** to omoimasu. It's expensive, so I don't think I'll buy it. (… I think I won't buy it.)

✓ Giving advice with *hó ga ii*

To give advice on a course of action, add **hō ga ii** ('It's best to …') after the plain form of a verb.

O-sake wa ni takusan **nomanai hō ga ii** desu. It's best not to drink a lot of sake.

Yoru osoi toki, takushii de **kaeru hō ga ii** desu. Late at night it's best to go home by taxi.

Kyō wa kibun ga warui kara, kaisha ni **ikanai hō ga ii** to omoimasu. I don't feel well today, so I think it's best if I don't go to work.

ACTIVITY 14

What would you suggest to someone who …

1 … has put on weight because she eats too much?
2 … has hurt her leg but plans to drive tomorrow?
3 … has exams soon but doesn't study at all?
4 … plans to buy a new car but can't really afford it?

Now do activities 15 and 16 on the recording.

(13.4) Japanese Culture
Nihon no bunka

THE JAPANESE BATH

Taking a long, relaxing Japanese-style bath every day is generally considered to be one of the most important elements in maintaining a happy and healthy outlook on life. The bath itself is not for getting clean – this is done before getting into the bath – but for relaxing after washing. If you are staying in a **ryokan** (inn) or with a Japanese family, then take the opportunity to experience the pleasures of the **furo** (Japanese-style bath), and soak away the troubles of the day.

Most Japanese homes now have their own baths, but in some areas the **sentō**, or public bath house, still exists, and it is not uncommon to see people walking through the streets in their **yukata** with a plastic bowl and bottles of shampoo and soap tucked under their arms, heading for an evening bath at the **sentō**. Here the baths are large and communal (though segregated into men's and women's) and neighbours chat happily while soaking in the tub, and parents and children scrub each other's backs.

If you go to a **sentō**, leave your clothes in the basket provided in the changing area. In the bathroom you'll find taps set very low in the wall and a tiny stool to sit on while washing. Use the bowl to pour water from the taps over yourself and scrub yourself squeaky clean before getting into the bath. Everyone uses the same water, so make sure you get rid of all traces of soap and shampoo before getting in. The water in the bath is often scalding hot, so take care. The bath is small but deep, so you can sit comfortably with the water right up to your neck while the water does its job of soothing away your cares. You'll emerge pink and steaming, and if you're staying in a **ryokan** you'll be able to put on the crisp cotton **yukata** provided. It is perfectly acceptable to wander around the **ryokan** in your **yukata**. If the weather is cold, a heavier top jacket will also be provided.

ACTIVITY 17

In the unfortunate case of getting aches and pains while in Japan, you may need to describe just where you're hurting. Look at the following figure and find out the names for the various parts of the body. Then match the **romaji** words below to their meanings.

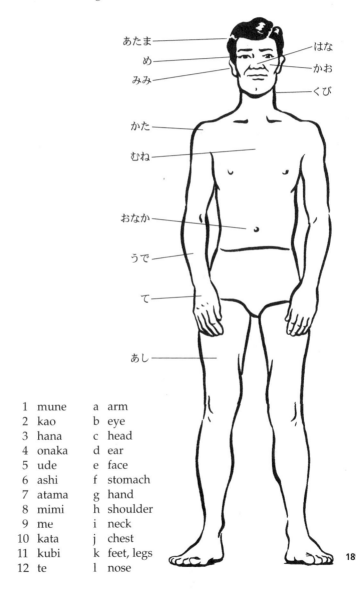

1	mune	a	arm
2	kao	b	eye
3	hana	c	head
4	onaka	d	ear
5	ude	e	face
6	ashi	f	stomach
7	atama	g	hand
8	mimi	h	shoulder
9	me	i	neck
10	kata	j	chest
11	kubi	k	feet, legs
12	te	l	nose

13.5 Midori-ya

FEELING SAD
SABISHII YO

It's evening and Ikeda san has just arrived at Midori-ya for a drink and something to eat. She starts chatting to Harada san.

dareka	someone
zuibun yopparatte imasu	fairly drunk
sabishii	lonely
oshiete kudasai	tell us
misete kuremashita	he showed me
eiga suta	film star

ACTIVITY 18

Listen for these topics of conversation and arrange them in the order they occur.

1 __ the content of a letter is described
2 __ someone is told to go home
3 __ someone orders food
4 __ someone is described as being drunk

ACTIVITY 19

Listen to the dialogue again and complete this summary.

Ikeda san orders tofu, (1) _____ and some beer.

Outside, they hear the sound of someone (2) _____. Itō san says it's Hayashi san, who is feeling (3) _____ and has drunk too much. Harada san tells Hayashi to (4) _____.

Itō san says that Hayashi san showed him (5) _____ from (6) ____. It said she didn't want to marry him because (7) _____.

Hayashi san was so drunk he fell over and hurt his (8) _____, ____ and _____.

Ikeda	Masutā, yakidōfu to yakitori o 2-hon kudasai.
Itō	Hai. O-nomimono wa?
Ikeda	Biiru o kudasai.
Harada	Are wa nan deshō. Dareka utatte imasu ne.
Itō	Hayashi san da to omoimasu.
Harada	A, Hayashi san. Zuibun yopparatte imasu ne. Hayashi san, mō uchi e kaeru hō ga ii desu yo.
Hayashi	Harada san? Konbanwa.
Itō	Hayashi san wa konban chotto sabishii kara nonde iru to omoimasu.
Ikeda	Dō shita n' desu ka.
Itō	Sō desu ne...
Ikeda	Masutā, oshiete kudasai yo. Hayashi san wa dō shite sabishii desu ka.
Itō	Jitsu wa, kesa Hayashi san wa Morita san kara tegami o moraimashita.
Ikeda	Kyūshū no Morita san desu ka. O-miai no aite?
Itō	Hai, sō desu. Watashi ni sono tegami o misete kuremashita.
Ikeda	Haaa.....
Itō	Kanojo wa, Hayashi san no hanashi wa eiga bakari da kara, kekkon wa dame da to kakimashita. Hayashi san wa eiga sutā to kekkon suru hō ga ii to kakimashita.
Ikeda	Sō desu ka.
Hayashi	Tsuki ga deta deta, tsuki ga deta (a yoi yoi)
	Miike no tanko no ue ni deta
	Anmari entotsu ga takai no de
	Sazoya otsuki san kemutakaro (sano yoi yoi)
Ikeda	Hayashi san, daijōbu desu ka.
Hayashi	Itai! Atama ga itai! Ashi ga itai! Ude ga itai!

Test

It's time to test your progress in Unit 13.

1 Complete this table with appropriate forms of the verbs.

-masu	plain positive	plain negative	meaning
1 ikimasu	iku	...	go
2 kaerimasu	...	kaeranai	return
3 naorimasu	...	naoranai	recover
4 shimasu	suru	...	do
5 kimasu	...	...	come
6 arimasu	aru	...	have, exist
7 tabemasu	....	tabenai	eat
8 nomimasu	...	...	drink

10

2 Match these sentences to the situations when you might use them.

1 O-daiji ni.
2 Kao iro ga warui desu ne.
3 Kawatte imasen.
4 Kibun ga warui desu.
5 Shitsumon shimasu.
6 Sonna koto dekinai to omoimasu.
7 Mochiron desu.
8 Shinai hō ga ii desu yo.

a A friend doesn't look well.
b Someone asks about something which you think is obvious.
c A friend is going to do something you don't agree with.
d You're going to question someone.
e A friend is recovering from an illness.
f You weigh yourself, and find you haven't lost any weight.
g You don't feel well.
h Someone asks if you could run a half-marathon.

8

3 Make up sentences to describe this person's health plan.

1 jog three times a week
2 go to gym once a week
3 play tennis twice a month
4 eat fruit every morning
5 lose 20 kg in a year

10

4 Choose the appropriate word from those in brackets to complete these sentences.

1 Sonna ni takusan tabako o (**suu** / **suwanai**) hō ga ii desu yo.

2 Ano hito wa Ishii san (**ja nai** / **nai**) to omoimasu yo.

3 Shū ni nan-kai jimu de (**unten** / **undō**) shimasu ka.

4 Itsu made ni ashi ga (**naorimasen** / **naoru**) to omoimasu ka.

5 Kyō wa kaze desu kara, chotto (**kao** / **kibun**) ga warui desu.

6 Yoru osoi kara, aruite (**kawanai** / **kaeranai**) hō ga ii desu yo.

| | 6 |

5 Put these sentences in the correct order to make a conversation between two acquaintances in a doctor's waiting room.

1 Ē, totemo itai desu.

2 Kinō jogingu shite imashita ga, kōen de korobimashita.

3 Sonna koto dekimasen yo. Futorimasu kara!

4 Sō desu ka. Ashi ga itai desu ka.

5 Dō shimashita ka.

6 Ja, mō undō o shinai hō ga ii desu ne. Jogingu o yamete kudasai.

| | 6 |

6 Answer these questions about yourself.

1 Maishū undō o shimasu ka. Nani o shimasu ka.

2 Sukii ga dekimasu ka.

3 Taijū wa nan-kiro desu ka. Shinchō wa nan-senchi desu ka.

4 Nen ni nan-kai gurai gaikoku e ikimasu ka.

5 Kyonen kara futorimashita ka. Yasemashita ka.

| | 10 |

TOTAL SCORE | 50 |

If you scored less than 40, look at the Language Building sections again before completing the Summary on page 194.

Summary 13

 Now try this final test summarizing the main points covered in this unit. You can check your answers on the recording.

How would you:
1 comment that someone doesn't look well?
2 ask someone how many times a week she exercises?
3 ask someone if he can speak English?
4 say you think that's Takeda san over there?
5 say you go jogging every morning, but your weight hasn't really changed?
6 suggest to someone that he should go home by taxi?
7 say you don't think you'll go to the gym tomorrow.
8 suggest to someone that she shouldn't drink so much coffee?
9 say you don't feel well?
10 say you can speak a little Japanese?

REVISION

Think about the various things you do to keep healthy. Do you think it's a good idea to exercise regularly? What do you eat and drink, or avoid eating and drinking? What forms of exercise do you do, and how often? See how long you can keep talking about this in Japanese!

Use the verb list in the Grammar Summary to make sure you're familiar with the plain forms of the most commonly used verbs. Get someone to test you, if possible.

High days and holidays
Omedetō!

OBJECTIVES

In this unit, you'll learn how to:

- ✓ ask about experiences
- ✓ describe events
- ✓ talk about festivals
- ✓ express yourself when giving and receiving

And cover the following grammar and language:

- ✓ the plain form of past tense verbs
- ✓ **-ta koto ga arimasu ka** ('Have you ever …?') to ask about experiences
- ✓ **-te** form verbs in joining sentences
- ✓ the **-kute** form of **-i** adjectives in joining sentences
- ✓ verbs of giving and receiving

LEARNING JAPANESE 14

Now that you've completed this course, what can you do to continue your learning? There are several useful suggestions throughout the Learning Japanese sections at the beginning of each unit and the Introduction contains a summary of learning strategies.

In particular, keep developing your vocabulary lists and reviewing them regularly. Dip into the course again from time to time to refresh your memory. Listen to the recordings and practise speaking as much as you can: ideally, try to find native Japanese speakers to talk to. An adult education Japanese class in a local college is also a good resource. And, of course, a visit to Japan would give you the perfect opportunity to try out your Japanese.

🎧 Now start the recording for Unit 14.

Gaikoku e itta koto ga arimasu ka

ACTIVITY 1 is on the recording.

ACTIVITY 2

Correct the statements which are false.

1	The man wants to honeymoon abroad.	T / F
2	He's never been on a plane.	T / F
3	Neither of them has been to Hawaii.	T / F
4	The woman was at university in Canada.	T / F
5	The woman wants to go to Okinawa.	T / F

DIALOGUE 1

○ Hanemūn wa doko ni ikimashō ka. Okinawa wa dō desu ka.

■ Iie, watashi wa gaikoku e itta koto ga arimasen kara, gaikoku e ikimashō. Hikōki ni mo notta koto ga arimasen yo. Hawai wa dō desu ka.

○ Iie, Hawai wa kyonen ikimashita.

■ Sō desu ka. Ja, Ōsutoraria e mo itta deshō.

○ Ē, Shidonii ni ryūgaku shite imashita.

■ Ja, Kanada e itta koto ga arimasu ka.

○ Ē, daigakusei no toki ikimashita. Oji to oba ga Ontario ni sunde imasu kara.

■ Ja, doko ga ii desu ka.

○ Okinawa ga ii ja nai desu ka. Atsui shi ….

VOCABULARY	
hanemūn	honeymoon
Okinawa	*Japanese island to the south of Kyushu*
itta koto ga arimasen	I've never been to … [*also* I've never been there]
notta koto ga arimasen	I've never ridden, I've never travelled on
Shidonii	Sydney
ryūgaku	study abroad
oji to oba	(my) uncle and aunt
ii ja nai desu ka	(it) would be good, wouldn't it?

✓ Plain form of past tense verbs

There are plain forms of verbs in the past tense as well as the present tense, and these too can be used in the middle of a sentence without affecting the overall polite tone as long as the final verb is in the polite **-masu/-mashita** form. The positive ('went', 'did', 'came', etc.) is formed in the same way as the **-te** form, but ends in **-ta** instead of **-te**.

Present	-te form	Past	English
iku	**itte**	**itta**	went
kaeru	**kaette**	**kaetta**	went home
taberu	**tabete**	**tabeta**	ate
miru	**mite**	**mita**	saw

Ishii san wa mō **kaetta** to omoimasu. I think Ishii san has already gone home.

Sono eiga o kinō **mita** deshō. You saw that film yesterday, right?

To form the negative ('didn't go, didn't eat', etc.), replace the **-nai** of the present negative with **-nakatta**.

Present positive	Present negative	Past negative	English
iku	**ikanai**	**ikanakatta**	didn't go
iru	**inai**	**inakatta**	wasn't in
kuru	**konai**	**konakatta**	didn't come
au	**awanai**	**awanakatta**	didn't meet

The comparable forms of **desu** are **datta** and **ja nakatta**.

Kinō denwa shimashita ga, uchi ni **inakatta** deshō. I called you yesterday, but you weren't in, were you?

Itō san ni **awanakatta** deshō. You didn't meet Itō san, did you?

✓ Describing experiences with *-ta koto ga arimasu*

To ask about things people have or haven't done, use the plain past form of the verb + **koto ga arimasu ka** ('Have you ever ...?'). **koto** means 'experience', so the literal meaning is 'Do you have the experience of ....?'

Nihon no matsuri o **mita koto ga arimasu ka**. Have you ever seen a Japanese festival?

Sake o **nonda koto ga arimasen**. I've never drunk sake.

ACTIVITY 3

How would you ask and reply? Have you ...?

1 been to Europe?
2 travelled on the Shinkansen?
3 eaten sashimi?
4 met any famous people?

🎧 Now do activities 4 and 5 on the recording.

Matsuri o mimashita

ACTIVITY 6 is on the recording.

ACTIVITY 7

Which of the following topics were mentioned?

1 The man went to Hamamatsu at the weekend.
2 It was the first time he'd seen the kite festival.
3 It was very interesting.
4 It's a famous festival.
5 The kites are all hand-made.
6 The kites are large and it takes a lot of people to fly each one.

DIALOGUE 2

○ Shūmatsu wa, nani o shimashita ka.
■ Hamamatsu e itte, tako-age matsuri o mimashita.
○ Sō desu ka. Dō deshita ka.
■ Omoshirokatta desu yo. Yamada san wa mita koto ga arimasu ka.
○ Iie, arimasen ga, kiita koto ga arimasu. Yūmei-na matsuri desu ne.
■ Sō desu. Tako wa kirei de, totemo ōkii desu. Ni-jū-nin de agemasu. Tako o agete, hoka no tako to kenka shimasu. Sugoi desu yo. A, kore wa o-miyage desu.
○ Chiisai tako desu ka. Kawaii desu ne. Arigatō.

VOCABULARY	
shūmatsu	weekend
Hamamatsu e itte, ...	I went to Hamamatsu, and ...
tako	kite
tako-age matsuri	kite-flying festival
kiita koto ga arimasu	I've heard of it
kirei de, ...	they're beautiful, and ...
agemasu	fly (a kite) [also raise]
tako o agete ...	they raise up the kite, and ...
kenka shimasu	fight, quarrel
sugoi	amazing, wonderful
kawaii	cute, sweet

✓ Joining sentences with *-te* forms

When linking several sentences together to describe a sequence of events, the **-te** form of the verb is used at the end of each clause. The **-te** form can be used in the middle of the sentence regardless of whether the meaning is past, present, or future, because it's the final verb that indicates the tense.

Pabu ni ikimashita. + Takusan nomimashita. =

Pabu ni **itte**, takusan nomimashita. I went to the pub and drank a lot.

Matsuri o mimashita. + Shashin o takusan torimashita. =

Matsuri o **mite**, shashin o takusan torimashita. I watched the festival and took a lot of photos.

Konban uchi ni imasu. + Terebi o mimasu. =

Konban uchi ni **ite**, terebi o mimasu. This evening I'm going to stay in and watch TV.

The equivalent form for **desu** is **de**.

Ashita wa watashi no tanjōbi **de**, asatte wa shujin no tanjōbi desu. Today is my birthday and tomorrow is my husband's birthday.
Yama wa kirei **de**, tanoshikatta desu. The mountains were beautiful and I had a good time.

ACTIVITY 8

Look at this person's brief diary notes for last week. Use the **-te** form to describe what he did each day.

1 Mon:	went to Yokohama – bought new jacket
2 Tue:	stayed in – watched video
3 Wed:	joined new French class – studied hard!
4 Thur:	tennis in morning – went to gym in afternoon
5 Fri:	birthday – had a party; drank a lot of beer had quarrel with girlfriend
6 Sat/Sun:	went to mountains with Yamada san – hiking

 Now do activities 9 and 10 on the recording.

199

O-toshi dama o moraimashita

 ACTIVITY 11 is on the recording.

ACTIVITY 12

Number the topics in the order they are mentioned.

1 going to a large shrine for the first time
2 receiving New Year gifts of money
3 visiting grandparents
4 the crowds of people at the shrine
5 the weather
6 eating New Year food at home
7 aching feet

DIALOGUE 3

Akemashite omedetō gozaimasu. Nihon no o-shōgatsu wa samui desu ga, Ōsutoraria wa atsui deshō. Kinō, Meiji Jingū ni itte, o-saisen o agemashita. Uchi no chikaku no o-tera e wa itta koto ga arimasu ga, Meiji Jingū wa hajimete desu. Taihen konde imashita yo. Jū-man-nin gurai imashita! Watashi wa kimono o kite ikimashita ga, ashi ga itakute, taihen deshita. Sore kara uchi e kaette, o-sechi ryōri o tabemashita. O-toshi dama o moraimashita. Ashita sofu to sobo no uchi e itte, mata o-sechi ryōri o tabemasu. O-shōgatsu wa itsumo futorimasu ne!

VOCABULARY	
akemashite omedetō gozaimasu	Happy New Year!
omedetō gozaimasu	congratulations
o-shōgatsu	New Year's Day, the New Year
o-saisen	*a money offering at a temple/shrine*
o-saisen o agemashita	gave offering of money
o-tera	temple
konde imashita	was crowded [*from* **komu** be crowded]
ashi ga itakute...	my feet hurt and ...
o-sechi ryōri	*special New Year dishes*
o-toshi dama	*money given to youngsters at New Year*
sofu to sobo	(my) grandfather and grandmother

✓ Verbs of giving and receiving

There is no single equivalent of the verb 'to give' in Japanese – it depends on who is doing the giving. When the speaker (or someone whose relationship with the speaker is close) gives something, **agemasu** is used. The person who's receiving is marked by the particle **ni**. As it is obvious who is doing the giving because of the verb used, it isn't necessary to include **watashi**.

> Tomodachi ni purezento o **agemashita**. I gave a present to my friend.
> O-miyage o katte, haha ni **agemashita**. I bought a souvenir and gave it to my mother.

There are other verbs used when someone else is giving to the speaker (**kuremasu, kudasaimasu**), depending on the relationship between the giver and the receiver. However, the complications of choosing which verb to use are generally avoided, as it is much more common to express such exchanges in terms of receiving rather than giving. The verb **moraimasu** means 'receive', 'get', and the person giving is marked by **ni**.

> Chichi ni kamera o **moratte**, ane ni fuirumu o **moraimashita**. I got a camera from my father and I got some film from my older sister.
> Yamada san ni nani o **moraimashita** ka. What did you get from Yamada san?

✓ Joining -*i* adjectives

To link an -**i** adjective to another adjective ('a small, cheap car'), replace the final -**i** with -**kute**.

> Ano kuruma wa **chiisakute, yasui** desu. It's a small, cheap car.
> Meiji Jingu wa **hirokute, rippa** desu. Meiji Shrine is large and it's wonderful.

When a -**na** adjective is linked to another adjective, it needs to be followed by **de**.

> Meiji Jingu wa **rippa de, hiroi** desu. Meiji Shrine is wonderful, and it's huge.

ACTIVITY 13

How would this Japanese woman describe her trip to London?

London interesting, really fun! Hotel expensive, not very good. Weather cold, horrible. My birthday yesterday – got beautiful watch from Yamaguchi san. Bought lots of souvenirs. Will give handbag to mum and sweater to dad. Going to Paris tomorrow, back to Japan on Thursday. Emiko

 Now do activities 14 and 15 on the recording.

201

CULTURE

GIVING GIFTS

Japan is a gift-giving society and presents are exchanged not only at festive times such as birthdays and weddings, but also at two other special gift-giving times, **o-chūgen** in the summer and **o-seibo** at the year end. The giving of gifts at these times is for strengthening relationships not only between individuals and families, but also between businesses. Gifts are exchanged at **o-chūgen** and **o-seibo** in thanks for favours or business done in the past, and also to bind relationships in anticipation of future transactions. In other words, they are gifts given from a sense of obligation, or **giri**.

A great deal of business is done by department stores during **o-chūgen** and **o-seibo**, and takings may increase by 20 percent during these times of year. Practical items such as soap, tea, biscuits, seaweed, sake, and cooking oil are generally chosen, and whole departments are given over to selling special gift packs of these items. The way of giving presents, the items chosen, and the relative costs are all governed by rules of etiquette, and many people keep records of gifts given and received to refer to when choosing the next round of gifts the following year.

The wrapping of a gift is also important and staff in department stores are trained to wrap presents with exquisite perfection, using special paper, ribbons, and carrier bags. Even gifts of money are never given unwrapped – special envelopes are available depending on whether the money is given at a birthday, a wedding, New Year, or a funeral.

Small gifts are usually taken when visiting someone's home, generally an item of food such as biscuits or fruit, and handed over with an expression of modesty such as **Tsumaranai mono desu ga** … ('It's just a small thing, but … '). Do not be offended if a present you give is put to one side unopened – traditionally gifts are not opened until after the visitor has left, although this custom is gradually changing and younger people eagerly open presents when they receive them.

ACTIVITY 16

Work out the names of these five annual festivals.

1 せつぶん　2月3日または4日　The day before the beginning of spring, according to the old calendar. In the evening, families go outside the house and throw beans to drive demons and bad luck out of the house and to let good luck in.

2 ひなまつり　3月3日　Festival of Dolls, also know as Girls' Day Festival: an occasion for wishing for the future health and happiness of girls. Homes are decorated with a display of dolls in ancient court dress.

3 たんごのせっく　5月5日　Boys' Festival, for the future health and happiness of boys. Homes are decorated with dolls in traditional warrior costume and huge streamers in the shape of fish are flown outside the house.

4 おぼん　8月　Festival of Souls, in mid-August, to remember and pray for the spirits of ancestors. People return to their home towns for family get-togethers. Yukata are worn for outdoor traditional dances known as **bon-odori**.

5 しちごさん　11月15日　Seven-five-three festival, when five-year-old boys and three- and seven-year-old girls are dressed in their finest clothes – often tiny kimono – and taken to shrines to wish for good futures for the children.

ACTIVITY 17

Here are a few lines from a young girl's diary, describing what she did on New Year's Day. Using the hiragana and katakana charts on page viii, see how much you can read and understand.

きのうのあさ きものをきて、おかあさんと おとうさんと いっしょに
めいじじんぐうに いった。たいへん こんでいた！ おかあさんに
おかねを もらって、おさいせんを あげた。さむかったから、すぐうちへ
かえった。ごご おじさんと おばさんが うちへ きて、おとしだまを
もらった！
たいへん たのしい いちにちだった。

HAYASHI SAN AND THE NURSE
HAYASHI SAN TO KANGOFU SAN

Ikeda san called a taxi and took Hayashi san to hospital after his fall outside Midori-ya. She's just returned.

kangofu	nurse
futsuka-kan	a period of two days
o-mimai ni iku	go to visit a sick person
kibun wa dō desu ka	how do you feel?
daibu naorimashita	considerably, much
taiin shimasu	come out of hospital
mi ni ikimasu	go to see

ACTIVITY 18

Listen to the dialogue and find words for

1 a part of the body   3 two jobs
2 two kinds of transport

ACTIVITY 19

Put a tick by the events which are mentioned in the dialogue and a cross by those which aren't.

1 Someone sang in a taxi.
2 Someone is having dinner.
3 Someone spoke on the phone today.
4 Two people visit the hospital.
5 Someone is watching a video.
6 Someone takes some medicine.

ACTIVITY 20

Listen for the Japanese equivalent of these sentences and put them in the order you hear them.

1 ___ Please come this way.
2 ___ Your friends have come to see you.
3 ___ What did the driver say?
4 ___ Is about 4.00 OK?

ACTIVITY 21

Correct these statements.

1 Hayashi san should stay in hospital for a week.
2 He fell asleep in the taxi to the hospital.
3 Hayashi san tells Ikeda san he's leaving hospital tomorrow.
4 The nurse likes sports.
5 Hayashi san is going to see a movie with Ikeda san tonight.

STORY TRANSCRIPT

Itō	Hayashi san wa daijōbu desu ka.
Ikeda	Hai, daijōbu da to omoimasu. Demo kangofu wa, Hayashi san wa futsuka-kan gurai byōin ni ita hō ga ii to iimashita.
Harada	Hayashi san wa yopparatte imashita deshō.
Ikeda	Sō desu ne. Takushii no naka de mo utatte imashita.
Itō	Untenshu wa nan to iimashita ka.
Ikeda	Untenshu wa uta ga suki da kara, issho ni utatte imashita... Tokorode, Itō san, ashita byōin ni o-mimai ni iku kara, issho ni ikimasen ka.
Itō	Hai, ii desu yo.
	...
Ikeda	Sumimasen, kangofu san?
Nurse	Hai.
Ikeda	Hayashi san wa ....?
Nurse	A, Hayashi san desu ne. Dōzo, kochira e. Ima bideo o mite imasu ga...
Itō	Mata eiga desu ka. Hayashi san wa eiga bakari desu ne.
Nurse	Totemo omoshiroi eiga o ima mite imasu. Watashi mo sono eiga o san-kai mimashita.
Itō	Sō desu ka.
Nurse	Hayashi san, o-tomodachi ga o-mimai ni kimashita.
Hayashi	A, arigatō. A, Itō san, Ikeda san, ohayō gozaimasu.
Ikeda	Ohayō gozaimasu. Kibun wa dō desu ka.
Hayashi	Un, atama wa daibu naorimashita yo. Kyō no gogo taiin shimasu.
Ikeda	Yokatta desu ne. Nan-ji ni? Watashi ga kuruma de kimasu kara... 4.00 goro de ii desu ka.
Hayashi	Iie, kekkō desu yo. Konban Yamaguchi san to issho ni eiga o mi ni ikimasu kara.
Ikeda	Ē? Yamaguchi san? Yamaguchi san wa donata desu ka.
Hayashi	Ano kangofu san desu. Yamaguchi san no shumi mo eiga desu.
Ikeda/Itō	Haaaa....

Test

Now it's time to test your progress in Unit 14.

1 Read these sentences and then say who gave what to whom.

   1 Tanjōbi ni gakusei ga Yamaguchi sensei ni hana o agemashita.
   2 Tanaka san wa Hayashi san ni sukāfu o moraimashita.
   3 Ane ga haha ni kirei-na saifu o agemashita.
   4 Tomodachi ni Kyōto no o-miyage o agemashita.

	What?	Given by?	Received by?
1			
2			
3			
4			

`12`

2 Complete these sentences with an appropriate form of the word in brackets.

   1 Shūmatsu ni yama e (ikimasu) ____, haikingu o shimashita.
   2 Kinō wa tanjōbi (desu) ___, iroiro-na purezento o moraimashita.
   3 Jonson san wa sumō o (mimasu) ____ koto ga arimasu ka.
   4 Fuji Hoteru wa (takai) ____, heya wa kirei ja nai desu.
   5 Nihon no matsuri wa (omoshiroi) ____, tanoshii desu.
   6 O-sechi ryōri o (tabemasu) ____ koto ga arimasu ka.

`6`

3 Rearrange the words to form sentences.

   1 o / ga / o-sake / koto / ka / arimasu / nonda
   2 shimashita / de / kenka / resutoran / to / bōifurendo
   3 de / tanjōbi / mokuyōbi / shujin no / agemashita / wa / shii dii / o
   4 ban / ni / no / deshō / kino / inakatta / uchi
   5 moraimashita / tanjōbi / tokei / ni / ni / kanai / o

`5`

4 How would you express your thoughts in Japanese?

1 This film's famous, but it's not very good.

2 He's never been abroad.

3 He bought that jacket in Harrods.

4 I've met her before.

5 He's going to Nagoya tomorrow and coming back the next day.

`10`

---

5 Rearrange these lines to make a dialogue between two friends.

1 __ Iie, daigakusei no toki Nyū Yōku e ryūgaku shite imashita.
2 __ Nyū Yōku e itte, myūjikaru o mimashita.
3 __ Mochiron desu yo. A, o-miyage o dōzo.
4 __ Ii desu ne. Nyū Yōku wa hajimete deshita ka.
5 __ O-shōgatsu wa dō deshita ka.
6 __ Sō desu ka. Kaimono o takusan shimashita ka.

`6`

---

6 Answer these questions about yourself.

1 Nihon no matsuri o mita koto ga arimasu ka.
2 Kyonen no tanjōbi ni, nani o moraimashita ka.
3 Anata no kuni ni, yūmei-na matsuri ga arimasu ka.
4 Gaikoku e ryūgaku o shita koto ga arimasu ka.
5 Kimono o kita koto ga arimasu ka.
6 Kodomo no toki, yoku tako o agemashita ka.

`12`

TOTAL SCORE `51`

If you scored less than 41, look at the Language Building sections again before completing the Summary on page 208.

Summary 14

Now try this final test summarizing the main points covered in this unit. You can check your answers on the recording.

How would you:
1 ask someone if he's ever been to New York?
2 say you got some CDs and a camera for your birthday?
3 say the kabuki in Kyoto was beautiful and it was really interesting?
4 ask someone what he did at New Year?
5 say it's really hot and horrible in Tokyo at the moment?
6 say you're going to give a yukata to your younger sister and a kite to your younger brother?
7 say you came back from Kyoto on 2 January and worked from the 3rd?
8 ask a friend who she got those flowers from?
9 say you've heard of the kite festival, but you've never seen it?
10 say you stayed in last night and watched TV?

REVISION

Have you ever watched or taken part in a festival? Where, and when? What did you see, and what did you do? Was there any special festive food? How many people were there? Think about how you would explain the festival to a Japanese friend. What festivals from other countries have you heard of? Could you describe them?

The final section of the book is the review, so this is a good time to do some general revision. Go back and dip into the book at random, and make a note of any vocabulary you may have forgotten. Read over the Revision notes at the end of each unit and make sure you followed up the ideas suggested there.

Review 4

VOCABULARY

1 List the items of clothing, etc., under the appropriate verbs.

zubon, yukata, nekutai, iyaringu, sētā, kutsushita, megane, bōshi, sangurasu, jiinzu, burausu, sukāfu

kaburimasu kimasu   hakimasu kakemasu shimasu

_____   _____   _____   _____   _____

_____   _____   _____   _____   _____

_____   _____   _____   _____   _____

2 Which are the odd ones out in the following groups?

1 kiite / yonde / mite / asatte / katte / shite
2 kachō / kakarichō / shutchō / buchō / fuku-shachō
3 o-naka / hashi / ude / atama / kao / ashi
4 sofu / otona / oba / sobo / oji / ane
5 shū / tsuki / nen / fun / jikan / mai

3 What do you say to …

1 … someone who has just announced he's to be married soon?
2 … someone you meet on New Year's Day?
3 … someone who is unwell, hoping he gets better soon?
4 … someone who looks pale?
5 … someone with a broken leg when you want to know what happened?

GRAMMAR AND USAGE

4 Complete these sentences with one of the following particles: **wa, ga, ni, no, o.**

1 Sensei _____ denwa bangō _____ shitte imasu ka.
2 Saitō san, kono shorui _____ Ōsaka shisha _____ okutte kudasai.
3 Tsuki _____ yon-kai gurai tenisu ___ shimasu.
4 Takahashi san _____ eigo _____ dekimasu ka.
5 Nihon no matsuri _____ mita koto _____ arimasu ka.
6 Oji to oba _____ o-toshi dama _____ moraimashita.

5 Below are the cues for some typical questions you might be asked if you go to Japan. What are the questions and how would you respond?
Example: ever heard Japanese songs?
Nihon no uta o kiita koto ga arimasu ka. Hai, arimasu.

Have you ever ....
1 .... drunk sake?
2 .... eaten raw fish?
3 .... made a Japanese meal?
4 .... been to Kyoto?
5 .... worn a kimono?
6 .... seen sumo?

6 Complete these sentences with an appropriate form of the verb in brackets.

1 Takahashi san wa ima Nyū Yōku de Nihongo o (oshiemasu) _____ imasu.
2 O-namae to go-jūsho o koko ni (kakimasu) _____ kudasai.
3 Ude wa itsu goro (naorimasu) _____ to omoimasu ka.
4 Mada wakai kara, sake o amari (nomimasu) _____ hō ga ii to omoimasu.
5 Sono kamera wa takai kara, Itō san wa (kaimasu) ____ to omoimasu.
6 Ishii san wa mō Tōkyō e (kaerimasu) _____ deshō.

🔊 LISTENING

7 Listen to a student telling her friend about a blind date she had last night and complete the following description of the man she met.

Profile

Name: Yukio Terada

Age:

Height:

Weight:

Interests:

Appearance/clothes:

---

8 Listen to this **buchō** as he talks to some of the staff in his department about their schedules for the next few days, then answer the questions below.

1 Where is Suzuki san going tomorrow and how long will she stay there?
2 What does the buchō ask her to do while she's there?
3 Why is she going alone?

🔊 SPEAKING

9 Imagine you are the person described below, a foreign student in Japan, and you have just gone to have a health check. Listen to the questions and use the information below for the answers.

Name: Susan Carter

Nationality: English

Age: 24

Exercise: play badminton twice a week; occasionally go to gym

Smoking: quit about 5 years ago

Drinking: not much – a little beer about once a week

---

10 And finally a general knowledge test in English. You will find answers to all the questions in the Culture sections of the units.

    1 What is pachinko?
    2 When is the rainy season in Japan?
    3 Is there a national holiday on the Emperor's birthday?
    4 What is often used instead of a signature on official documents?
    5 Name one of the English-language newspapers in Japan.
    6 At what time of the year do people often wear kimono?
    7 What is the approximate distance from the northernmost to the southernmost islands of Japan?
    8 What can usually be found outside restaurants to help you choose your meal?
    9 What is the difference between sushi and sashimi?
  10 What happens during the periods of o-chūgen and o-seibo?

Well done, you've completed the final test of the course. Don't forget to review any points you're unsure of, but above all good luck and go for it! **Ganbatte kudasai**.

Answers

Unit 1

2 1 b, 2 c, 3 a

3 *Free answers.* Choose 1 if it's nice weather, 2 if it's horrible, 3 if it's cold and 4 if it's hot.

7 Kimura san, Shimada san, Yoshida san

8 (your name) desu. Dōzo yoroshiku.

9 1 b, 2 a, 3 c (if you matched 1 with a, remember that you don't used san with your own name)

13 *Woman*: orange juice and cheese sandwich; *Man*: lemon tea

14 tomato juice, coffee, ice cream, mixed sandwiches, cream soda, tea with milk, pizza, spaghetti, Coca Cola, beer, hamburger, salad

17 *Drink*: coffee, coke, ice cocoa, soda; *Food*: toast, cake, cheesecake,sausages

18 2, 4, 5, 1, 3

19 1 T, 2 DK (it isn't mentioned if they're friends or not), 3 T, 4 F (he gives the newcomer a beer), 5 DK

20 6

21 onegai shimasu, atsui, arigatō, dōmo, oishii

Test

1 1 d, 2 f, 3 a, 5 b, 6 c, 7 e

2 1 Kōhii to aisu kuriimu o kudasai, 2 Mikkusu sando to kōra o kudasai, 3 Hanbāgā to orenji jūsu o kudasai, 4 Biiru to piza o kudasai, 5 Sarada to tomato jūsu o kudasai.

3 *Food*: hanbāga, orenji, sarada, chiizu; *Drink*: kōhii, miruku, biiru, mizu, tii; Exception: mizu (water)

4 1 Shimada san desu ka, 2 Ii tenki desu ne, 3 Ohayō gozaimasu, 4 Hai, Kimura san desu, 5 Sumimasen.

5 Koyama, ka; Hai, desu; Ross desu, yoroshiku; yoroshiku.

Summary 1

1 Ohayō gozaimasu, Konnichiwa, Konbanwa. *2* Ii tenki desu ne. *3* Sō desu ne, Samui desu ne. *4* Koyama san desu ka. *5* Dōzo yoroshiku *6* Kōhii to orenji jūsu o kudasai *7* Arigatō.

Unit 2

2 1 8 o'clock, 2 iced coffee, 3 it's hot, 4 the film is just starting

4 1 (Eiga wa) hachi-ji han desu, 2 (Konsāto wa) shichi-ji desu, 3 Iie, (nyūsu wa) ku-ji desu.

8 3.30, 8.30, 9.00

9 1 Hai, sō desu, 2 Iie, sō ja arimasen (Shichi-ji han made desu), 3 Iie, sō ja arimasen (Jū-ichi-ji kara desu)

13 1 T, 2 F (it's 3.15pm in New York), 3 T, 4 F (today is his day off)

14 1 e, 2 d, 3 a, 4 c, 5 b

17 Star Wars (Sutā Wōzu), Lion King (Raion Kingu), Superman (Sūpāman), Psycho (Saiko)

18 soro soro x 3, shigoto x 3, ashita x 7, onegai shimasu x 2

19 1 Ikeda (Ja, mata ashita. Oyasumi nasai), 2 Itō (Jū-ichi-ji han desu), 3 Hayashi (E? Yasumi desu ka), 4 Itō (Ja, Hayashi san mo dōzo), 5 Ikeda (Osoi desu ne)

2, 5, 1, 3, 4

20 1 Ikeda san leaves at ~~11.00~~ 11.30, 2 Harada san is ~~shopping~~ working tomorrow morning, 3 Hayashi san decides not to have another beer, 4 Hayashi san isn't busy; he accepts the invitation to the picnic.

Test

1 1 c, 2 f, 4 e, 5 d, 6 b, 7 a

2 1 asa ichi-ji han, 2 asa yo-ji jū-go-fun, 3 asa shichi-ji, 4 gogo hachi-ji ni-jup-pun, 5 gogo jū-ji yon-jup-pun, 6 gogo jū-ichi-ji go-jū-go-fun

3 1 Depāto wa (asa) jū-ji kara (gogo) hachi-ji made desu, 2 Ginkō wa (asa) ku-ji kara (gogo) san-ji made desu, 3 Supōtsu sentā wa (asa) hachi-ji han kara (gogo) ku-ji yon-jū-go-fun made desu (You can omit asa and gogo if it's obvious from the context that the times are a.m or p.m.)

4 1 Kyō wa yasumi ja arimasen. 2 Konsāto wa nan-ji kara desu ka, 3 Depāto wa asa 10.00 kara desu, 4 Pūru wa gogo 7.00 made desu, 5 Ashita wa shigoto desu ka

5 1 Asa desu or Gogo desu, 2 (time) desu, 3 Hai, sō desu or Iie, shigoto desu

6 1 Konsāto wa nan-ji kara desu ka. 2 Shigoto wa ku-ji kara go-ji han made desu. 3 Kyō wa chotto samui desu ne. 4 Konsāto wa kyō ja arimasen. Ashita desu. 5 Mō ichido, onegai shimasu.

Summary 2

1 ichi, ni, san, yon or shi, go, roku, shichi or

213

nana, hachi, kyū, jū. *2* Ima nan-ji desu ka.
3 Eiga wa shichi-ji jū-go-fun kara desu.
4 Pūru wa go-ji made desu. *5* Ashita wa
shigoto ja arimasen. *6* Mō ichido, onegai
shimasu. *7* Tōkyō wa ima asa desu ka. Gogo
desu ka. *8* Hayai desu ne. or Osoi desu ne.

Unit 3

2   1 to England, 2 ¥150, 3 three

3   1 Hagaki wa hyaku en desu. 2 Earoguramu
       wa hyaku roku-jū en desu. 3 Aisu kuriimu
       wa ni-hyaku san-jū en desu.

7   1, 2, 3

8   1 Furansu no wain wa dō desu ka. 2 Jazu
       no shii dii wa dō desu ka. 3 Nihon no tokei
       wa dō desu ka. 4 Tōkyō no o-miyage wa
       dō desu ka.

12 1 T, 2 T, 3 F (there are lots of smaller
       purses), 4 T, 5 T

13 Kitte wa arimasu ka. Tōkyō no hagaki wa
       arimasu ka. Firumu wa arimasu ka.
       Kodomo no T-shatsu wa arimasu ka.

14 1 Hoteru no hagaki ni shimasu. 2 'Gojira'
       no T-shatsu ni shimasu.

17 *B1* fruit (furūtsu), coffee (kōhii), tea (tii);
       1 accessories (akusesarii), handkerchiefs
       (hankachiifu), neckties (nekutai), belts
       (beruto); *2* blouses (burausu), jeans (jiinzu),
       nightwear (naito uea), aprons (epuron);
       3 suits (sūtsu), coats (kōto), shatsu (shirts);
       4 tennis wear (tenisu uea), golf wear
       (gorufu uea); *5* art gallery (āto gyararii),
       restaurants (resutoran); *Roof* game corner
       (gēmu kōnā), beer garden (biya gāden)

18 1 c, 2 d, 3 a, 4 b

19 4, 6, 3, 7, 1, 5, 2

20 1 Everyone drinks some beer (Mina san,
       biiru wa dō desu ka ... Kanpai!). 2 Harada
       san thinks it's too early to drink beer
       (Biiru? Chotto hayai desu ne). 3 Ikeda san
       thinks picnics are fun (pikunikku wa
       tanoshii desu ne). 4 Hayashi san seems like
       a strange person (Hen-na hito).

Test

1   1 Firumu wa hap-pyaku go-jū en desu.
     2 Kodomo no T-shatsu wa san-zen yon-
     hyaku go-jū en desu. 3 Chiisai saifu wa
     kyū-sen go-hyaku en desu, 4 Ōkii saifu wa
     ichi-man yon-sen ni-hyaku en desu. 5 Itaria
     no sangurasu wa ni-man yon-sen hap-
     pyaku en desu.

2   1 o, 2 arimasen, 3 no, 4 arimasu,
     5 ja arimasen, 6 dō

3   1 c, 2 d, 3 f, 4 a, 5 b

4   5, 1, 4, 6, 3, 2

5   1 Kamera wa chotto takai desu ne.
     2 T-shatsu wa chotto chiisai desu ne.

3 Sangurasu wa chotto ōkii desu ne.
4 Yūbinkyoku wa chotto atsui desu ne.

6   1 Sumimasen ga, motto chiisai saifu wa
     arimasu ka. 2 Are wa ikura desu ka.
     3 Earoguramu o san-mai kudasai. 4 Kore
     wa Fukuda san no sangurasu desu ka.
     5 Sore wa Furansu no wain desu ka.
     6 Nihon no tokei ja arimasen.

Summary 3

1 Hyaku ni-jū en kitte o ni-mai kudasai.
2 Hagaki wa Igirisu made ikura desu ka.
3 Ni-man go-sen en. *4* T-shatsu wa dō desu ka.
5 Chotto takai desu ne. *6* Chigaimasu. *7* Kore
wa Nihon no kamera desu ka. *8* Firumu wa
arimasu ka. *9* Chiisai tokei ni shimasu.
10 Motto ōkii T-shatsu wa arimasu ka.

Review 1

1 *Greeting*: ohayō gozaimasu, konnichiwa,
      konbanwa; *Goodbye*: mata ashita, oyasumi
      nasai

2 1 T, 2 F (ni-hyaku hachi-jū en desu), 3 F
      (san-byaku ni-jū en desu), 4 T, 5 T, 6 F (san-
      byaku ni-jū en desu)

3 1 hanbāgā (the others are all drinks),
      2 ima (the others are all question words),
      3 kodomo (the only one which isn't a
      building), 4 tegami (the only one which
      isn't an adjective), 5 to (the others are all
      numbers)

4 1 a, 2 b, 3 a, 4 a, 5 a

5 1 arimasu, 2 desu, 3 arimasen, 4 desu,
      5 arimasu, 6 ja arimasen, desu

6 1 desu, 2 kudasai, 3 kara, 4 no, 5 nan

7 1 Hoteru (*Hotel*), 2 Twice, 3 9.30 am (the
      second one is at 5.30 pm), 4 Amerika no
      yasumi (*American Holiday*), 5 4.45 pm (the
      first one is at 10.20 am)

8 B: ~~Ii~~ Sō desu ne, A: ~~Kore~~ Sore wa dō desu
      ka, B: Ikura desu ka. ~~¥5,000?~~ Y6,000?
      Chotto takai desu ne ne, A: ~~¥2,350~~ Y2,450
      desu ne.

10 1 Fukuda san, ohayō gozaimasu. 2 Hai, sō
      desu. 3 Tenisu desu ka. Chotto samui desu
      ne. 4 *Hotel* wa ii eiga desu ne. Nan-ji kara
      desu ka. 5 Sumimasen, mō ichido, onegai
      shimasu. 6 Fukuda san, daijōbu desu ka.
      7 Sō desu ne.

11 *Example, following order on recording*:
      1 Iie, kyō wa atsui desu. 2 Hai, asa desu.
      3 Iie, kamera wa arimasen. 4 Hai, yasumi
      desu. 5 50-mai arimasu. Maiku Morisu
      desu.

Unit 4

2   1 T, 2 F (she shows him the address),
       3 T, 4 T

3   1 Maruzen made, onegai shimasu.

2 Wakarimasen. 3 Jūsho wa koko ni arimasu. 4 Maruzen wa asoko ni arimasu. 5 Hidari ni arimasu.

7 police box: A , Nakano Hall: D

8 1 Kōen wa eki no ushiro ni arimasu. 2 Kōban wa eki no mae ni arimasu. 3 Kissaten wa depāto no naka ni arimasu. 4 Resutoran wa depāto no tonari ni arimasu. 5 Eigakan wa depāto no mukai ni arimasu.

12 1 Yes, 2 Yes, 3 A supermarket and a cinema, 4 Traffic lights (in front of the supermarket) and a police box (in front of the cinema).

13 *Example*: 1 Ima uchi ni imasu. 2 Iie, kodomo wa imasen. 3 Hai, neko ga imasu. Namae wa 'Snowy' desu. 4 Rondon ni arimasu. 5 Sūpā ga arimasu. Hoteru mo arimasu. Kōen wa arimasen.

16 1 Sapporo, 2 Tokyo, 3 Yokohama, 4 Kawasaki, 5 Nagoya, 6 Ōsaka, 7 Kyōto, 8 Kōbe, 9 Hiroshima.

17 1 a, 2 c, 3 d, 4 b

18 1 ~~koko~~ doko 2 ~~Mō~~ Mada 3 ~~kore~~ sore 4 ~~Igirisu~~ watashi

19 1 Harada (Hen-na hito desu ne), 2 Harada (Mada 5.30 desu), 3 Hayashi (Kore wa watashi no bideo desu), 4 Harada (Koko wa kōen desu. Eigakan ja arimasen), 5 Harada (O-sake, dōzo), 6 Harada (Kaban no naka ni nani ga arimasu ka), 7 Hayashi (Ii desu ka)

Test

1 1 T, 2 T, 3 F (Supōtsu sentā wa hoteru no mukai ni arimasu), 4 T, 5 F (Pūru wa, supōtsu sentā no ushiro ni arimasu)

2 1 Depāto no, 2 no tonari or no hidari, 3 no mukai ni, 4 Depāto wa.

3 1 c, 2 b, 3 d, 4 a, 5 g, 6 e, 7 f

4 1 imasu (subject is 'cat'), 2 sono, 3 asoko, 4 arimasu (subject is 'house'), 5 wakarimasen.

5 *Example*: 1 Kaisha ni imasen. Daigaku ni mo imasen. Uchi ni imasu, 2 Iie, arimasen. 3 Iie, imasen. Kodomo wa ima kōen ni imasu. 4 Hai, arimasu. Koko ni arimasu. Saifu no naka ni 15 pondo ('pounds') arimasu.

Summary 4

1 Tōkyō eki made onegai shimasu.
2 Wakarimasen. *3* Hoteru wa Nakano ni arimasu. *4* Meiji Jingu wa doko ni arimasu ka. *5* Kono chikaku ni yūbinkyoku wa arimasu ka. *6* Uchi no mukai ni kōen ga arimasu. *7* Ima doko ni imasu ka. *8* Chotto matte kudasai.

Unit 5

2 1 to Yokohama, 2 one, 3 three, 4 Platform 3

3 Yokohama made, 3-mai kudasai. Iie, otona 2-mai to kodomo 1-mai desu. Yokohama yuki wa nan-ban sen desu ka.

7 1 T, 2 F (The Kyoto train leaves from platform 3), 3 F (The next stop is Otsu. Kyōto is the stop after next), 4 T

8 1 Tōkyō kara Kyōto made, san-jikan kakarimasu, 2 Ōsaka kara Hiroshima made, ichi-jikan kakarimasu, 3 Hiroshima kara Nagoya made, 2-jikan jū-go-fun kakarimasu.

12 3

13 *Example*: Kyō wa yasumi desu. Shinkansen de Ōsaka e ikimasu. Jū-ji ni-jup-pun ni tsukimasu. Takushii de Koyama san no uchi e ikimasu. Ashita Ōsaka ni imasu. Asatte hikōki de Tōkyō e kaerimasu.

16 The kanji is pronounced **guchi** when it appears as part of a word, or **kuchi** when it stands alone. It means 'mouth', 'opening', 'entrance/exit'.

17 joggingu shimasu x 2, ikimasu x 4, kakarimasu x 3, kaerimasu x 1, tsukaremasu x 1

18 1 Ikeda: Doko made ikimasu ka, 2 Itō: Kōen wa tōi desu yo, 3 Ikeda: Ja, kaeri wa?, 4 Itō: Tsukaremasu yo.

19 jogging from home to shops, walking from shops to park, home from park by bus

20 1 Itō san started jogging ~~today~~ yesterday, 2 He's going to ~~run~~ walk from here to the park, 3 Ikeda san thinks it should take about ~~40~~ 30 minutes to the park, 4 Harada san is ~~driving~~ riding a bicycle.

Test

1 1 b, 2 e, 3 f, 4 a, 5 c, 6 d

2 ikimasu, ikimasu, kakarimasu, tsukimasu, kaerimasu

3 1 Otona no kippu wa, kono botan desu ka. 2 Kono densha wa, Ōsaka yuki desu ka. 3 Tōkyō yuki no densha wa, san-ban sen desu ka. 4 Basu no kippu wa, ni-hyaku en desu ka. 5 Wada san wa asatte kaerimasu ka.

4 1 b, 2 d, 3 c, 4 f, 5 a

5 A Kono basu wa Nakano e ikimasu ka.
B Iie, kono basu wa Meguro yuki desu.
A Nakano yuki no basu wa nan-ban desu ka.

6 *Example*: 1 Kaisha e ikimasu. 2 Uchi kara eki made jū-go-fun kakarimasu. 3 Iie, yasumi ja arimasen. 4 Iie, mainichi ikimasen. 5 Hai, arimasu. 'Mini' ga arimasu, 6 Ima hitori dake imasu. 7 Chikatetsu de kaisha e ikimasu.

Summary 5

1 Kōbe made san-mai kudasai. 2 Tōkyō yuki wa nan-ban sen desu ka. 3 Otona futari to kodomo hitori desu. 4 Kono densha wa Kyōto e ikimasu ka. 5 Tsugi wa Yokohama desu ka. 6 Uchi kara eki made jū-go-fun kakarimasu. 7 Ashita shinkansen de Hiroshima e ikimasu. 8 Nan-ji ni tsukimasu ka.

Unit 6

2 1 evening, 2 evening, 3 afternoon, 4 evening, 5 morning.

3 *Example*: 1 'Times' o yomimasu. 2 Shichi-ji han ni asa-gohan o tabemasu. 3 Iie, mainichi ja arimasen. 4 Hai, sukoshi hanashimasu.

4 Getsuyōbi ni, Ōsaka e ikimasu. Kayōbi ni, Tōkyō e kaerimasu. Suiyōbi wa yasumi desu. Mokuyōbi no asa, Furansugo o benkyō shimasu. Kinyōbi no yoru, eiga o mimasu.

8 1 never, 2 often, 3 always, 4 not often, 5 often

9 *Example*: 1 Tokidoki tenisu o shimasu. 2 Sakana o amari tabemasen. 3 Yoku resutoran e ikimasu. 4 Terebi o yoku mimasu. 5 Nichiyōbi ni, shigoto o zenzen shimasen. 6 Shinbun o yoku yomimasu.

13 1 T, 2 T, 3 F (He has a swimming pool at home), 4 F (He goes to work in his Mercedes)

14 1 Kono sakana wa amari oishiku nai desu ne. 2 Kono resutoran wa yasuku nai desu ne. 3 Eki wa chikaku nai desu ne. 4 Kono hoteru wa ōkiku nai desu ne. 5 Kono supagetti wa atsuku nai desu ne. 6 Pikunikku wa tanoshiku nai desu ne.

17 1 c, 2 f, 3 a, 4 e, 5 b, 6 d

18 *Order of days*: Monday, Tuesday, Wednesday, Thursday, Friday, Saturday, Sunday
Activities: flower arranging, karate, shopping

19 3, 1, 4, 2

20 1 T, 2 DK (He hurts her leg somehow, but it's not clear how), 3 T, 4 DK (She watches TV, but we don't know if she watches films), 5 T

21 1 Watashi ~~wa~~ mo ... 2 ... ~~zenzen~~ amari genki ja arimasen ne, 3 ...itsu made ~~koko~~ byōin ni ..., 4 Shokuji wa ~~eishii~~ dō ...

Test

1 1 c, 2 h, 3 g, 4 c, 5 f, 6 b, 7 a, 8 d (*Mainichi Shinbun* is the name of one of the daily Japanese newspapers)

2 1 wa, 2 o, 3 wa, 4 ni, 5 o, 6 o

3 1 Itariago o benkyō shimasu. 2 Resutoran e ikimasu. 3 Kinyōbi ni Yokohama e ikimasu. 4 Eiga o mimasu. 5 Iie, nichiyōbi ni hakubutsukan e ikimasu. 6 Doyōbi no asa, kaimono o shimasu.

4 4, 3, 6, 2, 1, 5

5 *Example*: 1 Nan-ji ni asa-gohan (or ban-gohan) o tabemasu ka. 2 Nan-yōbi ni Kōbe (or other place) e ikimasu ka. 3 Kaisha (or other object) wa ōkii desu ka. 4 Furansugo (or other language) o hanashimasu ka. 5 Asa-gohan wa, nani o tabemasu ka. 6 Yoku supōtsu o shimasu ka.

6 *Example*: 1 Iie, wain o amari nomimasen ga, biiru o yoku nomimasu. 2 Iie, mainichi ja arimasen. Doyōbi to nichiyōbi ni benkyō shimasu. 3 Furansugo o sukoshi hanashimasu ga, Itariago o zenzen hanashimasen. 4 Getsuyōbi kara kinyōbi made, 7.30 ni asa-gohan o tabemasu. 5 Hai, tokidoki kinyōbi ni eiga o mimasu. 6 Supōtsu o amari shimasen. Tokidoki tenisu o shimasu.

Summary 6

1 getsuyōbi, kayōbi, suiyōbi, mokuyōbi, kinyōbi, doyōbi, nichiyōbi. 2 Yoku Ōsaka e ikimasu ka. 3 Doyōbi ni shigoto o shimasu ka. 4 Tenki wa yoku nai desu ne. 5 Asa-gohan wa nani o tabemasu ka. 6 Sakana o zenzen tabemasen. 7 Shinbun wa, nani o yomimasu ka. 8 Tokidoki Nihon no terebi o mimasu. 9 Mainichi benkyō shimasu. 10 Ashita nani o shimasu ka.

Unit 7

2 The man likes classical music and golf; the woman likes rock music and wrestling, she doesn't really like classical music, and she dislikes golf.

3 1 Saitō san wa kabuki ga suki desu ga, Fukuda san wa amari suki ja arimasen. 2 Tanaka san wa eiga ga dai-suki desu ga, Saitō san wa amari suki ja arimasen. 3 Tanaka san wa, haikingu mo eiga mo dai-suki desu. 4 Fukuda san wa, haikingu mo kabuki mo amari suki ja arimasen.

7 1 In the morning, 2 At an old pub, 3 Watch tennis at Wimbledon, 4 At an Indian restaurant in Soho, 5 Because after dinner they're going to see a musical.

8 1 Yūbinkyoku de kitte o kaimasu. 2 Supōtsu sentā de badominton o shimasu. 3 Kaisha de shigoto o shimasu. 4 Eigakan de eiga o mimasu. 5 Gekijō de myūjikaru o mimasu. 6 Kissaten de kōhii o nomimasu.

12 1 T, 2 T, 3 F (They're going by train), 4 F (Both the fish and the beer are good), 5 T

13 1 Mokuyōbi no yoru, supōtsu sentā de

badominton o shimasen ka. 2 Kinyōbi no yoru, eiga o mimasen ka. 3 Doyōbi no asa, Yokohama de kaimono o shimasen ka. 4 Doyōbi no gogo, kōen de pikunikku o shimasen ka.

14 1 Shichi-ji han ni supōtsu sentā de aimashō. 2 Watashi ga nomimono o kaimashō.

17 1 K, 2 K, 3 H, 4 H, 5 K, 6 H, 7 H, 8 H

18 1 gorufu (golf), 2 sukii (skiing), 3 yakyū (baseball), 4 ikebana (flower arranging), 5 tenisu (tennis), 6 eiga (films), 7 karate (karate), 8 shōgi (a kind of chess)

19 3: okimashō (let's put in, install), utaimashō (let's sing), dashimashō (let's serve)

20 1 T, 2 F (She thinks it's a bad idea because Midori-ya is small), 3 DK, 4 F (He suggests installing a video player), 5 T, 6 DK, 7 F (She insists that things stay the same as they are)

21 1 Ikeda, 2 Hayashi, 3 Itō 4 Ikeda

Test

1 dai-suki desu, suki desu, mā-mā suki desu, amari suki ja arimasen, kirai desu, dai-kirai desu

2 1 ni (no action is involved), 2 ja arimasen ('amari' is always followed by a negative), 3 Donna ('Dō' means 'how about?'), 4 shimasu (meaning is 'do shopping', not 'buy'), 5 shimashō (an offer, not an invitation), 6 de (studying is an action)

3 1 a, 2 b, 3 b, 4 b, 5 a

4 1 amari, 2 ni, 3 to, 4 arimasu, 5 doko, 6 de.

5 1 mimashō, 2 tabemashō, 3 shimashō, 4 ikimashō, 5 nomimashō.

6 *Example:* 1 Watashi wa rokku ga dai-suki desu. 2 Hai, tokidoki ikimasu. 3 Rondon de shigoto shimasu. 4 Iie, resutoran de amari tabemasen, 5 Hai, suki desu. 6 Shumi wa tenisu to haikingu to ryōri desu. 7 Iie, doyōbi to nichiyōbi ni ryōri o shimasu.

Summary 7

1 Konban, konsāto e ikimasen ka. *2* Nihon ryōri ga dai-suki desu. *3* Takushii de kaerimashō. *4* Sumō wa suki desu ka. *5* Ashita no gogo, doko de kaimono o shimasu ka. *6* Shichi-ji han ni aimashō. *7* Donna ongaku wa suki desu ka. *8* Daigaku de Nihongo o benkyō shimasu.

Review 2

1 *Free answers.* Activities are: eat breakfast, eat lunch, drink tea or coffee, return home, read the paper, watch TV, go to work, study Japanese

2 hobbies/interests: ikebana, ryōri, sukii, yakyū, buildings: sūpā, uchi, ryokan,

depāto, eki, eigakan, transport: chikatetsu, hikōki, densha, kuruma, jitensha, question words: dare, itsu, nanyōbi, donna, doko

3 1 d, 2 e, 3 g, 4 f, 5 h, 6 b, 7 a, 8 c

4 1 wa, de, 2 wa, ni, 3 o, 4 e/ni, 5 ni, o, 6 de, e/ni

5 *Example:* 1 Ikeda san wa, se ga takai desu ka. 2 Uchi kara kaisha made, dono gurai kakarimasu ka. 3 Yamada san wa doko ni imasu ka. 4 Ongaku wa, nani ga suki desu ka. 5 Takushii de kaerimasu ka, 6 Tōkyō wa ima atsui desu ka.

6 1 c, 2 a, 3 e, 4 f, 5 b, 6 d

7 *Tue–Sat:* work at large department store; *Tue evening:* play badminton; *Wed and Fri evening:* study English; *Sun afternoon:* play tennis with boyfriend, sometimes watch baseball

8 1 at 6.30, 2 on Friday evening, 3 near her house, 4 it's a new Italian restaurant, and the spaghetti is good, 5 in front of the restaurant at 7.30

9 1 Nagano e ikimasu. 2 Iie, kuruma de ikimasu. 3 Yo-jikan gurai kakarimasu. 4 Doyōbi no asa ikimasu. Getsuyōbi no gogo made imasu. 5 Haikingu wa suki desu ka. 6 Issho ni ikimasen ka.

10 *Example, following order on recording:* 1 Iie, mainichi yomimasen. 2 Hai, tokidoki resutoran de bangohan o tabemasu. 3 Itaria ryōri ga suki desu. 4 Eiga ga suki desu. 5 Iie, mainichi ja arimasen. 6 Haikingu to badominton ga suki desu. 7 Hai, yoku mimasu.

Unit 8

2 1 T, 2 F (She got back yesterday morning), 3 F (She went with her friend, Kimura san), 4 T, 5 T

3 1 Atarashii kutsu o kaimashita. 2 Ginkō e ikimasen deshita. 3 Konsāto no kippu o kaimesen deshita. 4 Eigo o benkyō shimashita or Eigo no benkyō o shimashita. 5 Fukuda san to tenisu o shimashita. 6 Yoru, jogingu shimasen deshita.

7 Sapporo, 36 years old, married, taxi driver, worked in a Sapporo restaurant

8 umaremashita, sotsugyō, hatarakimashita, toki, narimashita, kekkon, kaerimashita

12 1 Saturday, 2 She gave her earrings, but Ishii san soon lost them, 3 She gave up smoking last month, 4 She's on a diet.

13 1 jū-ni-gatsu ni-jū-go-nichi, 2 shi-gatsu tsuitachi, 3 ni-gatsu jū-yokka, 4 *free answer*

14 1 Kinō wa yasumi deshita kara, umi e

ikimashita (It was a holiday yesterday, so I went to the sea). 2 Daietto-chū desu kara, hanbāgā o yamemashita (I'm on a diet, so I've stopped eating hamburgers). 3 O-sake ga kirai desu kara, nomimasen (I don't drink sake because I don't like it). 4 Saifu o nakushimshita kara, o-kane ga arimasen (I've lost my purse, so I don't have any money).

17 ichi-gatsu tsuitachi (January 1), ichi-gatsu jū-go-nichi (January 15), ni-gatsu jū-ichi-nichi (February 11), san-gatsu ni-jū-ichi-nichi (March 21), shi-gatsu ni-jū-ku-nichi (April 29), go-gatsu mikka (May 3), go-gatsu yokka (May 4), go-gatsu itsuka (May 5), shichi-gatsu hatsuka (July 20), ku-gatsu jū-go-nichi (September 15), ku-gatsu ni-jū-san-nichi (September 23), jū-gatsu tōka (October 10), jū-ichi-gatsu mikka (November 3), jū-ichi-gatsu ni-jū-san-nichi (November 23), jū-ni-gatsu ni-jū-san nichi (December 23)

18 5, 2, 4, 1, 3

19 ... Arrived on ~~Monday~~ Thursday, ... Hotel is very ~~large~~ expensive, ... Yesterday ~~morning~~ evening, ... Brad Brown, ~~35~~ 25, ... ~~Today's~~ Tomorrow's the last day, ... June ~~13th~~ 23rd

Test

1 1 ku-gatsu ni-jū-roku-nichi 2 shi-gatsu muikka, 3 jū-ichi-gatsu tsuitachi, 4 roku-gatsu hatsuka, 5 san-gatsu jū-roku-nichi, 6 hachi-gatsu jū-yokka

2 1 c, 2 a, 3 d, 4 b, 5 e, 6 f

3 e ikimashita, kara kaerimashita, kaimono shimashita, kaimasen deshita, tsuitachi, o mimashita, wakarimasen deshita, kimashita kara, tsukurimashita, mikka, Itaria ryōri, shimashita

4 1 kara, 2 ga, 3 ga, 4 kara, 5 ga, 6 kara

5 *Example*: 1 Hitori de Yōroppa e ikimashita ka. 2 Itsu Nihon e kimashita ka. 3 Nani o kaimashita ka. 4 Nan-sai desu ka. 5 Kinō nani o shimashita ka.

6 *Example*: 1 Rondon de umaremashita. 2 32-sai desu. 3 Supōtsu ga suki deshita. 4 Ku-gatsu mikka desu. 5 Supein e ikimashita. 6 Kaimono shimashita. Sore kara eiga o mimashita.

Summary 8

1 Kyonen, Yōroppa e ikimashita. *2* Hitori de Nihon e kimashita. *3* Ni-jū-san-sai no toki, kekkon shimashita. *4* Tanjōbi wa go-gatsu, ni-jū-yokka desu. *5* Itsu daigaku o sotsugyō shimashita ka. *6* Doko de eigo o benkyō shimashita ka. *7* Sen kyū-hyaku kyū-jū nana-nen ni Supein e ikimashita. *8* Daietto-chū desu kara, kēki o tabemasen. *9* Rondon de

umaremashita. *10* Kyō ginkō e ikimasen deshita.

Unit 9

2 1 T, 2 T, 3 F (Only their father played golf), 4 T

3 1 Imōto wa daigakusei desu. 2 Chichi wa eigo no sensei deshita. 3 Haha wa Itaria ryōri ga dai-suki desu. 4 Okāsan mo otōsan mo Tōkyō ni irasshaimasu ka. 5 Otōtosan to imōtosan wa o-ikutsu desu ka.

7 1 Last month, 2 American, 3 Two children, 4 He's a reporter for an American newspaper

8 1 Haha ni denwa shimashita. 2 Eki de Katō san to go-shujin ni aimashita. 3 Yamada san no musukosan ni tanjōbi no purezento o agemashita. 4 Ikeda san ni tegami o kakimasen deshita. 5 Sensei ni shashin o agemasen deshita.

12 1 plain, 2 fat, 3 short, 4 bad

13 1 Kirei-na musumesan desu ne.
2 Hansamu-na bōifurendo desu ne.
3 Benri-na kamera desu ne. 4 Iya-na tenki desu ne. 5 Taihen-na shigoto desu ne.

16 Uchi: 1, 5, 6, 8; Soto: 2, 3, 4, 7, 9, 10

17 1 h, 2 d, 3 f, 4 a, 5 i, 6 b, 7 j, 8 g, 9 c, 10 e

18 1 shiroi; 2 biiru, kōra; 3 bōshi, būtsū, shatsu; 4 musuko, okāsan, otōsan

19 3, 4

20 1 Hayashi san, 2 Hayashi san, 3 Itō san, 4 Hayashi san's mother, 5 Hayashi san

Test

1 1 c, 2 d, 3 f, 4 e, 5 a, 6 b

2 1 haha, 2 imōto, 3 ani, 4 musuko, 5 musume

3 1 Futari imasu. 2 Ni-jū issai desu, 3 Nana-sai desu.

4 1 irasshaimashita, 2 chichi, 3 hito, 4 o-ikutsu, 5 shinsetsu-na, 6 donata

5 desu, desu, o-genki, okage sama, genki

6 *Example*: 1 Hai, arimasu. Kuroi desu. 2 Hai, imōto ga imasu. 22-sai desu. 3 Senshū tomodachi ni hagaki o kakimashita. 4 Kiiro to murasaki ga suki desu. 5 64-kiro desu or arimasu. 6 Hai, watashi no kamera wa totemo benri desu. Chiisai desu. Shashin o yoku torimasu.

Summary 9

1 Okāsan mo otōsan mo Tōkyō ni irasshaimasu ka. *2* Otōtosan wa o-ikutsu desu ka. *3* Ani wa kōkō no sensei desu. *4* Kirei-na shashin desu ne. *5* Ano akai kuruma ga suki desu. *6* Atarashii konpyūtā wa totemo benri desu. *7* Kinō Ishii san to okusan ni aimashita. *8* Nihongo no sensei no go-shujin wa Igirisu-jin desu. *9* Hisashiburi desu ne. *10* Hai, o-kage sama de.

Unit 10

2 1 T, 2 T, 3 F (Mr Johnson has the grilled fish), 4 T

3 1 Kōhii o futatsu to kōra o hitotsu kudasai. 2 Tempura teishoku o mittsu to biiru o sanbon kudasai. 3 Hanbāgā o futatsu to biiru o ippon kudasai.

7 1 He likes Japanese and Chinese food, so he often uses chopsticks. 2 In Japanese restaurants in New York. 3 He thinks kanji is difficult.

8 *Example*: 1 Iie, amari tsukaimasen. 2 Furansu ryōri ga dai-suki desu. 3 'Chopsticks' to iimasu.

9 1 c, 2 f, 3 e, 4 d, 5 a, 6 b

13 1 c, 2 e, 3 d, 4 a, 5 b (f is not mentioned)

14 1 Hoteru no heya wa amari kirei ja nakatta desu *or* Kirei ja arimasen deshita. 2 Tenki wa samukatta desu. 3 Atama ga itakatta desu. 4 Terebi wa omoshiroku nakatta desu. 5 Resutoran wa takakatta desu. 6 Sakana wa shinsen ja nakatta desu *or* Shinsen ja arimasen deshita.

17 1 tenpura, 2 sushi, 3 sashimi, 4 yakizakana, 5 misoshiru, 6 gohan, 7 soba, udon, 8 oden, 9 yakitori, 10 o-bentō, 11 sukiyaki, 12 okonomiyaki

18 1 mittsu, 2 rop-pon, 3 ¥650, 4 ¥710, 5 ¥290, 6 ni-jū-roku-sai

19 1 F (She gives him ¥1000), 2 F (He's with both his parents), 3 DK, 4 T, 5 DK, 6 F (She's 26), 7 T

20 1 It's Saturday morning, not afternoon. 2 Harada san doesn't buy a pineapple. 3 Hayashi san was embarrassed because all the customers in Midori-ya saw the o-miai photos. 4 He goes to see new films on Sundays.

Test

1 1 d, 2 c, 3 f, 4 e, 5 b, 6 a (b could also be said last, when leaving the restaurant)

2 1 Tonkatsu teishoku o futatsu, hanbāgā teishoku o hitotsu, biiru o san-bon kudasai. 2 Kōhii o mittsu, orenji jūsu o hitotsu, mikkusu sando o yottsu kudasai. 3 Yakitori o hap-pon, tenpura o futatsu, biiru o yon-hon kudasai.

3 1 Watashi wa supagetti ni shimasu. 2 Jonson san wa nihongo ga jōzu desu. 3 Konsāto wa amari yoku nakatta desu. 4 Ano hito wa dare deshō ka. 5 Sashimi wa hontō ni oshikatta desu. 6 Sakana, wa amari shinsen ja nakatta desu.

4 1 b, 2 a, 3 a, 4 b, 5 b, 6 a

5 6, 4, 5, 2, 3, 7, 1

6 1 Sakana wa amari shinsen ja nakatta desu kara, tabemasen deshita. 2 Sono resutoran wa takai deshō ka. 3 Iie, kekkō desu. 4 Biiru mo ippon, kudasai. 5 Watashi wa ryōri ga heta desu. 6 Tōkyō wa tanoshikatta desu ga, takakatta desu.

Summary 10

1 ip-pon, ni-hon, san-bon, yon-hon, go-hon, rop-pon, nana-hon, hap-pon, kyū-hon, jup-pon. *2* hitotsu, futatsu, mittsu, yottsu, itsutsu, muttsu,nanatsu, yattsu, kokonotsu, tō. *3* 'Fish' wa nihongo de nan to iimasu ka. *4* Iie, mada heta desu. *5* Itadakimasu. *6* Go-chisō sama deshita. *7* Kekkon shite irasshaimasu ka. *8* Kekkō desu. *9* Sakana wa oishikatta desu.

Review 3

1 1 asatte, 2 ashita, 3 kesa, 4 kinō, 5 ototoi, 6 senshū, 7 sengetsu, 8 kyonen

2 1 kirei (not a colour), 2 futatsu (not a date), 3 onna (not a family member), 4 shatsu (not a number), 5 shinsen (not food)

3 1 b, 2 c, 3 d, 4 e, 5 h, 6 g, 7 f, 8 a

4 2 Takahashi san wa nihon-jin desu. 3 Shigatsu tōka ni umaremashita, 4 Ōsaka de umaremashita. 5 Sen kyū-hyaku hachi-jū-roku nen ni Kyōto daigaku o sotsugyō shimashita. 6 Repōtā desu. 7 Sen kyū-hyaku kyū-jū-ichi nen ni kekkon shimashita.

5 1 a, 2 a, 3 b, 4 a, 5 b, 6 b

6 1 kara, 2 imōtosan (the verb shows that the speaker is being polite), 3 burū no, 4 atsukatta desu, 5 ikutsu, 6 donata (the use of **kata** shows that the tone of the sentence is polite)

7 1 at university, 2 sport – tennis and jogging, 3 there were lots of American students there, 4 in 1991, 5 Tatsuo lives in Sapporo now, 6 in June last year

8 1 Four – Yamada san's father, mother, older sister, and her sister's husband, 2 Yamada san, 3 last year

9 *Example*: 1 Pari to Roma e ikimashita. 2 Roma wa totemo atsukatta desu. 3 Hoteru wa takakatta desu ga, hontō ni kirei deshita. 4 Ē, oishikatta desu. 5 Ē, wain o takusan nomimashita. 6 Pari wa takakatta desu kara, nani mo kaimasen deshita. 7 Ni-jū-ichi-nichi ni kaerimashita.

10 *Example, following order on recording*: 1 Kanada desu. 2 (your birthday) desu. 3 Nyū Yōku de umaremashita. 4 Hai futari imasu. 5 Kino kaisha de hatarakimashita. Kinō no yoru, uchi de bideo o mimashita.

Unit 11

2 1 d, 2 a, 3 b

3 *Free answers*. Activities are: watching TV, listening to music, drinking coffee, studying, eating a sandwich, cooking

4 1 Imōto wa, atama ga itai desu kara, nete imasu. 2 Yoshida san wa, raishū Amerika e ikimasu kara, eigo o benkyō shite imasu. 3 Kimura san wa ryōri ga dai-suki desu kara, kēki o tsukutte imasu. (Don't forget that the first part of the sentence with **kara** (because) gives the reason and the second part gives the result.)

8 1 F (She's standing in front of the entrance), 2 T, 3 T, 4 T, 5 F (They moved because her husband works in the Kyoto branch office)

9 1 Doko ni sunde imasu ka. 2 Kekkon shite imasu ka. 3 Doko ni tsutomete imasu ka.

10 1 Hai, Amerika-jin ja arimasen. or Iie, Amerika-jin desu. 2 Hai, muzukashiku nai desu. or Iie, muzukashii desu. 3 Hai, daigakusei ja arimasen. or Iie, gakusei desu.

14 1 Ishii , 2 Ishii, 3 Katō, 4 Katō, 5 Ishii, 6 Katō

15 *Example*: Ima burū no shatsu to jaketto o kite imasu. Kuroi jiinzu o haite imasu. Kutsu mo kuro desu.

16 *Example*: 1 Shikago ni sunde imashita. 2 Kuroi kutsu o haite imashita. 3 Ima kekkon shite imasu ga, 10-nen mae wa kekkon shite imasen deshita. 4 Hai, nete imashita.

19 1 c, 2 h, 3 k, 4 f, 5 a, 6 j, 7 d, 8 l, 9 b, 10 e, 11 g, 12 i

20 sūtsu, handobaggu, bōshi, kutsu, kōto

21 1 T, 2 T, 3 DK (The colour of her shoes isn't mentioned), 4 T, 5 F (This is only the second time – she doesn't like Tokyo), 6 T, 7 F (She wants to stay in Midori-ya to talk to Harada san), 8 DK (It isn't mentioned)

Test

1 asonde, tabete, nomimasu, tsukutte, mimasu, nete, kikimasu, yonde, tatte, shite

2 1 shite imasu 2 haite imasu 3 kabutte imashita 4 kite imasen 5 kakete imasu

3 1 c, 2 f , 3 d, 4 b, 5 e, 6 a

4 1 Mō Tōkyō ni sunde imasen ka. 2 Gakkō no jūsho o shitte imasu ka. 3 Dō shite Kōbe e hikkoshi shimashita ka. 4 Daigaku de nani o benkyō shite imasu ka. 5 Dono ongaku o kiite imasu ka.

5 1 Chichi wa Katō san to tenisu o shite imashita. 2 Ani wa konpyūta de asonde imashita. 3 Haha wa Yokohama de kaimono o shite imashita. 4 Otōto wa uchi de bideo o mite imashita. 5 Ane wa tomodachi no uchi de ongaku o kiite imashita. 6 Watashi wa nani mo shite imasen deshita.

6 *Example*: 1 Akai kutsu o haite imasu. 2 Manchesutā ni sunde imasu. 3 Daigaku de bankyō o shite imashita. 4 Iie, zenzen kaburimasen. 5 Ima nihongo o benkyō shite imasu. Sore kara kōhii o nonde imasu. 6 Hai, ikimasen deshita.

Summary 11

1 Ima Rondon ni sunde imasu. *2* Ishii san wa kekkon shite imasu. *3* Doko de eigo o benkyō shite imasu ka. *4* Yon-kagetsu mae ni Tōkyō e hikkoshi shimashita. *5* Ii sūtsu o kite imasu ne. *6* Nihon no kaisha ni tsutomete imasu. *7* Dono hon o yonde imasu ka. *8* Terada san no kaisha no denwa bangō o shitte imasu ka. *9* Kinō, tomodachi no uchi de bideo o mite imashita. *10* Kyō megane o kakete imasen.

Unit 12

2 1 To the Osaka branch, 2 Take them to the buchō to get his name stamp on them, 3 Make him some green tea, 4 Sending an e-mail

3 1 Ikeda san, kono shorui o Kōbe shisha ni okutte kudasai. 2 Katō san, kaigi no repōto o kaite kudasai. 3 Yamada san, kono shorui ni, shachō no hanko o moratte kudasai. 4 Ishii san, Kōbe no hoteru o yoyaku shite kudasai. 5 Mina san, atarashii naisen bangō o oshiete kudasai.

7 1 T, 2 F (He'll stay for two nights from Wednesday), 3 T, 4 F (The New Ginza Hotel is closer to the office), 5 F (He'll go by shinkansen, the bullet train)

8 A Papiyon to Pasutarando to, **dochira no hō ga** ii desu ka. B Sō desu ne. , **Papiyon no hō ga** takai desu ga, **Pasutarando no hō ga** hiroi desu. A Papiyon mo Pasutarando mo Shinjuku ni arimasu ne. B E, demo **Papiyon no hō ga** eki ni chikai desu. Tokorode, Furansu ryōri to **Itaria ryōri** to, **dochira ga** suki desu ka. A Watashi wa Furansu ryōri **ga suki** desu ne.

12 3 (... rippa desu ne ... heya wa hiroi shi, akarui shi ... mae no shokudō yori, oishii desu)

13 *Example*: 1 Wain wa, biiru yori takai desu. Wain yori, biiru no hō o yoku nomimasu. 2 Pari wa, Tōkyō yori furui desu. Pari yori, Tōkyō no hō ga ōkii desu. 3 Kinō wa, kyō yori atsukatta desu. Kinō yori, kyō no hō ga zutto isogashii desu.

14 1 Fuji-san desu. 2 Tōkyō desu. 3 Shinkansen desu. 4 Honshū ga ichiban ōkii desu.

17 1 Yamanaka, 2 Tanaka, 3 Kawamoto,
4 Kida, 5 Kawamura, 6 Kitagawa,
7 Kimura, 8 Kitayama, 9 Nishimura,
10 Nishiyama, 11 Yamamoto
18 2 tables, 3 chairs, 5 clock, 7 TV
19 1 Itō, 2 Ikeda, 3 Harada, 4 Ikeda
20 Incidents which do not occur: 3 Itō san
offers the delivery man some tea, 6 Ikeda
san tells her boss what time she will be at
the office tomorrow morning, 8 Harada
san invites Ikeda san for coffee

Test

1 shachō, fuku-shachō, buchō, kachō,
kakarichō
2 a shite, b shite imasu, c okutte, d
wakarimashita, e shimashita, f shite,
g hanashite kudasai
3 1 F (May is warmer than January), 2 T, 3 T,
4 F (Osaka is the biggest), 5 F (Mount Fuji
is the tallest mountain in Japan), 6 T (most
people would probably agree!)
4 1 a, 2 b, 3 a, 4 a, 5 b 6 a
5 1 Resutoran wa akarui shi, kirei desu. 2 Bā
wa chiisai shi, urusai desu. 3 Heya wa hiroi
shi, sutereo mo bideo mo arimasu.
4 Hoteru wa gekijo ni chikai shi, mise mo
chikai shi, totemo benri desu.
6 Example: 1 Ichiban suki-na tabemono wa
tenpura desu. 2 Watashi ga ichiban se ga
takai desu. 3 Tokidoki Rondon e shutchō
shimasu. 4 Yama no hō ga suki desu.
5 E-mēru no hō o yoku tsukaimasu.
Fakkusu wa amari tsukaimasen. 6 Ichiban
takai biru wa Hiruton Hoteru desu.

Summary 12

1 Kaisha no jūsho o oshiete kudasai. 2 Shachō
wa ashita Nyū Yōku e shutchō shimasu.
3 Kono shorui o honsha ni okutte kudasai.
4 Densha to kuruma to, dochira no hō ga
hayai desu ka. 5 Atarashii biru wa, mae no
biru yori zutto ii desu. 6 Hiru-gohan no ato
de, Rondon shisha ni denwa shimasu. 7 Tōkyō
de ichiban takai biru wa nan desu ka.
8 Namae to jūsho o koko ni kaite kudasai.
9 Chotto matte kudasai. 10 Atarashii shigoto
wa omoshiroi shi, kyūryō mo ii desu.

Unit 13

2 1 she eats too much, 2 she has a cold,
3 she fell down the station steps
3 1 Kaze da to omoimasu. 2 San-ji ni uchi e
kaeru to omoimasu. 3 E-mēru was benri da
to omoimasu. 4 Ishii san wa ashita Nagoya
ni iku to omoimasu. 5 Ano hito wa buchō
no okusan da to omoimasu.
7 95 kgs, 175 cms, 5 bottles of beer per day,
approx 20 per day

8 Example: 1 Tsuki ni ni-kai gurai tegami o
kakimasu. 2 Shū ni ni-kai undō o shimasu.
3 Nen ni ik-kai Nihon ryōri o tabemasu.
4 Ni-nen ni ik-kai gaikoku e ikimasu.
5 Mainichi shinbun o yomimasu. 6 Shū ni
san-kai Nihongo o benkyō shimasu.
9 Example: 1 Watashi wa ryōri ga amari
dekimasen. 2 Furansugo ga sukoshi
dekimasu. 3/4 Gorufu mo sukii mo zenzen
dekimasen. 5 Tenisu ga dekimasu. 6 Unten
ga dekimasu.
13 1 T, 2 F (He's still drinking beer), 3 T,
4 F (He shouldn't eat hamburgers or
spaghetti), 5 T
14 Example: 1 Sonna ni takusan tabenai hō
ga ii desu. 2 Ashita unten shinai hō ga ii
desu. 3 Motto benkyō o suru hō ga ii desu.
4 Atarashii kuruma o kawanai hō ga ii
desu.
17 1 j, 2 e, 3 l, 4 f, 5 a, 6 k, 7 c, 8 d, 9 b, 10 h,
11 i, 12 g
18 3, 4, 2, 1
19 1 yakitori, 2 singing, 3 lonely, 4 go home,
5 a letter, 6 Morita, 7 he only ever talks
about films, 8 head, leg, and arm

Test

1 1 ikanai, 2 kaeru, 3 naoru, 4 shinai, 5 kuru,
konai, 6 nai, 7 taberu, 8 nomu, nomanai
2 1 e, 2 a, 3 f , 4 g, 5 d, 6 h, 7 b, 8 c
3 1 Shū ni san-kai jogingu o shimasu. 2 Shū
ni ik-kai jimu ni ikimasu. 3 Tsuki ni ni-kai
tenisu o shimasu. 4 Maiasa kudamono o
tabemasu. 5 Ichi-nen ni 20 kiro yasemasu.
4 1 suwanai , 2 ja nai, 3 undō, 4 naoru,
5 kibun, 6 kaeranai
5 5, 2, 4, 1, 6, 3
6 Example: 1 Watashi wa shū ni ni-kai
badominton o shimasu. 2 Iie, sukii wa
zenzen dekimasen. 3 Taijū wa 61 kiro
desu. Shinchō wa 179 senchi desu. 4 Nen ni
san-kai gurai Yōroppa e ikimasu. 5 Kyōnen
kara 5 kiro futorimashita.

Summary 13

1 Kao iro ga warui desu ne. 2 Shū ni nan-kai
undō shimasu ka. 3 Eigo ga dekimasu ka.
4 Ano hito wa Takeda san da to omoimasu.
5 Maiasa jogingu shimasu ga, taijū wa amari
kawatte imasen. 6 Takushii de kaeru hō ga ii
desu. 7 Ashita jimu ni ikanai to omoimasu.
8 Kōhii o sonna ni takusan nomanai hō ga ii
desu yo. 9 Kibun ga warui desu. 10 Nihongo
ga sukoshi dekimasu.

Unit 14

2 1 T, 2 T, 3 F (The woman has been to
Hawaii), 4 F (She was a university student
at the time she visited Canada), 5 T

3 *Suggested responses in brackets*:
1 Yōroppa e itta koto ga arimasu ka (Hai, kyonen Itaria to Furansu e ikimashita).
2 Shinkansen ni notta koto ga arimasu ka (Iie, arimasen). 3 Sashimi o tabeta koto ga arimasu ka (Hai, sashimi ga dai-suki desu). 4 Kabuki o mita koto ga arimasu ka (Iie, mita koto ga arimasen).

7 1, 3, 4, 6

8 1 Getsuyōbi, Yokohama e itte, atarashii jaketto o kaimashita. 2 Kayōbi, uchi ni ite, bideo o mimashita. 3 Suiyōbi, atarashii Furansugo no kurasu ni haite, takusan benkyō shimashita. 4 Mokuyōbi no asa wa tenisu o shite, gogo wa jimu ni ikimashita. 5 Kinyōbi wa watashi no tanjōbi de, pātii o shimashita. Demo biiru o takusan nonde, gārufurendo to kenka shimashita.
6 Shūmatsu ni, Yamada san to issho no yama ni itte, haikingu shimashita.

12 5, 1, 4, 7, 6, 2, 3

13 *Example*: Rondon wa omoshirokute tanoshii desu. Hoteru wa takakute, amari yoku nai desu. Samukute, iya desu. Kinō wa tanjōbi de, Yamaguchi san ni kirei-na tokei o moraimashita. O-miyage o takusan kaimashita. Haha ni handobaggu o agete, chichi ni sētā o agemasu. Ashita Pari ni itte, mokuyōbi ni Nihon e kaerimasu. Emiko

16 1 Setsubun, 2 Hina Matsuri, 3 Tango no Sekku, 4 O-bon, 5 Shichi Go San

17 Kinō no asa kimono o kite, okāsan to otōsan to issho ni Meiji Jingū ni itta. Taihen konde ita! Okāsan ni okane o moratte, osaisen o ageta. Samukatta kara, sugu uchi e kaetta. Gogo, ojisan to obasan ga uchi e kite, otoshi dama o moratta! Taihen tanoshii ichi-nichi datta! (Yesterday morning I wore a kimono and went to Meiji Shrine with mother and father. It was really crowded! Mother gave me some money, and I made an offering at the shrine. It was cold, so we soon came home again. In the afternoon aunt and uncle came to the house, and gave me some New Year money! It was a really enjoyable day!).

18 1 atama, 2 takushii, kuruma, 3 untenshu, kangofu

19 Events which aren't mentioned: 2, 3, 6

20 (Untenshu wa nan to iimashita ka),
1 (Dōzo, kochira e), 2 (O-tomodachi ga o-
mimai ni kimashita), 4 (4.00 goro de ii desu ka)

21 1 He should stay in hospital for two days.
2 He continued to sing in the taxi. 3 He says he's leaving this afternoon. 4 She likes

films. 5 He's going to see a film with the nurse.

Test

1 1 flowers, from students to teacher, Yamaguchi san, 2 scarf, from Hayashi san to Tanaka san, 3 purse, from older sister to my mother, 4 souvenir from Kyoto, from me to friend

2 1 itte, 2 de, 3 mita, 4 takakute, 5 omoshirokute, 6 tabeta

3 1 O-sake o nonda koto ga arimasu ka.
2 Resutoran de bōifurendo to kenka shimashita. 3 Mokuyōbi wa shujin no tanjōbi de, shii dii o agemashita. 4 Kinō no ban uchi ni inakatta deshō. 5 Tanjōbi ni kanai ni tokei o moraimashita.

4 1 Kono eiga wa yūmei desu ga, amari yoku nai to omoimasu. 2 Kare wa gaikoku e itta koto ga nai to omoimasu. 3 Kare wa Harodzu de sono jaketto o katta to omoimasu. 4 Kanojo ni atta koto ga aru to omoimasu. 5 Kare wa ashita Nagoya e itte, asatte kaeru to omoimasu.

5 5, 2, 4, 1, 6, 3

6 *Example*: 1 Hai, Kyōto no Gion Matsuri o mita koto ga arimasu. 2 Shii dii to hon to sētā o moraimashita. 3 Yūmei-na matsuri ga arimasen ga, iroiro-na chiisai matsuri ga arimasu. 4 Iie, arimasen. 5 Hai, arimasu.
6 Hai, tako ga dai-suki deshita. Yoku tako o agemashita.

Summary 14

1 Nyū Yōku e itta koto ga arimasu ka.
2 Tanjōbi ni shii dii to kamera o moraimashita. *3* Kyōto no kabuki wa kirei de, totemo omoshirokatta desu. *4* O-shōgatsu wa nani o shimashita ka. *5* Ima Tōkyō wa taihen atsukute, iya desu. *6* Imōto ni yukata o agete, otōto ni tako o agemasu. *7* Ichi-gatsu futsuka ni Kyōto kara kaette, 3-ka kara shigoto ni shimashita. *8* Sono hana o dare ni moraimashita ka. *9* Tako-age matsuri o kiita koto ga arimasu ga, mita koto ga arimasen. *10* Kinō no ban uchi ni ite, terebi o mimashita.

Review 4

1 kaburimasu: bōshi; kimasu: yukata, sētā, burausu; hakimasu: zubon, kutsushita, jiinzu; kakemasu: megane, sangurasu; shimasu: nekutai, iyaringu, sukāfu

2 1 asatte (not a -te form of verb), 2 shutchō (not a job title), 3 hashi (not a part of the body), 4 otona (not a relative), 5 mui (not a period of time)

3 1 Omedetō gozaimasu. 2 Akemashite omedetō gozaimasu. 3 O-daiji ni. 4 Kao iro ga warui desu ne. 5 Dō shimashita ka. or Dō shita n' desu ka.

4 1 no, o, 2 o, ni, 3 ni, o, 4 wa, ga, 5 o, ga, 6 ni, o

5 1 Sake o nonda koto ga arimasu ka.
2 Sashimi o tabeta koto ga arimasu ka.
3 Nihon ryōri o tsukutta koto ga arimasu ka. 4 Kyōto e itta koto ga arimasu ka.
5 Kimono o kita koto ga arimasu ka.
6 Sumō o mita koto ga arimasu ka.

6 1 oshiete, 2 kaite, 3 naoru, 4 nomanai, 5 kawanai, 6 kaetta

7 Age: 28, Height: 170 cm, Weight: 80 kg, Interests: sport – jogs every morning, plays tennis three times a week, watches baseball on Saturdays, Appearance/ clothes: green suit, green shirt, blue necktie.

8 1 She's going to head office tomorrow, and will be there until Thursday. 2 He asks her to get the president's name stamp on some documents. 3 Matsuda san was supposed to be going with her, but he's developed a bad cold.

9 Susan Carter desu. Igirisu desu. Ni-jū-yon-sai desu. Hai, shū ni ni-kai badominton o shimasu. Tokidoki jimu e ikimasu. Iie, go-nen gurai mae ni yamemashita. Amari nomimasen. Shū ni ik-kai gurai biiru o sukoshi nomimasu.

10 1 Pachinko is a game similar to upright pinball, 2 From around mid-June to mid-July, 3 Yes, it's on December 23rd, 4 A hanko, or name stamp, 5 *Japan Times*, *Daily Yomiuri*, *Asahi Evening News*, 6 At New Year, 7 Approximately 3000 miles, 8 Wax models of the dishes served in the restaurant, 9 Sashimi is raw fish; sushi is pieces of raw fish or shellfish on small balls of rice, often wrapped around with seaweed, 10 Gifts are exchanged between households and companies.

Grammar summary

All grammatical terms used in this summary are defined in the Glossary of Grammatical Terms, pp. 242–3.

Word order

The word order in Japanese sentences is very different from that of English. In general, the main topic of the sentence is stated first and the specific details follow on. The verb comes at the end of the sentence.

Ikeda san wa / kinō / Yokohama e / ikimashita.
[Regarding Mr Ikeda / yesterday / to Yokohama / he went.]
Ikeda san went to Yokohama yesterday.

Kono akai sētā wa / ikura / desu ka.
[About this red sweater / how much / is it?]
How much is this red sweater?

Omission of words and phrases

It is very common to omit words or phrases from sentences if the meaning can be understood from the context. For example, the word **anata** ('you') is rarely used when talking directly to someone as it is generally obvious to whom you are referring.

(Anata wa) Doko e ikimasu ka. Where are you going?
(Watashi wa) Yokohama e ikimasu. I'm going to Yokohama.

The subject of a verb is usually omitted if it has already been established in the conversation.

Ikeda san wa Amerika e ikimashita yo. Mr Ikeda has gone to America.
Sō desu ka. (Kare wa) Itsu ikimashita ka. Really? When did he go?

Verbs

Unlike English, Japanese verb endings stay the same regardless of the subject. If the subject is obvious from the context, then it is not necessary to state it. Hence **ikimasu** may mean 'I go', 'you go', 'he/she/it goes', 'we go', or 'they go'.

Present and past tense verbs have a 'plain' form and a 'polite' form, and the choice of which to use generally depends on the degree of formality required by the situation. The plain form is used within the family and between very close friends, while the polite form is generally used for more formal everyday conversation.

Present/future tense

The present plain form and **-masu** form are used both for present actions and also to refer to events happening in the future. If it is not clear from the context which is intended, then a phrase indicating the time, such as 'tomorrow afternoon', 'at 2.00', etc., is used.

Most of the plain form verbs which end in **-iru** or **-eru** drop the final **-ru** to form the basic stem, to which **-masu/-masen** can be added to form the polite present. The plain negative is formed by adding -**nai** to the stem.

plain positive	stem	-masu	plain negative	English
taberu	tabe-	tabemasu	tabenai	eat
miru	mi-	mimasu	minai	see

The other, much larger group includes all the verbs which do not end in **-iru/-eru** and also a small number that do. These verbs drop **-u** to form the basic stem, and add **-imasu/-imasen** to form the present polite form. For the plain negative, add **-anai** to the stem (or **-awanai** if the stem ends in a vowel).

plain positive	stem	-masu	plain negative	English
nomu	nom-	nomimasu	nomanai	drink
kiku	kik-	kikimasu	kikanai	hear, listen
kau	ka-	kaimasu	kawanai	buy

Maiasa shinbun o **yomimasu**. I read the paper every morning.

There are only two verbs which are slightly irregular in the way they form the basic stem.

plain positive	stem	-masu	plain negative	English
suru	shi-	shimasu	shinai	do
kuru	ki-	kimasu	konai	come

Plain past

To form the plain past tense, with **-ru** verbs, add **-ta** (positive) or **-nakatta** (negative) to the stem.

plain positive	stem	plain past	plain negative	English
taberu	tabe-	tabeta	tabenakatta	eat
miru	mi-	mita	minakatta	see

With **-u** verbs, the plain past form depends on the last letters of the plain present.

-tsu, -ru, or **-u**:	add **-tta** (**matsu** – **matta**, wait; **futoru** – **futotta**, get fat; **kau** – **katta**, buy)
-su:	add **-shita** (**hanasu** – **hanashita**, talk)
-ku:	add **-ita** (**kaku** – **kaita**, write)
-gu:	add **-ida** (**oyogu** – **oyoida**, swim)
-mu, -bu, -nu:	add **-nda** (**yomu** – **yonda**, read; **asobu** – **asonda**, play)

Kinō atarashii kamera o **katta** deshō. You bought a new camera yesterday, is that right?

To form the plain past negative, add **-nakatta** to the stem (or **-awanakatta** if the stem ends in a vowel).

plain positive	plain negative	plain past negative	English
nomu	nomanai	nomanakatta	drink
kiku	kikanai	kikanakatta	hear, listen
au	awanai	awanakatta	meet

Ishii san ni **awanakatta** deshō. You didn't meet Ishii san, did you?

-te form:

The **-te** form is used with **kudasai** to make requests, with **iru** to make the present progressive tense, and alone to join sentences. It is formed by replacing the final **-ta** of the plain past with **-te**.

plain positive	plain past	-te form	English
taberu	tabeta	tabete	eat
kaku	kaita	kaite	write
shimasu	shita	shite	do

Koko ni o-namae o **kaite kudasai**. Please write your name here.
Doko de nihongo o **benkyō shite imasu** ka. Where are you studying Japanese?

Following is a list of the principal parts of the main verbs which occur in this course.

Verbs which drop -ru

plain positive	-masu form	plain negative	-te form	meaning
ageru	agemasu	agenai	agete	give
dekiru	dekimasu	dekinai	dekite	be able to
ireru	iremasu	irenai	irete	put in
iru	imasu	inai	ite	be, exist
kimeru	kimemasu	kimenai	kimete	decide
kiru	kimasu	kinai	kite	wear
kureru	kuremasu	kurenai	kurete	give
miru	mimasu	minai	mite	see
miseru	misemasu	misenai	misete	show
neru	nemasu	nenai	nete	sleep
taberu	tabemasu	tabenai	tabete	eat
tsukareru	tsukaremasu	tsukarenai	tsukarete	get tired
tsutomeru	tsutomemasu	tsutomenai	tsutomete	be employed
umareru	umaremasu	umarenai	umarete	be born
wasureru	wasuremasu	wasurenai	wasurete	forget
yameru	yamemasu	yamenai	yamete	quit, stop
yaseru	yasemasu	yasenai	yasete	get thin

Verbs which drop -u

plain positive	-masu form	plain negative	-te form	meaning
au	aimasu	awanai	atte	meet
aru	arimasu	nai	atte	be, exist
asobu	asobimasu	asobanai	asonde	play
dasu	dashimasu	dasanai	dashite	put out
futoru	futorimasu	futoranai	futotte	get fat
hanasu	hanashimasu	hanasanai	hanashite	talk
hairu	hairimasu	hairanai	haitte	enter, go in
harau	haraimasu	harawanai	haratte	pay
hataraku	hatarakimasu	hatarakanai	hataraite	work
iku	ikimasu	ikanai	itte	go
iu	iimasu	iwanai	itte	say
kau	kaimasu	kawanai	katte	buy
kaeru	kaerimasu	kaeranai	kaette	return, go home
kaku	kakimasu	kakanai	kaite	write
kiku	kikimasu	kikanai	kiite	hear, listen
morau	moraimasu	morawanai	moratte	receive
naru	narimasu	naranai	naratte	become
nomu	nomimasu	nomanai	nonde	drink
okuru	okurimasu	okuranai	okutte	send
omou	omoimasu	omowanai	omotte	think
toru	torimasu	toranai	totte	take
tsukau	tsukaimasu	tsukawanai	tsukatte	use
tsuku	tsukimasu	tsukanai	tsuite	arrive
tsukuru	tsukurimasu	tsukuranai	tsukutte	make
wakaru	wakarimasu	wakaranai	wakatte	understand
yomu	yomimasu	yomanai	yonde	read

Irregular verbs

plain positive	-masu form	plain negative	-te form	meaning
suru	shimasu	shinai	shite	do
kuru	kimasu	konai	kite	come

Particles

Japanese uses short words called particles to show the function of a word or phrase in a sentence. In English it is often the word order which shows the subject and the object of a verb ('John ate the bear. The bear ate John.'), but word order can be more flexible in Japanese as the particle makes the meaning clear. Particles always come after the word or phrase to which they refer.

wa: indicates the topic of the sentence. This may or may not be the grammatical subject of the verb.

> **Watashi wa** gakusei desu. **I'm** a student.
> **Kono hon wa** mō yomimashita ka. Have you read **this book**?
> [*literally* regarding this book – have you read it?]

ga: indicates the subject of the verb, especially when it is being introduced into the conversation for the first time. It is always used with question words when they are the subject.

> Kono hoteru ni, **ii resutoran ga** arimasu. There's **a good restaurant** in this hotel.
> Kono resutoran ni, **nani ga** oishii desu ka. **What's** good in this restaurant?

o: indicates the object of the verb.

> Mainichi **sakana o** tabemasu. I eat **fish** every day.
> Konban **bideo o** mimashō ka. Shall we watch **a video** tonight?

ka: is added to the end of a sentence to form a question.

> Doko e **ikimasu ka**. Where **are you going**?

ni (1): indicates the point in time at which an action occurs.

> **3.00 ni** kaerimashita. I got home **at 3.00**.
> **3-gatsu 15-nichi ni** umaremashita. I was born **on 15 March**.

ni (2): shows the place where something is or exists.

> Haha wa ima **uchi ni** imasu. My mother is **at home** now.
> Eki wa **asoko ni** arimasu. The station is **over there**.

ni (3): shows the direction of movement towards a place.

> Ashita **Tōkyō ni** ikimasu. I'm going **to Tokyo** tomorrow.
> Kinō Tanaka san ga **uchi ni** kimashita. Yesterday Tanaka san came **to my house**.

ni (4): points out the indirect object of a verb, often the person who is on the receiving end of an action.

> Watashi wa **tomodachi ni** purezento o agemashita. I gave a present **to my friend**.
> Kono shorui o **honsha ni** okutte kudasai. Please send these documents **to head office**.

e: like **ni** (3), also shows the direction of movement towards a place.

Kyonen **Yōroppa e** ikimashita. Last year we went **to Europe**.
11.30 ni **uchi e** kaerimashita. I went **home** at 11.30.

de: shows the place where an action occurs.

Depāto de kaimashita. I bought it **at the department store**.
Rondon de eigo o benkyō shimashita. I studied English **in London**.

no (1): shows possession.

Watashi no kaban wa doko ni arimasu ka. Where's **my** bag?
Amerika no kaisha desu ka. Is it an **American** company?

no (2): joins two nouns where the first gives information about the second.

Tomodachi no Ikeda san mo kimasu. **My friend, Ikeda san**, is also coming.
Basu no kippu wa ikura desu ka. How much is **a bus ticket?**

Numbers and counting objects

There are various ways of counting things in Japanese, depending on the type of objects being counted. This occurs in English to some extent (e.g. three bars of chocolate, one spoonful of sugar, two slices of bread), but far more so in Japanese, as every object needs a so-called 'counter'. Below you will find some of the most commonly used counters.

-hon: used for long, thin objects such as pens, bottles, bananas

1	ip-pon	6	rop-pon
2	ni-hon	7	nana-hon
3	san-bon	8	hap-pon
4	yon-hon	9	kyū-hon
5	go-hon	10	jup-pon

Banana o **san-bon** kudasai. Three bananas, please.

-mai: used for thin, flat objects such as CDs, pieces of paper, stamps

1	ichi-mai	6	roku-mai
2	ni-mai	7	nana-mai
3	san-mai	8	hachi-mai
4	yon-mai	9	kyū-mai
5	go-mai	10	jū-mai

Kesa shii dii o **san-mai** kaimashita. I bought three CDs this morning.

-nin: used to count people

1	hitori	6	roku-nin
2	futari	7	nana-nin
3	san-n	8	hachi-nin
4	yo-ni	9	kyū-nin
5	go-ni	10	jū-nin

Tomodachi **san-nin** to issho ni ikimashita. I went with three friends.

-kai: used for counting the number of times something occurs

1	ik-kai	6	rok-kai
2	ni-kai	7	nana-kai
3	san-kai	8	hachi-kai
4	yon-kai	9	kyū-kai
5	go-kai	10	juk-kai

Shū ni **ni-kai** tenisu o shimasu. I play tennis **twice** a week.

-tsu: for abstract nouns and objects which have no special counter

1	hitotsu	6	muttsu
2	futatsu	7	nanatsu
3	mittsu	8	yattsu
4	yottsu	9	kokonotsu
5	itsutsu	10	tō

Supagetti o **futatsu** to hanbāgā o **hitotsu** kudasai. Two spaghettis and **one** hamburger, please.

Levels of formality and politeness

The style of speech used in a conversation differs according to the degree of formality, politeness, and respect dictated by the situation, and the relationship between the speakers (e.g. doctor–patient, teacher–student, boss–employee, customer–sales assistant). This may involve different verb or adjectival forms, and the use of 'honorific' terms to refer to others and 'humble' terms to refer to oneself. In some cases completely different words are used (e.g. **haha** – my mother, **okāsan** – your mother; **agemasu** – I give to you, **kuremasu** – you give to me). With certain nouns, the prefixes **o-** or **go-** can be added to indicate politeness: such words are never used to refer to oneself (**namae** – my name, **o-namae** – your name; **shujin** – my husband, **go-shujin** – your husband).

Go-shujin wa mada Igirisu ni **irasshaimasu** ka. Is **your husband** still in England?
Hai, **shujin** wa 3-gatsu made Igirisu ni **imasu**. Yes, **my husband** is in England until March.

Adjectives

Adjectives can be divided into two distinct types, **-i** adjectives and **-na** adjectives.

The **-i** adjectives all end in **-ai**, **-ii**, **-ui**, or **-oi**. They are similar to verbs in that they have negative and past forms. These are formed by the addition of various endings after dropping the final **-i**.

Present	Present negative	Past	Past negative	English
atsui	atsuku nai	atsukatta	atsuku nakatta	hot
ōkii	ōkiku nai	ōkikatta	ōkiku nakatta	big
yasui	yasuku nai	yasukatta	yasuku nakatta	cheap
ii/yoi	yoku nai	yokatta	yoku nakatta	good

Kyonen no natsu wa amari **atsuku nakatta** desu. Last summer **wasn't very hot**.

Ano depāto wa **ōkii** desu ga, amari **yoku nai** desu. That department store **is big**, but it **isn't very good**.

The **-na** adjectives behave more like nouns. They do not change their form in the negative or the past. When they describe a noun by coming directly before it, they need the addition of **-na**.

Ano hoteru wa **yūmei** desu ne. That hotel is **famous**, isn't it?

Are wa **yūmei-na** hoteru desu ne. That's a **famous** hotel, isn't it?

Vocabulary

All verbs in the Vocabulary are listed by their **-masu** form, as this is the form you will be most familiar with. The plain form is also shown (in brackets). Note that this is the form under which verbs are listed in dictionaries.

A

abunai	look out! danger!
agemasu (ageru)	fly (a kite); raise
agemasu (ageru)	give
aimasu (au)	meet
aisatsu	greetings
aisu kuriimu	ice cream
aite	partner
akai	red
akarui	bright, light
akemashite omedetō gozaimasu	Happy New Year!
aki	autumn, fall
amari	not very [with negative]
ame	rain
Amerika	America, USA
ane	(my) older sister
ani	(my) older brother
ano	that ... over there
anō	uh, um
aoi	blue-green
apāto	flat, apartment
are	that one over there
arigatō	thank you
arimashita	got it, here it is
arimasu (aru)	there is/are, have
aruite	on foot, walking
arukōru	alcohol
asa	morning, a.m.
asa-gohan	breakfast
asatte	the day after tomorrow
ashi	leg, foot
ashita	tomorrow
asobimasu (asobu)	play [verb]
asoko	over there
atama	head
atama ga ii	clever
atarashii	new
ato	after, later
atsui	hot

B

bā	bar
badominton	badminton
bakari	only, nothing but
ban	evening
ban-gohan	dinner, evening meal
banana	banana
-banchi	house/lot number [in addresses]
basu	bus
bēkon-eggu	bacon and eggs
benkyō shimasu (suru)	study
benri(-na)	handy, useful
(o-)bentō	boxed meal
Bentsu	Mercedes-Benz
bideo	video
biiru	beer
biru	building
bōifurendo	boyfriend
bōshi	hat
botan	button
buchō	departmental manager
bunka	culture
burausu	blouse
burū	blue
butaniku	pork
būtsu	boots
butsukarimasu (butsukaru)	collide with, bump into
butsukemasu (butskeru)	bump, hit
-byaku	hundred
byōin	hospital

C

cha no yū	tea ceremony
chairoi	brown
chokku	check design
chichi	(my) father
chigaimasu (chigau)	be different or incorrect
chiisai	small

chiizu	cheese
chikai	close
chikaku	nearby, the local area
chikatetsu	underground, subway
chizu	map
-chō, -chōme	division of area, in addresses
chōdo ii	just right
chotto	a little, rather
chotto matte kudasai	just a moment, please
chotto matte!	hold on! just a minute!
chūgakkō	middle school, junior high school
chūka ryōri	Chinese food

D

da	is [plain form of desu]
dai-kirai desu	hate
dai-suki desu	like very much
daibu	considerably, much
daietto-chū	on a diet
daigaku	university
daigakusei	university student
daijōbu	all right
daishumi	great interest
dake	only
dame desu	it's no good, useless; don't do that!
dare	who?
dareka	someone
dashimasu (dasu)	put out, serve
de	by, by means of
de	in, at [+ location]
de gozaimasu	is, are [polite equivalent of desu]
deguchi	exit
dekimasu (dekiru)	can, be able to
demo	but, however
densha	train
denwa	telephone
depāto	department store
deshō	right? isn't it?
deshō ka	I wonder
desu (da)	am, is, are
dēta	data
dewa ...	well ... [polite equivalent of ja]
dioru	Dior
dō	how about?
dō itashimashite	you're welcome, think nothing of it
dō shita n' desu ka	what's happened?
dō shite	why?

dochira	where? [polite]
dochira no hō	which (of the two)?
doko	where?
dokushin	unmarried
dōmo	thanks
dōmo arigatō	thank you very much
dōmo arigatō gozaimashita	thank you very much [polite]
dōmo arigatō gozaimasu	thank you very much [polite]
donata	who? [polite]
donna	what kind of?
dono	which?
dono gurai	how long?
doyōbi	Saturday
dōzo	here you are, here it is, go ahead
dōzo yoroshiku	pleased to meet you

E

ē	yes [informal]
e	to, towards
e-mēru	e-mail
earōbikkusu	aerobics
eiga	film/movie
eigakan	cinema/movie theatre
eiga sutā	film/movie star
eigo	English language
eigo de	in English
eki	train station
en	yen
enjinia	engineer
earoguramu	aerogram
ēto	um, uh

F

fakkusu	fax
firumu	film [for camera]
Fuji-san	Mt Fuji
fuku-shachō	vice-president
fun (pun)	minute
Furansu	France
furō	Japanese-style bath
furui	old
futari	two (people)
futatsu	two (objects)
futorimasu (futoru)	get fat
futsū	ordinary, regular
futsuka	second of the month
futsuka-kan	two-day period
fuyu	winter

G

ga	but
ga	*particle indicating subject of verb*
gaikoku	abroad, foreign country
ganbatte kudasai	good luck, go for it
-gatsu	*counter for months*
gekijo	theatre
genki(-na)	healthy, well
getsuyōbi	Monday
ginkō	bank
giri	obligation
-go	language of a country
go	five
go-chisō sama deshita	*set phrase said after eating*
go-kyōdai	brothers and sisters
go-shujin	husband
gogo	afternoon, p.m.
gohan	rice
gokurō sama desu	sorry you've had so much trouble
gomen kudasai	excuse me [*to get someone's attention*]
gomen nasai	I beg your pardon; sorry
gorufu	golf
gozaimasu	there is/are, have [*polite equivalent of* **arimasu**]
gurai	about, approximately
gurē	grey

H

hachi	eight
hagaki	postcard
haha	(my) mother
hai	yes
haikingu	hiking
hairimasu (hairu)	go in, enter
hajimete	first time
haka	grave
hakimasu (haku)	wear, put on [*clothes pulled on, e.g. shoes, jeans, skirts*]
-haku	overnight stay [*stating number of nights*]
hakubutsukan	museum
han	half, half past [*with time*]
hana	flower
hana	nose

hanashimasu (hanasu)	speak
hanbāgā	hamburger
handobaggu	handbag
hanemūn	honeymoon
hanko	name stamp, seal
hansamu(-na)	handsome
haraimasu (harau)	pay
Hariuddo	Hollywood
Harodzu	Harrods
haru	spring [*season*]
hashi	chopsticks
hatachi	20 years old [*of people*]
hatarakimasu (hataraku)	work
hayai	early, quick
hazukashi-sō	look embarrassed
hen(-na)	strange, peculiar
heta(-na)	unskilful
heta desu	be poor at
heya	room
hi	day
hidari	left side
hikkoshi shimasu (suru)	move house, move
hikōki	airplane
hina matsuri	Festival of Dolls [*3 March*]
hiroi	spacious
(o-)hiru-gohan	lunch, midday meal
hisashiburi desu ne	it's been a long time!
hito	person
hitori	one (person)
hitori de	alone, by oneself
hitotsu	one (object)
hō ga ii	it's best to
hoka no	other, another
Hokkaido	*the northernmost of the four main Japanese islands*
-hon	*counter for long thin objects*
hon	book
honsha	head office
Honshu	*the largest of the four main Japanese islands*
hontō ni	really, very
hoteru	hotel
hyaku	hundred

I

ichi	one
ichi nichi	one day
ichiban	the number one, the most, -est

Igirisu	England, Britain	-ji	o'clock
ii desu ka	is it OK? [*asking permission*]	ji	characters, handwriting
ii	nice, good	jiinzu	jeans
iie	no	jikan	hour, time
iimasu (iu)	say	jimu	gym
ikaga	how about? [*polite equivalent of* **dō**]	-jin	-person [*indicating nationality*]
ikebana	flower arranging	jitensha	bicycle
ikimasu (iku)	go	jitsu wa	the fact is
ikura	how much?	jiyū-seki	unreserved seat
ikutsu	how many?	jogingu shimasu	
(o-)ikutsu	how old?	(suru)	go jogging
ima	now	jōzu(-na)	skilful
imasu (iru)	be, exist [*for people*]	jū	ten
		jūsho	address
imōto	(my) younger sister	jūsu	juice
imōtosan	(another person's) younger sister		

K

Indo	India
irasshai!	welcome! [*variation used in informal situations*]

ka	*sentence-ending indicating a question*
irasshaimase!	welcome!	kaban	bag
irasshaimasu (irassharu)	go, come, be [*polite*]	kabuki	kabuki theatre
		kaburimasu (kaburu)	wear, put on (hat)
iremasu (ireru)	put in, make [*coffee, tea*]	kachō	section manager
		kaeri	return journey, round trip
iriguchi	entrance	kaerimasu (kaeru)	return, go home
irimasu (iru)	need	-kagetsu	*counter for months*
iro	colour	kaidan	steps, stairs
iroiro(-na)	all kinds of, various	kaigi	meeting
isogashii	busy	kaimasu (kau)	buy
issho ni	together	kaimono	shopping
isu	chair	kaisatsuguchi	ticket barrier
itadakimasu	*set phrase said before eating*	kaisha	company, office
		kakarichō	section manager
itai	hurting, painful; ouch!	kakarimasu (kakaru)	take, last [*with time expressions*]
Itaria	Italy	kakemasu (kakeru)	wear (glasses, sunglasses)
itsu	when?		
itsuka	fifth [*of the month*]	kakimasu (kaku)	write
itsumo	always	kakunin	confirmation
itsutsu	five (objects)	kamera	camera
iya(-na)	horrible	kami	hair
iyaringu	earrings	-kan	*counter for periods of time, e.g. months, years*
izakaya	bar		

J

		Kanada	Canada
ja	well, in that case	kanai	(my) wife
ja arimasen	isn't, aren't	(o-)kane	money
ja nai	isn't, aren't [*alternative form of* **ja arimasen**]	kangae	thought, idea
		kangofu	nurse
		(o-)kanjō	bill, check
... ja nai yo!	it isn't ...! [*very informal*]	kanojo	she, her [*pronoun*]
		kanpai!	cheers!
jaketto	jacket	kao	face
jazu	jazz	(o-)kanemochi	rich person

235

kara	because
kara	from
kare	he, him
karē raisu	curry with rice
kasa	umbrella
kashikomarimashita	certainly, of course [*polite*]
kata	shoulder
kata	person [*polite*]
katakana	*syllabary for writing words of non-Japanese origin*
kaubōi	cowboy
kawaii	cute, sweet
kawarimasu (kawaru)	change, be altered
kayōbi	Tuesday
kaze	a cold
(go-)kazoku	family
keiken	experience
keizai	economics
kēki	cake
kekkō desu	I've had enough
kekkon shimasu (suru)	get married
-ken	prefecture
kenka shimasu (suru)	fight, quarrel
kesa	this morning
ki	tree
kibun	feeling, mood
kiiroi	yellow
kikai	machine
kikimasu (kiku)	hear, listen
(o-)kimari	decision, agreement
kimasu (kiru)	wear, put on [*e.g. shirts, jackets, coats*]
kimemasu (kimeru)	decide
kinō	yesterday
kinyōbi	Friday
kippu	ticket
kippu uriba	ticket window
kirai desu	dislike
kirei(-na)	pretty, beautiful, clear
kiro	kilogram
kissaten	coffee shop
Kita-Kyūshu	*city in Kyushu*
kitte	stamp
kōban	police box
kōcha	tea
kochira e	this way [*polite*]
kodomo	child, children
kōen	park
kōhii	coffee
koko	here, this place
kōkō	senior high school
kokonoka	ninth of the month
kokonotsu	nine (objects)
kōkūbin	air mail
komimasu (komu)	be crowded
konban	this evening
konbanwa	good evening!
kondo	next time
kongetsu	this month
konna	such as this, like this
konnichiwa	hello, good afternoon
kono	this
konpyūtā	computer
konsāto	concert
kopii	photocopy
kōra	cola
kore	this one
korobimasu (korobu)	fall over, fall down
koto	thing, fact, topic
-ku	*division of city, in addresses*
kubi	neck
kudamono	fruit
kūkō	airport
(o-)kuni	country
kurabu	club
kurashikku	classical music
kurasu	class
kuriimu soda	cream soda
kuroi	black
kuruma	car
kutsu	shoes
kutsushita	socks
(o-)kyaku san	customer, guest
kyō	today
(go-)kyōdai	brothers and sisters
kyonen	last year
kyū, ku	nine
kyūkō	express train
kyūryō	salary
Kyūshū	*the southernmost of the four main Japanese islands*

M

mā-mā	so-so
machi	town, city
machigaimasu (machigau)	make a mistake
mada	not yet
made	until, as far as
mae	in front, before
maguro	tuna
-mai	*counter for flat objects*
maiasa	every morning
maiban	every evening
mainen	every year
mainichi	every day
maishū	every week
maitsuki	every month

mājan	mah jong
mama	as it is, as it stands
man	ten thousand
masutā	master [*term of address to owner of bar*]
mata	again
mata ashita	see you tomorrow
matsuri	festival
me	eye
megane	glasses
mi ni ikimasu (iku)	go to see
(o-)miai	meeting with a view to marriage
michi	street
midori	green
migi	right side
mikka	third [*of the month*]
mikkusu sando	mixed sandwiches
mimasu (miru)	watch, see
mimi	ear
mina san	everyone
minna	everything, everyone
minna de	altogether
miruku	milk
mise	shop, store; premises
misemasu, miseru	show
misete kuremasu (kureru)	show (me)
miso shiru	miso soup
mittsu	three (objects)
mizu	water
mo	too, also; as much as
... mo, ... mo	both ... and ...
mō	already
mō ichido	once more
mochiron	of course
mokuyōbi	Thursday
mono	thing, object
moraimasu (morau)	receive
moshi moshi	hello? [*on phone*]
motte kimasu (kuru)	bring
motto	more
muika	sixth [*of the month*]
mukai	opposite
mune	chest
murasaki	purple
musuko	(my) son
musukosan	(someone else's) son
musume	(my) daughter
musumesan	(someone else's) daughter
muttsu	six (objects)
muzukashii	difficult
myūjikaru	a musical

N

naisen bangō	extension number
naka	in, inside
nakushimasu (nakusu)	lose
namae	name
nan, nani	what?
nan-ban sen	which platform?
nan-ban	what number?
nan-bon	how many? [*long, thin objects*]
nan-ji	what time?
nan-jikan	how many hours?
nan-kai	how many times?
nan-nin	how many people?
nan-sai	how old?
nana	seven
nanatsu	seven (objects)
nani mo	nothing [+ *negative*]
nanoka	seventh [*of the month*]
nanyōbi	what day?
naorimasu (naoru)	get better, recover
narimasu (naru)	become
natsu	summer
ne	isn't it? aren't they? etc. [*indicates tag question*]
neko	cat
nekutai	necktie
nemasu (neru)	sleep
nen	year; *counter for years*
ni	at [*time*]
ni	in, at [*place*]
ni	two
... ni shimasu	decide on, have [*when ordering*]
-nichi	*counter for days of the month*
ni-kai-me	second time
nichiyōbi	Sunday
Nihon	Japan
niku	meat
-nin	*counter for people*
no	Noh theatre
no	of, belonging to, 's
nomimasu (nomu)	drink
nomimono	drinks
notte imasu (iru)	is riding
nyūsu	news

O

o	*particle indicating object of verb*
... o kudasai	I'd like ...; could I have ...?

o-bentō	boxed meal	ojisan	(someone else's)
o-bon	Festival of Souls		uncle
	[*mid-August*]	okage sama de	fine, thank you
o-cha	green tea	okāsan	(someone else's)
o-chūgen	*summer gift-giving*		mother
	season	ōkii	big
o-daiji ni	please take care of	okimasu (oku)	place, put, install
	yourself	Okinawa	*Japanese island to*
o-genki desu ka	how are you?; are		*the south of Kyushu*
	you well?	okonomiyaki	*thick pancake made*
o-hiru-gohan	lunch, midday meal		*with meat or*
o-ikutsu	how old?		*vegetables*
o-kaeri nasai	welcome back	okurimasu (okuru)	send
o-kage sama de	I'm fine, thank you	okusan	(someone else's)
o-kane	money		wife
o-kanemochi	rich person	omedetō gozaimasu	congratulations
o-kanjō	bill/check	omoimasu (omou)	think
o-kimari	decision, agreement	omoshiroi	interesting
o-ko-san	(someone else's)	onaji	similar to, like
	children	onaka	stomach
o-kuni	country	onegai shimasu	please [*when asking*
o-kyaku san	customer, guest	(suru)	*a favour*]
o-miai	meeting with a view	onēsan	(someone else's)
	to marriage		older sister
o-mimai ni ikimasu	go to visit a sick	oniisan	(someone else's)
(iku)	person		older brother
o-miyage	souvenir	ongaku	music
o-saisen	a money offering at	onna	woman, female
	a temple or shrine	onsen	hot springs
o-sake	sake, rice wine	orenji	orange
o-sechi ryōri	*special dishes eaten*	oshibori	moist hand towel
	at New Year	oshiemasu (oshieru)	teach
o-seibo	*year-end gift-giving*	osoi	slow, late
	season	otoko	man, male
o-shōgatsu	New Year's Day, the	otona	adult
	New Year	otōsan	(someone else's)
o-taku	your house		father
o-tearai	toilets	otōto	(my) younger
o-tera	temple		brother
o-toshi dama	*money given to*	ototoi	the day before
	youngsters at New		yesterday
	Year	otōtosan	(someone else's)
o-tsuri	change [*money*]		younger brother
o-yome san	bride	oyasumi	night!
oba	(my) aunt	oyasumi nasai	goodnight
obasan	(someone else's)		
	aunt	**P**	
obāsan	(someone else's)		
	grandmother	pabu	pub, bar
oden	fish and vegetables	pachinko	pinball game
	in a fish-based stock	painappuru	pineapple
ohayō	Morning! [*informal*]	pātii	party
ohayō gozaimasu	good morning!	pikunikku	picnic
oishi-sō	looks delicious	pinku	pink
oishii	delicious	piza	pizza
oji	(my) uncle	-pon	*counter for long*
ojiisan	(someone else's)		*thin objects*
	grandfather	purezento	present
		puru resu	wrestling

pūru	swimming pool
-pyaku	hundred

R

raishū	next week
raitā	lighter
ramen	*a type of noodle*
remon	lemon
repōtā	reporter
repōto	report
ressun	lesson
resutoran	restaurant
ringi	decision-making process
ringo	apple
rippa	wonderful, superb
rokku	rock music
roku	six
ryokan	inn
ryōri	cooking, cuisine
ryōshin	parents
ryūgaku shimasu (suru)	study abroad

S

sabishii	lonely
sadō	tea ceremony
-sai	-years old
saifu	purse, wallet
saigo	last, final
saikin	recently
sakana	fish
(o-)sake	sake, rice wine
sakura	cherry blossom
sama	*polite form of* san
samui	cold
san	Mr, Mrs, Ms
san	three
sando	sandwich
sangurasu	sunglasses
sarada	salad
sashimi	raw fish
sauna	sauna
sawaranaide kudasai	please don't touch
sayōnara	goodbye
se ga takai	tall [*of a person*]
sekai	world
sen	(train) line
sen	thousand
senchi	centimetre
sengetsu	last month
sensei	teacher
senshū	last week
sentō	public bath house
sētā	sweater
setsubun	spring festival [*3 or 4 February*]
shachō	company president

shain	employee
shashin	photograph
shatsu	shirt
-shi	city
shi	four
shi	and what's more, moreover
shichi	seven
shichi-go-san	Seven-Three-Five Festival [*15 November*]
Shidonii	Sydney
shigoto	work, job
shii dii	CD
shika	only, nothing but [+ *negative*]
Shikoku	*the smallest of the four main Japanese islands*
shimasu (suru)	do, play [*sports*]
shimasu (suru)	wear [*with accessories, e.g. jewellery, neckties, belts*]
shinbun	newspaper
shinchō	(person's) height
shingo	traffic signals
shinjimasu (shinjiru)	believe
shinjiraremasen	unbelievable; I can't believe it
shinkansen	Bullet Train
shinsen(-na)	fresh
shinsetsu(-na)	kind, gentle
shirimasu (shiru)	know
shiroi	white
shisha	branch office
shita	under; bottom
shitei-seki	reserved seat
shitsumon	question
shitsurei shimasu	excuse me
shizuka(-na)	quiet, peaceful
shodō	calligraphy
(o-)shōgatsu	New Year's Day, the New Year
shōgi	*a kind of chess*
shokudō	dining room, canteen, cafeteria
shokuji	meal
shorui	papers, documents
(go-)shujin	husband
shū	week
shūmatsu	weekend
shumi	interests, hobbies
shutchō	business trip
sō desu	that's right; it's so
sō desu ka	is that right? really?
soba	*a type of noodle*
sobo	(my) grandmother

239

sofu	(my) grandfather	taiin shimasu (suru)	come out of hospital
sokkusu	socks		
soko	there	taijū	(person's) weight
sonna ni	that much, to that extent	taka-sō	looks expensive
		takai	expensive
sono	that [*adjective*]	tako	kite
sono tsugi	the one after that	tako-age	kite-flying
sore	that one	(o-)taku	your house
sore de?	so what?	takusan	many, lots of
sore kara	and also, then	takushii	taxi
sore ni	and also; and on top of that	tana	shelf
		tango no sekku	Boys' Day Festival [*5 May*]
soro soro	it's time I was leaving	tanjōbi	birthday
soto	outside	tanoshii	fun, enjoyable
sotsugyō shimasu (suru)	graduate	te	hand
		(o-)tearai	toilets
sugoi	amazing, wonderful	tēburu	table
sugoku	incredibly, extremely	tegami	letter
sugu	soon, immediately	teishoku	set meal
suimasu (suu)	smoke, inhale	tenisu	tennis
suiyōbi	Wednesday	tenki	weather
sukāto	skirt	tenpura	tempura [*deep-fried fish and vegetables in batter*]
sukejūru	schedule		
suki desu	like		
sukii	skiing	(o-)tera	temple
sukiyaki	one-pot dish of thin slices of beef and vegetables	terebi	television
		tii	tea
		to	and
sukoshi	a little, small amount	… to iimasu	it's called …
		tō	ten (objects)
sukunai	few	tōi	far, a long way
sumāto(-na)	slim, stylish	toire	toilet
sumimasen	excuse me, sorry	tōka	tenth [*of the month*]
sumimasen ga …	excuse me, but … ; I'm sorry, but …	tokei	watch
		toki	time, hour
sumimasu (sumu)	reside, live	tokidoki	sometimes
sumō	sumo wrestling	tokkyū	limited express (train)
sunde imasu (iru)	be living [*in a place*]		
sūpā	supermarket	tokorode	by the way
supagetti	spaghetti	tokui	good at
supōtsu	sport	tomato	tomato
supōtsu sentā	sports centre	tomodachi	friend
supōtsuman	sportsman	tonari	next to, beside
sushi	bite-sized delicacies served on vinagered rice	tonkatsu	pork cutlet
		torimasu (toru)	take
		totemo	very
suteki	great, wonderful	tsugi	next
sūtsu	suit	tsuitachi	first [*of the month*]
suwaranaide kudasai	please don't touch	tsukaimasu (tsukau)	use
		tsukaremasu (tsukareru)	get tired

T

T-shatsu	T-shirt	tsuki	month
tabako	cigarette	tsukimasu (tsuku)	arrive
tabemasu (taberu)	eat	tsukurimasu (tsukuru)	make
tabemono	food		
tachimasu, tatsu	stand	tsumaranai	trifling,
taihen(-na)	awful, terrible		

	uninteresting
tsumori desu	intend to
tsutomemasu	
(tsutomeru)	be employed, work
tsuyoi	strong
tsuyu	rainy season

U

uchi	house, home
uchi	inside; our [*of our group*]
ude	arm
udon	*a type of noodle*
ue	above, on top
umaku	well, skilfully, successfully
umaremasu	
(umareru)	be born
umi	sea
undō shimasu (suru)	do exercise
unten shimasu (suru)	drive
untenshu	driver
unyu	transport, conveyance
uōkuman	personal stereo
urusai	noisy
ushiro	behind
utaimasu (utau)	sing

W

wa	*particle indicating topic of sentence*
wain	wine
wakai	young
wakarimashita	I see, I understand
wakarimasu (wakaru)	know, understand
wanpiisu	dress [*woman's*]
warui	bad
wasuremasu	
(wasureru)	forget, leave behind
watashi	I, me
Winburudon	Wimbledon

Y

ya	and, or
yakidōfu	deep-fried tofu
yakitori	*pieces of barbecued chicken*
yaki-zakana	grilled fish
yakyū	baseball
yama	mountain
yamemasu (yameru)	stop, quit
yappari	so it is! no doubt about it!
yasai	vegetables
yasemasu (yaseru)	get thin, lose weight
yasui	cheap

yasumi	holiday, day off
yattsu	eight (objects)
yo	*sentence-ending for emphasis*
yoi	nice, good
yōka	eighth [*of the month*]
yokka	fourth [*of the month*]
yoku	often
(o-)yome san	bride
yomimasu, yomu	read
yon	four
yopparaimasu	
(yopparau)	be drunk
yori	than [*in comparisons*]
Yōroppa	Europe
yoroshiku	pleased to meet you [*informal*]
yoru	evening
yottsu	four (objects)
yoyaku	reservation
yūbinkyoku	post office
yukata	*light cotton kimono*
yuki	bound for, going to
yukkuri	slowly
yūmei(-na)	famous

Z

zenbu de	altogether
zenzen	never, not at all [*with negative*]
zubon	trousers, pants
zuibun	fairly, pretty much
zutto	by far, a great deal

Glossary of grammatical terms

Adjective: A word used to give information about a noun.

oishii kōhii **delicious** coffee
yūmei-na hito a **famous** person
Ano resutoran wa **takai** desu. That restaurant is **expensive**.

Adverb: A word used to give information about a verb, an adjective, or another adverb.

totemo kirei **very** beautiful
yukkuri hanashimasu speak **slowly**
yoku ikimasu **often** go

Article: In English 'the' is the *definite article* and 'a' and 'an' are the *indefinite articles*. There are no articles in Japanese.

Comparative: The forms used to express higher or lower degree. See also *Superlative*.

Motto yukkuri hanashite kudasai. Please speak **more slowly**.
Takushii **no hō** ga, densha **yori** hayai desu. A taxi is quicker than the train.
Kare ga okusan **yori** wakai desu. He's younger than his wife.

Direct object: The noun, pronoun, or phrase directly affected by the action of the verb.

Sakana o yoku tabemasu. I often eat **fish**.
Furansugo o benkyó shite imasu. He's learning **French**.

Future tense: The form of a verb used to express what will happen in the future. In Japanese the same form is used as for the present.

Ashita Yokohama e ikimasu. **I'll go** to Yokohama tomorrow.

Counter: A series of numbers for counting specific objects. Different counters are used depending on the item being counted. Often formed by adding a suffix (for example, **-mai, -nin, -bon**) to the cardinal numbers.

Hagaki o **san-mai** kakimashita. I wrote **three** postcards.
Tomodachi **san-nin** imashita. **Three** of my friends were there.
Banana o **san-bon** kaimashita. I bought **three** bananas.

Indirect Object: The noun, pronoun, or phrase indirectly affected by the action of the verb.

Haha ni tegami o kakimashita. I wrote a letter to **my mother**.
Tomodachi ni purezento o agemashita. I gave a present to **my friend**.

Intonation: The pattern of sounds made in a sentence as the speaker's voice rises and falls.

Irregular verb: A verb that does not follow one of the set patterns and has its own individual forms. Only **suru, shimasu** (do) and **kuru, kimasu** (come) are slightly irregular.

Negative: The form of a verb used to indicate that an action did not or will not occur. In Japanese, some adjectives also have negative forms.

Niku o **tabemasen**. I **don't eat** meat.
Kinō benkyō o **shimasen deshita**. I **didn't study** yesterday.
Ano resutoran wa **takaku nai** desu. That restaurant **isn't expensive**.

Noun: A word that identifies a person, thing, place, or concept.

densha (train), shinbun (newspaper), **Tanaka san** (Tanaka san), **sensei** (teacher), **uchi** (house), **keiken** experience

Object: The noun, pronoun, or phrase affected by the action of the verb. See *Direct Object* and *Indirect Object*.

Particle: A word such as **wa** which shows the relationship of nouns, pronouns, or phrases to the rest of the sentence. Particles function in the same way as to English prepositions (you may find them called prepositions or postpositions in other reference books).

Ikeda san **ga** ikimasu. Ikeda san will go.
Ikeda san **ni** denwa shimashita. I called Ikeda san.
Ikeda san **no** kuruma desu. It's Ikeda san's car.

Preposition: A word (e.g. at, by, from, etc.) or phrase (e.g. to the left of, next to, etc.) used with a noun or pronoun to show its relationship to the rest of the sentence.

Neko wa téburu **no shita ni** imasu. The cat is **under** the table.
Eki **no tonari ni** arimasu. It's **next to** the station.
Shichi-ji **ni** ikimasu. I'll go **at** 7.00.

Present tense: The form of a verb used to express something happening or in existence now, or as a habitual occurrence.

Maiasa 7.00 ni **okimasu. I get up** at 7.00 every morning.
Ikeda san wa eigo o **hanashimasu.** Ikeda san **speaks** English.

Pronoun: A word used to stand for a noun. Pronouns may refer to things or concepts (it, them), or people (she, him), and may be indefinite (someone, something).

Kore wa ii kamera desu ne. **This** is a nice camera, isn't it?
Kanojo wa nan-sai desu ka. How old is **she**?

Subject: The noun, pronoun, or phrase that performs the action indicated by the verb. Usually followed by the particle **wa** or **ga**.

Buchō **wa** Tōkyō e ikimashita. **The boss** has gone to Tokyo.
Kanojo wa jū-go-sai desu. **She**'s 15 years old.

Superlative: The form used to express the highest or lowest degree. See also *Comparative*.

Ichiban takai yama wa Eberesuto desu. The **highest** mountain is Everest.
Itō san ga **ichiban wakai** desu. Itō san is the **youngest**.

Syllable: A unit of pronunciation which forms either the whole or part of a word.

to (one syllable); **toki** (two syllables); **tokidoki** (four syllables)

Tense: The form of a verb which indicates when the action takes place, i.e. in the past, present, or future.

Topic: The word or phrase, usually indicated by **wa**, which shows what the sentence is about.

Natsu yasumi wa doko e ikimasu ka. Where are you going for your summer vacation? (literally: **About your summer vacation** where are you going?)
Kono kuruma wa dare no desu ka. Whose car is this? (literally: **This car** whose is it?)

Verb: A word or phrase used to express what is being done or what is happening. It can also be used to express a state.

Shinbun o **yonde imasu.** He **is reading** the paper.
Ikeda san wa **kaerimashita.** Ikeda san **has gone home**.
Kanojo wa ima Nyú Yóku ni **sunde imasu.** She **lives** in New York now.

Index

In addition to the Language Building pages listed below, see also the relevant section of the Grammar Summary.